The Anti-Capitalist Book of Fashion

Praise for *Stitched Up*

'Makes a strong case for nothing less than a revolution.'
—Emma Watson, actor

'An incredible accomplishment.'
—Susie Orbach, author of *Fat is a Feminist Issue*

'Interrogates today's fashion landscape with rigour - will make
you view your wardrobe through a different lens.'
—Lucy Siegle, author of *Turning the Tide on Plastic*

'Thoroughly researched with a reach extending both globally and
historically, the book is packed with interesting examples, and
Hoskins' engaging style makes it eminently readable.'
—*LSE Review of Books*

'A classic read for all fashion students, and of course those
interested in the politics of fashion. I will refer to my copy
for a long time to come.'
—Caryn Franklin MBE, fashion commentator and
body image activist

'A book that hangs like a garment on a coat-hanger. A garment
with many pockets. In the pockets numberless notes and remarks
about clothes and history. Take it off the hanger and put it on. By
which I mean – read it and walk through history.'
—John Berger

'A masterclass in unpicking the threads of injustice, exploitation and
oppression woven into our clothing. By joining the dots between
fashion and capitalism – this is a route map to weave a different story
for our clothing, our planet and its people.'
—Asad Rehman, Executive Director, War on Want

'This is a wonderful book, bursting at the seams with power,
passion and politics. Clothes will never look the same again!'
—John Hilary, former Executive Director of War on Want

The Anti-Capitalist Book of Fashion

Tansy E. Hoskins

Foreword by Andreja Pejić

PLUTO PRESS

First published 2022 by Pluto Press
New Wing, Somerset House, Strand, London WC2R 1LA

www.plutobooks.com

The Anti-Capitalist Book of Fashion is based upon *Stitched Up: The
Anti-Capitalist Book of Fashion*, published by Pluto Press in 2014.

British Library Cataloguing in Publication Data
A catalogue record for this book is available from the British Library

ISBN 978 0 7453 4662 5   Hardback
ISBN 978 0 7453 4661 8   Paperback
ISBN 978 0 7453 4665 6   PDF
ISBN 978 0 7453 4663 2   EPUB
ISBN 978 0 7453 4803 2   audiobook

This book is printed on paper suitable for recycling and made
from fully managed and sustained forest sources. Logging, pulping
and manufacturing processes are expected to conform to the
environmental standards of the country of origin.

Typeset by Stanford DTP Services, Northampton, England

Simultaneously printed in the United Kingdom and United States of
America

To my parents, Kay and Gareth,
with love and affection

And in loving memory of Neil Faulkner -
Workers of all lands unite

Contents

Foreword

Andreja Pejić

Almost 100 years ago, the Communist Revolutionary Leon Trotsky gave us these powerful words on art and a very fine vision of the future:

> Art then will become more general, will mature, will become tempered, and will become, the most perfect method of the progressive building of life in every field. It will not be merely 'pretty' without relation to anything else. All forms of life, such as the cultivation of land, the planning of human habitations, the building of theaters, the methods of socially educating children, the solution of scientific problems, the creation of new styles, will vitally engross all and every-body. People will divide into 'parties' over the question of a new gigantic canal, or the distribution of oases in the Sahara ... Such parties will not be poisoned by the greed of class or caste. All will be equally interested in the success of the whole. The struggle will have a purely ideologic character. It will have no running after profits, it will have nothing mean, no betrayals, no bribery, none of the things that form the soul of 'competition' in a society divided into classes. But this will in no way hinder the struggle from being absorbing, dramatic and passionate. ... The average human type will rise to the heights of an Aristotle, a Goethe, or a Marx. And above this ridge new peaks will rise.[1]

Foreword

This was Trotsky's vision for Soviet society in 1924. As we all know, this society did not come about. The Russian Revolution became isolated on the world stage, Stalin's theory of 'Socialism in One Country' prevailed and the state disintegrated into a bureaucratic dictatorship. Power was taken away from the working class, a political genocide ensued and most of the leaders of the Russian Revolution were eventually executed in the Great Purge. Trotsky himself was driven out of Russia and assassinated in Mexico in 1940 by one of Stalin's many assassins.

The same century also saw the successful rise of fascism in Germany and another major world war with untold death and destruction and an even more horrific genocide. Many movements across the world, from Africa to Asia to South America, fought for a better world and were betrayed in one way or another. The Soviet Union was dissolved in 1991, which meant that whatever remained of the achievements of the Russian Revolution was finally and fully betrayed. Capitalism as the world's main social system has survived to this day not necessarily because of a lack of revolutionary will or movement but because of a lack of genuinely principled revolutionary leadership. We have not reached the end of history, we are not living in some perfect new age, hyper-modern cyber world or some sugar-coated alternate reality or a third-wave feminist spiritual dawn. We have carried all the tragedies of the past century over to ours, minus the global war so far but one can't rule that out. Our environment is at the brink of ecological collapse. On this earth eight billionaires have more wealth than the bottom half of the world's population. Poverty, hunger, ignorance, depression, illness and epidemics have not been eliminated. Our technology has improved immeasurably but in so many ways we have undergone a great cultural and intellectual decline. My generation has grown up surrounded by social regression not progression.

Yes, there is now more diversity at the top and more minorities have representation in the upper echelons, but this is not *real* progress. Today we confuse personal career advancement with great social advancement, but a few people winning the lottery or even a hundred people or even a thousand people from all different backgrounds, genders and colours is not the same thing as millions and millions of people seeing a very real and tangible improvement in their standard of living. Radical wealth distribution would save transgender lives, not just a change of words or attitudes or a change in the casting of roles in film and television which identity politics often achieves through intimidation and attacking artistic freedom.

Still, when I read the above-quoted words it gives me great hope for art, fashion and our collective future. We also can't disregard the fact that even though the Russian Revolution did not deliver the society we would all hope for, it gave birth to remarkable principles as well as advancements in economic planning, science, art and culture.

I often surprise men on dates with my political education, or journalists or friends. To most people, modelling and Marxism live in two separate worlds and should never, ever mix. Tansy Hoskins has done a good job of applying Marxism to fashion. Trotsky was applying Marxism to the art of his times. Fashion might have built for itself an incredibly elitist, cold-hearted, overly polished and unnecessarily bitchy image, it might be, as Tansy quotes, 'capitalism's favourite child' and a ruthless, profit-hungry industry in its own right, but it is still an art form. The designer still creates. I would compare fashion most of all to architecture because feeling takes a back seat to technique, construction and outer aesthetic, whereas of course in music, theatre, film and painting feeling is central. However, feeling, empathy for the world, an understanding of the times, an understanding of history and a love for humanity

x

usually makes every art form and every person only better. The Bauhaus understood this. Too much of fashion today is about items of clothing and not enough about the human being clothed. As a result of the cultural decline and the domination of capitalist thinking, most creative fields today suffer from a lack of respect for humanity, but this is especially so in fashion. As a result, we have not produced great art or artists or thinkers. Where is the Shakespeare of our age? Where is the Shakespeare of fashion?

My 'new-age' spiritual friend tells me I'm not a real Marxist because I shop at Walmart. He was probably joking, but either way this type of thinking is indicative of a whole layer of 'radical' middle-class people. Progressive consumerism is where they begin and end. *The Anti-Capitalist Book of Fashion* clearly shows that the problem is bigger than one company or two or three or a dozen. Progressive consumerism is nice, if one doesn't lecture or judge working-class and poor people with much less buying power, but real structural change cannot happen without an organised and progressive assault on the whole system. That assault is only possible with the power of a conscious working class imbued with socialist goals. Creativity plays no small role in lifting and sensitizing consciousness.

As a result of Covid-19 I moved to New Mexico and got a part time job as a waitress. In America my position is that of a food runner, I am at the bottom of the restaurant hierarchy. Most people would find this shocking but what they don't understand is that selling clothes to millionaires does not nec-essarily make someone a millionaire. People have this image of models as being the ultimate 'elite'. No, just because rich men want to sleep with us does not automatically make us part of their class. Well, it can do, but a girl must put in a lot of dirty and degrading work, which is something I was never really interested in; at worst I entertained the idea.

There are so many models who come from very poor and difficult backgrounds, however, and it's true that the industry lifts us up out of our environment. The opportunity to model can be a golden ticket out of poverty, well maybe not for Kendall Jenner; however, it most often leads to an upper middle-class existence, and only a very small percentage enter the 'elite'.

I myself was given an incredible amount of media exposure but not a lot of money because I was always considered too artistic. There are models who are more 'editorial' or 'high fashion' and models who are more commercial. The commercial clients ran from the idea of a transgender supermodel like pigs away from a revolutionary bayonet. I guess I always went against the grain in one way or another, I was always biting the hand that feeds me, and this never helped my bank account. Celebrities were not exactly known to have public sex changes until I came along. Some backward person once messaged me on Instagram, 'you ruined everything, I can't even look at a Victoria's Secret model now without thinking she might be a man!!' Sue me but you won't get much money. A model's career is also notoriously short, it's easy to become the hot new face but it's very hard to maintain it. I was never the fashion elite's first choice, but they weren't exactly mine. I think I made enough of an impression to guarantee a comeback one day but I'm not holding my breath.

Last night, while this glamorous face was at work in the kitchen area, I was on my phone reading about Omicron as the restaurant was starting to get busy. My manager walked past me and screamed at me 'put that phone down Andreja!' I did what she said but I was thinking in my head, 'you property-loving, vicious lady, we are all risking our lives to keep your restaurant open! I work my ass off here, where is the respect?' She probably doesn't know that I am somewhat famous, so she treated me like any other worker, so I ask, where is the respect for a whole class of people who make our society run daily? We wouldn't have intellectuals or restaurants or modern technology or Elon Musk without this very class. Please stop treating the working masses like dogs, or less than dogs, or even as perpetual victims and start seeing them for what they really are, a mighty revolutionary force. Make art, develop aesthetics and morals that inspire people to reach for more, to fight for better for everyone. Enlighten and inspire or retire. To be frank, my manager is not that bad, she has her sweet moments, and she does much more work than Mr Musk.

It is important for all but especially for creatives to understand that people are not the problem or the main cause of all social evils; the system is the problem. The more I hate capitalism the more I fall in love with humanity. In my opinion, if we can put people on the moon, connect the whole world via the infamous internet and build robots we can also figure out how to live in a better socioeconomic system than the one we currently have. We can live in a liberated socialist non-dying highly artistic world where beautiful fashion is not just for the few. Where fashion loves humanity and humanity loves fashion. It's time to challenge the establishment, it's time to turn our backs on the devil who wears Prada and on the thinking that everyone longs to be as opportunistic as she is.

Acknowledgements

Writing a book is a social process. I remain indebted to everyone I thanked in the acknowledgments of *Stitched Up* in 2014 and the scholars, activists, revolutionaries, and everyone who has supported my work since then. While the bones of that first book remain, the following people helped this version grow new muscle, sinew, flesh, and skin.

For authoring the Foreword I am so happy to be able to thank luminous revolutionary Andreja Pejic. There really only ever was a shortlist of one for this role. For their kindness, comradeliness, exceptional work, and inspirational existence I would like to thank Nandita Shivakumar, Mayisha Begum, Asad Rehman, Ruth Ogier, Jody Furlong, Kirsty Fife, Amneet Johal, Bryn Hoskins, Janet Cheng, Laura Harvey, Bel Jacobs, Alice Wilby, Tegan Papasergi, Florent Bidios, Richard Kaby, Juan Mayorga, Dil Afrose Jahan, and Nidia Melissa Bautista. An extra large thank you to Riley Kucheran who worked with me on sections of this text and pushed me intellectually, right up to the dark, wintery finish line. For all the things I've lost on you, my love and affinity to Tom B. P. Sanderson – thank you will never be a big enough word.

During this time I also lost my friend, comrade and mentor the Marxist historian, archaeologist and author Neil Faulkner. Neil was the one who gave me the determination to write *Stitched Up* to the best of my ability. He once wrote to me 'the only thing worth doing is fighting to bring down the system, and one's humanity is central to that.' We miss you Neil.

Acknowledgements

Thank you Pluto Press – my star editor and friend David Castle, Emily Orford, Chris Browne, Kieran O'Connor, Robert Webb, Melanie Patrick, James Kelly, Sophie O'Reirdan, and Patrick Hughes. Thank you to Dan Harding and Dave Stanford for copy editing, proofreading, and typesetting, and to Janet Andrew for compiling the index. Thank you Babette Radclyffe-Thomas for notes on China. Thank you once again to Jade Pilgrom for the beautiful illustrations throughout this book. My thanks also to Andrew Gordon, and to David Evans and the entire team at David Higham. Plus an enormous shout out to everyone who continues to support independent radical publishing around the globe.

This book was written during the crisis of the Covid-19 pandemic, stalling for six weeks when I fell sick. While I am aware that gratitude is not enough, I am so thankful to the staff of the National Health Service and to health and public service workers across the globe.

Garment workers remain on the sharp end of capitalist exploitation and so were among those slammed hardest by the pandemic. I hope to have made a small contribution towards chronicling the injustices of the fashion industry, the violence it takes to sustain it, and the resistance that continues to fight.

Before you is a challenge that eclipses the pandemic. We must, each one of us, join the resistance and not allow our climate to crumble in the name of capitalism. John Berger once gave me a single word of advice which I pass on – Courage. Know that the movement for change is waiting for you. Come find us.

I don't know when the word fashion came into being, but it was an evil day. For thousands of years people got along with something called style and maybe, in another thousand, we'll go back to it.

—Elizabeth Hawes, 1937

Seeing nothing is as political an act as seeing something.

—Arundhati Roy

It is because being oppressed sometimes brings with it some slim bonuses that we are occasionally prepared to put up with it. The most efficient oppressor is the one who persuades his underlings to love, desire and identify with his power; and any practice of political emancipation thus involves that most difficult of all forms of liberation, freeing ourselves from ourselves. The other side of the story, however, is equally important. For if such dominion fails to yield its victims sufficient gratification over an extended period of time, then it is certain that they will finally revolt against it. If it is rational to settle for an ambiguous mixture of misery and marginal pleasure when the political alternatives appear perilous and obscure, it is equally rational to rebel when the miseries clearly outweigh the gratifications, and when it seems likely that there is more to be gained than to be lost by such action.

—Terry Eagleton

Introduction

Stories from Savar

Moushumi cannot sleep for the nightmares. Even during bright sunlit days she is haunted by memories. Young and pretty with a gold nose ring, Moushumi was two months into a job on the seventh floor, earning money to support her family. Now she sits at home, shoulders stooped and eyes haunted under the crease of a slight frown. Her small son stays close, not understanding why his mother no longer smiles. Four floors below Moushumi was Arisa, an experienced machinist in her early forties. She had migrated south from the city of Rangpur to ease her family's financial difficulties. Still in mourning for her death, her three children say they will never work in a garment factory. A woman named Rekha tells of her niece who was also killed – a bright young woman of 18 named Dulari who took a temporary job in garments to pay for an education so she could get an job in an office. Next to Rekha is six-year-old Shamim who will not let go of his father's trouser leg. After his mother Jaheda died in the collapse, his ten-year-old sister went to live with their grandmother in the village but Shamim is too distraught to leave his father's side for fear he will also be taken.

*　*　*

Situated in Savar, an industrial district on the outskirts of Dhaka, the Rana Plaza factory complex was an eight-storey building housing five garment factories. This overcrowded, poorly built complex became a symbol of global inequality when, on 24 April 2013, it collapsed in on itself – its straining internal pillars buckling and cracking under the weight of too many storeys, too many machines and bales of cloth, too many human beings packed in tight rows.

Considered the deadliest unintended structural failure of modern times, global trade unions called Rana Plaza a mass industrial homicide. An estimated 1,138 people were killed. Thousands more were trapped in the rubble – some of whom had to self-amputate their own limbs before they could be pulled free. For the world outside of Dhaka, when the TV screens lit up, the death of so many people and the brutal injury of thousands more exposed a truth: the world has been twisted to value objects more than human life and dignity.

As the wreckage was cleared away by day labourers with baskets of rubble on their heads, the catastrophe showed an industry out of control – where illegally constructed buildings crack under the weight of people and machinery while fashion brands make billions in profits. Where millions of impoverished women in the modern world work as machine operators and garment quality inspectors, pressing shirts and snipping loose threads six days a week while billionaires buy super-yachts.

Twenty-nine global brands were identified as having recent or current orders with at least one of the garment factories in the Rana Plaza building. These brands included Primark, Matalan, Benetton, Mango, C&A, Walmart, The Children's Place, and KiK.[1] Primark later admitted it had done two safety audits of Rana Plaza and given the building a clean bill of health. That the building was a death trap was common local knowledge. Major cracks had appeared the day before the collapse and workers did not want to go to work because of the danger. On that April morning workers argued with managers on the forecourt in front of the building, resisting the idea that they should even set foot inside. Their resistance led to arguments and finally to an ultimatum: go in and get to work or lose a month's pay. For a Bangladeshi garment worker, losing a month's pay represents hunger and eviction, it is a cruel impossibility. That moment on the forecourt should never be forgotten as it holds another eternal truth – the fashion industry places more value on the clothes it sells than on the lives of the people making them.

Rana Plaza is a catastrophe that belongs to those who died that day. To the mothers who never found the bodies of their daughters, the small children who spent the aftermath shadowing their remaining parent. The medics, rickshaw drivers, and students who rushed to help pull people from the rubble. The workers whose limbs were crushed and amputated, and those whose scars are not visible until you look into their eyes. Regardless of where you come from or who you are, however, there are two things everyone can understand and act upon: Rana Plaza was not an accident and the conditions that caused the death of at least 1,138 people are still with us today.

I wrote most of the first edition of this book in 2012 and completed it before the collapse took place. But even then, Bangladesh was the world's second-largest garment producer, churning out billions of pieces of clothing each year and attracting international brands with its super-low wages, lack of employment benefits, and poor health and safety. Prior to Rana Plaza there had already been a string of disasters in Bangladesh's garment industry, culminating in the Tazreen factory fire that killed 112 people six months earlier. Yet business continued as usual.

For campaigners and labour rights activists in Bangladesh, the horror of Rana Plaza had long been on the horizon. So, despite writing *Stitched Up* (my earlier book on which this book is based) before Rana Plaza collapsed, this book is, was, and will always be in one sense an attempt to answer the question – why did it collapse? This book looks at this question not just as one of building safety in Bangladesh, nor one of the problem of fast-fashion, nor one of single bad companies or evil billionaires. As much as this is a book about the fashion industry, this is also a book about capitalism: a vicious, unequal economic system whose depraved cruelty breeds violence and destruction. Fashion is so intertwined with capitalism that there would be no fashion industry without the capitalist exploitation of the Global South, of women, of migrant labour, of racist colonial trade practices. You cannot understand fashion until you comprehend capitalism.

Just as Rana Plaza was no accident, nor is it historical. It was supposed to be the watershed that changed the fashion industry forever and yet the attitude of fashion brands towards Rana Plaza is mirrored by their approach to the Covid-19 pandemic. In parallel with Rana Plaza we see the same truth in 2021, that clothes are more valued that human life. For all the fancy greenwashing brochures written by overpaid 'sustainability' executives, nothing has changed. Multinational corporations have responded to Covid-19 by bringing thousands of small factories to their knees with cancelled or withheld payments. Across the industry, in Guatemala, Honduras, India, Indonesia, Cambodia, and Myanmar, garment workers have sickened and died while stitching hoodies, leggings, jeans, T-shirts, and bras. Only last week, a question from a garment worker in India was relayed to me: 'Why do I have to die making clothes for foreigners?'

Eight years after Rana Plaza we still witness the expectation that risk, either in the global economy or on the factory floor, should be borne by the world's poorest people. As with Rana Plaza, those picked to be made so unbearably unsafe during Covid-19, those whose lives have been weighed and found to be worth less than profit, are overwhelmingly women in the poorest parts of the Global South. And as with Rana Plaza, they have faced the same ultimatum. Work in a death trap or starve. Before this crisis has even ended we are already bearing witness to the next planetary juggernaut of climate change which, if we do not act, will play out in the same fashion with billions of people across the Global South offered up as a human sacrifice. We must act collectively and act fast to reclaim our planet and categorically end this unequal, undignified, failure of a system once and for all.

* * *

There exists a conceptual impurity to the word 'fashion',[2] an impurity that some may accuse this book of contributing to. This book includes discussions of companies ranging from Chanel to Walmart, Louboutin to Tesco. I have not written separate books on 'high' fashion and 'high-street' fashion but have placed the two together. I have taken this approach for several reasons. First, there is a shrinking distinction between high fashion and high-street fashion. River Island, Topshop and Whistles have done shows at London Fashion Week. Similarly J.Crew has appeared at New York and Paris Fashion Week has seen H&M hold a show at the Musée Rodin.

Versace, Giambattista Valli, Stella McCartney, Lanvin, and Maison Martin Margiela have all done collections for H&M. Isaac Mizrahi, Marc Jacobs, Phillip Lim, and Prabal Gurung have designed for Target in the United States, and Jean Paul Gaultier and Karl Lagerfeld both spent time as creative directors for Coca-Cola. Famous couture houses rely more on sales of perfume and bath oils for their profits than $50,000 dresses.[3] Mass-produced sunglasses, 'It Bags', boxer shorts, cosmetics, designer T-shirts, and jeans with the word 'couture' printed on the label make up the majority of profits for the 'high fashion' industry. So why discuss only the pollution caused by high-street brands in China when It Bags are being made in the factory next door?[4] Why discuss only the issues of body image and race representation on the catwalks of Paris and Milan when the high street mimics the same exclusive aesthetics? Why pretend overconsumption is a problem only with regard to the cheapest brands?

Introduction

Fashion is a form of social production. All of the materials and skills that give rise to great works are socially produced. Just as the greatest pianist needs a socially produced piano to play on, so the most lauded designer needs socially produced pencils and paper, materials, a set of skills learned from teachers, and a history to both follow and rebel against, not to mention huge assistance in the form of design teams, administrators, financiers, and, often, domestic staff.[5] Numerous copyright lawsuits against brands like Zara show just how much inspiration the high street takes from high fashion. Yet high fashion houses also rely on the high street to popularise their ideas and their brand (as well as continually doing their own thieving).[6] Ignoring social production leads to the mystification of fashion. The point of this book is to unpick and demystify the fashion industry and its ideology not add to its carefully cultivated mystique. Therefore, 'high fashion' gets no special pedestal. Instead, this book uses a simple, workable definition of fashion: 'changing styles of dress and appearance adopted by groups of people'.[7] This is an immediately controversial position, one that some accuse of being Procrustean[8] (after the legend of Procrustes who chopped people's legs off to make them into an arbitrary size). Fashion, it is claimed, is purely a European concept indistinguishable from capitalism, with Burgundy in the 1400s named as the 'cradle of fashion'.[9] While I do not dispute this analysis of the origins of fashion, I do take issue with the way this definition has allowed 'fashion' to be historically guarded for a demographic that is rich and white. There is a prevalent myth that those outside this demographic do not 'do fashion'. That what Paris/Milan/London/New York produce is fashion but what everyone else produces is just clothing or apparel. Everybody else – the vast majority of the world – has been relegated to being 'people without fashion', which translates to 'people without history'.[10] Julius Nyerere, the first president of Tanzania, stated: 'Of the crimes of colonialism there is none worse than the attempt to make us believe we had no indigenous culture of our own; or that what we did have was worthless.' This racist approach allows for the dehumanisation, and therefore guiltless exploitation, of the Global South. As the Marxist art critic John Berger has written: 'The last need of imperialism is not for raw materials, exploited labour and controlled markets, it is for a mankind that counts for nothing.'[11]

'Global South' is a relatively recent term replacing the terms 'the Third World' or 'undeveloped countries'. It is a political term interlinked with globalisation and its problems. Anthropologist Thomas Hylland Eriksen says the term has come to represent countries that are 'subject to the forces of global neoliberalism' rather than the countries that impose it upon others. If a country benefits from the globalised neoliberal capitalist economy it is Global North, but if it suffers under this system it is Global South. But of course, inequality is not defined by borders – India has its billionaires and powerful elites, while Britain has its food banks, so 'Global South' should be taken more as a concept than a set of lines on a map.[12]

Defining fashion as 'Western' also looks woefully out of date with regard to design and production as it is today. Countries as diverse as China, Colombia, India, and Nigeria have vibrant industries, while neoliberalism and austerity have downgraded European wages to the point where corporations are scrabbling for the attention of Chinese consumers who are now the third-largest market for luxury goods and are predicted to overtake everyone else in the next few years.[13] For all of these reasons I have chosen a definition that is deliberately open and inclusive, material not ethereal, and which does not mystify the fashion industry.

The reality is far from mystical. The first time I came face to face with the reality of clothing production was in 2008, on

a research trip to Dharavi, Mumbai's infamous and impoverished city-within-a-city neighbourhood which houses over a
million people. We walked through overhung alleyways lined
with workshops filled with child workers losing their eyesight
as they stitched clothes. A lot of the workshops were live–work
units with rooms housing entire families perched on top. We
climbed a rickety ladder to speak to a line of children working
at a loom. Other children sat on the hard wooden planks of
the floor sewing beads onto luxury shawls. 'Small fingers for
difficult little beads', our guide said shaking his head sadly.[14]

Later, turning a corner, the smell of goat skins hung up to
dry in the searing sun hit the back of my throat and made me
gag – to the amusement of the tannery workers. Skins dripped
onto the dusty floor as around the courtyard people in workshops sewed bags and wove strips of leather into belts and
jewellery.

'Do you make things for international clients?' I asked one
of the workshop owners.

'Yes, of course', he laughed and pointed at me. 'For you.'

He was pointing at my belt, bought the evening before.
Woven leather sprayed blue and gold by people I now knew
worked without protective equipment or masks.

Since then, I have researched and visited textile, clothing,
and footwear production sites around the world, from Bangladesh and Macedonia to the Topshop warehouses in Solihull.
I have interviewed garment union leaders in Myanmar who
have served jail time for protesting, met with survivors of
factory fires as well as criminalised labour rights organisers,
and exposed multinational supply chains and human rights
abuses in fashion. I've watched the landscape become more
authoritarian and dangerous, watched the CEOs turn into
human dragons hoarding mountains of gold, and watched the
planet tremble at the point of no return.

This book, therefore, will not mystify the fashion industry because, above all, *The Anti-Capitalist Book of Fashion* takes the position that while items from the fashion industry can be viewed as signs of the times or products of social consciousness, they should also be seen as products of industry. A dress is not just a structure of meaning, it is also a commodity produced by a corporation and sold on the market for a profit at huge environmental cost. The designer is a worker whose work exists to enrich their company and earn them a wage – no matter how extravagant.[15] Paris Fashion Week is just an expensive sales pitch.[16] By analysing the fashion industry as an industry, *The Anti-Capitalist Book of Fashion* aims to keep the discussion of fashion firmly in the material world and to recognise that there is nothing academic about the struggles of those women and men seeking to free themselves from exploitation and oppression.

* * *

Early on, when I first started critiquing the fashion industry I was abruptly asked what right I had to write about an industry I had not worked in (other than the inevitable stints on various shop floors). My reply was that I *had* to write this book, that no one had adequately explained this omnipresent element of my life, that there was no single book on fashion that dealt with everything I wanted an end to: the terrible working conditions, the environmental destruction, the eating disorders I have watched friends fight, the racism that fashion promotes, the self-loathing and the black hole of wanting that exists and cannot be filled no matter how much you buy. I also reject the idea that only people who work in the upper echelons of the fashion industry should write about it. Fashion corporations purposefully work to have an effect on all of us – their ideas must be answered and, where necessary, rejected. The obligation to endure gives us the right to know,[17] but it also gives us the right – and the urgent need – to protest. Not working in fashion has blessed me with the freedom to write without worrying about future job prospects – a serious issue in an industry so devoid of criticism. As the photographer Nick Knight said: 'An art medium without a critical forum is not a healthy art medium.'[18]

After ten years of writing about fashion, I am more convinced than ever of the need for independent, critical, left-wing thought and action. I have not, however, written or rewritten this book simply in order to criticise. Writing *The Anti-Capitalist Book of Fashion* was possible only because I believe fashion truly is glorious and enthralling, as well as exasperating and terrible. The fashion industry's creations are inspiring and breathtaking. It is an incredibly skilled and demanding artform: 'In a society that expects from its authors and playwrights one or two great works in a lifetime, we take it in our stride when a designer does a magnificent collection each season.'[19] For every critical word in this book there exists a beautifully handcrafted item that captures the spirit of its time. But who made these clothes and why did they not get to wear them?

History is taught as if the only people that existed or mattered were monarchs and generals. Even now, in this deeply unequal world, it is drilled into us that it is 'royal' families, CEOs, and celebrities who are the wealth creators and that we cannot do without them. Within the fashion industry we see this as the outdated myth that beauty and design creativity is the preserve of a tiny clique. A good challenge to this is Bertolt Brecht's poem 'A Worker Reads History', which begins:

Who built the seven gates of Thebes?
The books are filled with names of kings.
Was it the kings who hauled the craggy blocks of stone?[20]

This poem is a reminder that all production is innately social, that the source of all wealth and beauty is human work and the biosphere, and that unknown craftspeople are more worthy of remembrance and respect than any celebrity. It is also an important reminder that we really don't need CEOs and monarchs – we already have all the knowledge, power, and resources we need to rebuild a society that is equitable and sustainable and that provides for all. Currently, however, the dreams and escape proffered in fashion are available only to the few, not the many. We suffer from 'possessive compulsive disorder'[21] rather than enjoyment, and fashion is, like the rest of art, tangled in a web of commerce and competition. Because I find fashion glorious as well as terrible, I write in the hope that it will one day be free from commerce and be experienced by everyone at unimaginable heights of creativity.

Finally, I write about fashion from an anti-capitalist perspective because for me there is no way of separating the issues in this book. There is no way to write about fashion's environmental impact without writing about the factories' impact on the people that staff them. Discussing the treatment of people necessitates an examination of racism and body issues, which also necessitates discussion of both alienation and consumption and the impact of the monopolised ownership of the industry and the media brands that support it. To divide up these issues would be an artificial act, which would ignore the overarching role of capitalism. As the feminist academic Audre Lorde said: 'There is no such thing as a single-issue struggle because we do not live single-issue lives.'[22]

* * *

Populations of exploited workers like those found in Savar, Bangladesh are replicated the world over, and this is a historically recent phenomenon created by colonialism and neoliberalism. Neoliberalism refers to an economic model championed by Margaret Thatcher and Ronald Reagan in the 1980s and Bill Clinton and Tony Blair in the 1990s. It emphasises the liberalisation of trade, the global integration of markets, the deregulation of state power, and the privatisation of public services, all of which are portrayed as inevitable, like gravity.[23] Neoliberalism drives down wages and pits workers in different countries and companies against each other in the so-called race to the bottom. To fill the spending gaps produced by falling wages, neoliberalism pushes personal credit – an issue particularly pertinent to fashion.

Neoliberalism has gone hand in hand with globalisation. 'Globalisation' appeared as a buzzword in 1983 to describe one of the most rapid yet precarious social and economic transformations in human history. It is a useful term to signpost a process of rapid industrial conquest prompted by technology from the internet modem to the oil refinery and the jet plane. As a result of this imbalanced system, we live in a global society where malnutrition contributes to 3.1 million under-five child deaths annually, yet in 2019, €281 billion was spent on luxury goods.[24]

The financial crisis that began in 2008 was the result of neoliberal strategies privileging deregulated financial services over manufacturing in Europe and the United States. This strategy saw the creation of a real estate bubble built on sub-prime mortgages. The bursting of this bubble brought bank bailouts – a forced transfer of wealth from the poor to the rich – on a scale never been seen before.

The disarray and uncertainty resulting from neoliberalism, financial crises, racism, and now the Covid-19 pandemic has led many people to look for answers elsewhere. Anti-capitalism as a movement most notably made headlines in 1999 when protesters in Seattle disrupted a World Trade Organization summit. This was followed by mass demonstrations in Genoa in 2001, World Social Forums in Brazil and India, gigantic anti-war campaigns, social movements across Latin America, Occupy Wall Street, and the Arab and African Uprisings of 2011 which were largely revolts against neoliberal conditions. More recently, Black Lives Matter and a burgeoning environmental movement have captured the global spirit of anti-capitalism, along with a resurgence in feminist protest, prison abolition, and animal rights activism. Anti-capitalism as a movement is vibrant and dynamic but not always cohesive.

The lack of a single anti-capitalist manifesto does not negate the need to work towards an alternative to capitalism. In *The Anti-Capitalist Book of Fashion*, anti-capitalist means the rejection of the capitalist system as a whole because it is the systemic cause of sweatshops, child labour, environmental devastation, and alienation. The problem is not simply one of bad companies or bad people at the top of society (though these exist) but of a bad system that produces destructive imperatives. Recurring crisis has shone a spotlight on the work of anti-capitalism's seminal thinker: Karl Marx. His work, and the work of those he influenced, plays a primary role in each of the chapters in this book.

But what does Karl Marx have to do with Karl Lagerfeld? What do neoliberalism or economic crisis have to do with the fashion industry? They are inextricably linked to the point that one cannot be understood without the other. Despite fashion being 'capitalism's favourite child',[25] the industry gets hit hard by crisis. In the economic crisis of 2008, ten million Chinese workers lost their jobs, and the shock waves were felt from the top to the bottom of the industry. The precarious nature of the fashion market led one fashion CEO to state: 'I feel like I'm having a black tie dinner on top of a volcano.'[26] Similarly, the Covid-19 pandemic shuttered shops and led to the obliteration of well-known brands while causing the luxury goods market to contract by 23 per cent.[27] More importantly, however, the industry's irresponsible reaction to the pandemic caused widespread suffering, hunger, and financial ruin for millions of garment workers. The fashion industry lays out in sharp relief all the ins and outs of capitalism – the drive for profit and its resulting exploitation, the power that comes from owning society's means of production, and the very real need to overhaul the unstable system we are currently living in.

Despite being unstable and unfair, capitalism is protected because it is often 'too close to the eyeball to be objectified'.[28] Like the traditional saying 'the fish do not talk about the water',[29] few people up until the financial crisis of 2008 ever talked about capitalism as a system. Instead, life just seemed like life, not life under capitalism. *The Anti-Capitalist Book of Fashion* is not an attempt to write a definitive book of fashion but an attempt to make capitalism visible by discussing its very real impact on the fashion industry and by showing how the very concept of fashion is part of the social process of capitalism. Along the way, some fundamental characteristics of capitalism are illuminated and explored.

Ideology

Trying to make sense of the world we live in means looking at the world around us. What people see when they look is not implicit; rather, it can be determined through the use of ideology: the ideas, values, and feelings that determine how people experience their societies at different times – how they see the very world around them.[30]

Take, for example, the coronation dress worn by Queen Victoria in 1837. Is this dress the symbol of the divine right of one family to rule all others; the legitimately accumulated wealth of a civilising empire and of a national, racial, and class hierarchy that brought order and allowed trade and exquisite fashion design to flourish? Or does this dress represent the tens of millions who died in famines across India in the late Victorian holocausts that created the inequality between the Global North and Global South?[31] Does it represent impoverished seamstresses going blind as they stitch by candlelight and mercantile capitalism siphoning off wealth to wrap racist, unelected, inbred figureheads in organza, pearls, and gold thread? Controlling which of these viewpoints is the accepted one is a powerful thing. Throughout history, it has allowed small groups to defend their property and their power without daily resort to armed suppression.[32] The essence of ideology is its ability to legitimate the power of the social class that is in charge.[33] Imagine for a moment how it feels to walk around the National Gallery, surrounded by giant paintings of monarchs and aristocracy. From the oil paint to the gilt frames and surrounding building, everything exudes authority, all pointing towards the divine right of the rich to rule as if it were 'inevitable'. This authority is also exuded by the fashion industry.

Fashion is a solid gold picture frame for its wearer. It also requires its own solid gold frame because, after all, we are talking here only about bits of cloth, no matter how artfully sewn. It is everything that *goes around* clothes that makes them fashion. Catwalks, media prestige and hype, and elaborate shops combine to produce a false religiosity.[34] The National Gallery feeling occurs in fashion museums and branches of Louis Vuitton or Chanel, where the buildings and clothes ooze with a sense of righteous power: no one but Chanel could produce such wonders, so Chanel *belongs* at the top. The role of ideology is to ensure that this power structure either feels natural or is simply not felt at all.[35]

Fashion is key to ideology. It so legitimates power that the mere fact of switching clothes can bestow a person with ruling-class prestige. Think, for example, of what occurs when poor clothes are swapped for rich ones in the films *The Prince and the Pauper*, *Aladdin*, *Pretty Woman*, *Maid in Manhattan*, *A*

Knight's Tale, *The Count of Monte Cristo*, *Cinderella*, or Ridley Scott's *Robin Hood*. Suddenly the protagonist is imbued with all the privileges of the ruling class. They have not changed, only their clothes have changed, causing Russell Crowe as Robin Hood to declare that 'there is no difference between a knight and any other man except what he wears'. The role of clothes is made clear in these films: they legitimate power and cement the idea that those in charge of society are *supposed* to be in charge. Does class make fashion? Certainly, it is a key way for the rich to signal and reproduce their power.[36] Once the masses gain access to a certain fashion (or close approximation of it) the ruling classes move on, leaving everyone else behind. As an art form, fashion plays a complicated role within ideology. Fashion can be both oppressive and emancipating, glorious and terrible, revolutionary and reactionary at the same time. It is inherently contradictory, as is all culture and indeed all social reality.[37] Dominant culture's ability to smooth over, and hide, the vast contradictions contained in this book is a key reason why people are not in continual revolt. Therefore, while fashion can be inspiring and prompt us to dream of a brighter future, it can also be deeply oppressive. If fashion resists power, it is also a compelling form of it.[38] Fashion is capable of summing up any given epoch, of bringing together time, society, and art. Art is therefore held within ideology at the same time as maintaining a distance from it. This means that art is one medium whereby the ideology that gives birth to art can be perceived.[39] In short, art does not simply reflect ideology. The experience of art – including fashion – gives you the experience of the situation it represents. This does not mean that fashion provides a literal interpretation of a given period. The playwright Bertolt Brecht described art as reflecting life with special mirrors, when it reflects it at all. Fashion distorts what it reflects, and often what is not shown tells us as much as what is.[40] If we can understand ideologies, we can understand both the past and the present more deeply – an understanding that is needed to achieve liberation.[41]

What Is Fashion For?

As you read this book, I invite you to keep in mind two central questions. The first is: *What kind of a society do you want to live in?* Does it look as it looks now, with some people starving while others hoard more money than can be spent in 1,000 lifetimes? Is the planet displaying signs of deep distress with wild fires, typhoons, and floods wreaking havoc? Have entire species gone extinct? Are the forests being raised to the ground? Is life hampered by prejudices like racism and homophobia? Is access to medicine, housing, education, leisure, and opportunity based upon access to wealth? Are the worst people in charge?

If this is not your ideal society, how would you change it for the better? Maybe it is a little different, with access to free healthcare and education assured. Maybe it is a radically different place where there is no such thing as a millionaire, let alone a billionaire; where people work only as much as their community needs and spend the rest of their time painting, gardening, writing, making music, and travelling the world on wind ships; where the means of production – from solar factories to hemp farms – are all collectively owned and everything is carefully organised to run in harmony with the biosphere; where there are no arms, meat, or fossil fuel industries and no prison industrial complex; and where racism, colonialism, sexism, homophobia, transphobia, ablism, and so on have been fought and banished. Where literature, art, music, and theatre has never been so widespread nor so magical.

How your ideal society would look is up to you. You are free to imagine. Once you have an answer, the second question is: *In this society, what is fashion for?* Is it for fun or to protect and enhance the body? Is it to act as a creative outlet, to represent culture and history, to seduce or repel, to showcase and celebrate difference, to express moods or the phases of the moon, to bring joy?

The point of this thought exercise is to reframe typical questions that are asked about fashion and to see it as a performance of deeper social issues.[42] The fashion industry looks as it does because of capitalism; what fashion is currently for is to make billions for a small cabal of people, to keep in place a system of subjugation, to restrict and control populations, and to distract from inequality and crisis. Fashion has been broken by capitalism and now exists as an excuse for the rich to exploit the poor. No matter the make-up of the ideal society you have dreamed up, I doubt you had this in mind as the purpose of clothing. We have, therefore, a great deal of work to do.

* * *

The Anti-Capitalist Book of Fashion unfolds as follows. Chapter 1 examines the monopolised ownership of fashion brands. It takes a historical look at the advent of fashion for the masses and examines the gargantuan sums of money being made. Chapter 2 explores the monopolised nature of the fashion media, both print and digital, and opens up the world of surveillance capitalism and social media.

Chapter 3 discusses the idea that the consumer is king and that the ills of the fashion industry are the fault of consumers. It puts into context the role of consumers by examining questions of class, debt and credit, advertising, alienation, and commodity fetishism. Chapter 4 is the flip side to this question – an investigation into fashion production and the violence, sexism, and racism that makes the factory system tick. It examines historical and present-day industrial struggles for change and critiques pro-sweatshop arguments by revealing who really benefits from exploitation. The fashion industry's ill-treatment of people is linked irrevocably to its ill-treatment of the planet. Chapter 5 explains why environmental destruction is inseparable from capitalism and colonialism and explores how we actively get out of this trap.

Chapter 6 looks at the links between the fashion industry and body image, eating disorders and women's rights. It shows the impact of fashion on women employed by the industry as models and on the general public. It explores why such a narrow version of beauty is propagated and how the use of digital enhancement makes reality unpalatable. Chapter 7 answers the question: Is fashion racist? It looks at the representation of people of colour in the industry, critiques the habit of cultural appropriation, and discusses why such racism exists and what its particular characteristics are during this time of neoliberalism and economic crisis. Chapters 8–10 examine attempts to change the fashion system. Chapter 8 looks at resisting the fashion industry. What happens when people use their clothing and appearance to defy fashion? Can fashion be reversed or refused? If you dress differently, does this count as rebellion? Is it possible to shock an industry that loves to shock? And is it possible to avoid co-option? Chapter 9 looks at both historical and present-day attempts to reform the fashion industry. Why do green fashion books suggest an ethical calculus to solve ethical dilemmas? Can corporations ever be green? Are trade unions or legislation the answer? And is there such a thing as just capitalism? Finally, Chapter 10 explores how we might dress in an ideal society. Who would design and make clothes? What would the world of fashion look like without class, race, or gender? Would it even exist?

I agree with the activist economist Michael Albert who wrote: 'Our negative or critical messages don't generate anger and action but only pile up more evidence that the enemy is beyond reach.'[43] While it is vital to expose the machinations of the fashion industry, I hope I have avoided the trap that Albert notes by writing about struggles that are seeking to change the fashion industry for the better. In addition, the last three chapters culminate in ideas for a brighter future. To combat hopelessness, I would like to reiterate that the fashion industry must be seen as part of capitalism. Capitalism is not a natural state of affairs; it is an economic system with a history, and what can be born can also die.[44] As Ursula Le Guin said: 'We live in capitalism, its power seems inescapable – but then, so did the divine right of kings. Any human power can be resisted and changed by human beings.'[45] I hope that *The Anti-Capitalist Book of Fashion* will bring capitalism into focus again instead of it being too close to the eyeball to be seen. My aim is to unpick one thread of the capitalist system and reveal what lies behind the clothes we wear. Hopefully, by the end of it, you will want to pull on the thread until the whole system unravels and we can restitch it into something new and beautiful.

CHAPTER ONE

Owning It

Linkenholt is a Hampshire village of meandering lanes lined by banks of daisies. Turkeys strut on manicured lawns and the village shop is run from the front room of a house. A bus only comes to the village if it is booked. The blacksmith can work for days without seeing another person and the story is still told of two sisters, now in their eighties, who cycled down the hill to a village dance where they met the two brothers who became their husbands.

In 2009, Linkenholt and its surrounding 2,000 acres were put up for sale. It was an unusual event that drew international attention – entire English villages do not often come on the market. The financial crisis cut Linkenholt's price tag to £25 million – far less than its actual worth. The sale passed the destiny of the land and the people who live and work on it into the hands of one man. The villagers met their new 'squire' the day after the sale was completed. He held a pit roast, shook hands with everyone, and, by all accounts, gave a good impression of himself. He has not, however, been seen there since and neither lives nearby nor drops in to shoot pheasant on the estate. The nearest clue to the wealth of this distant figure lies eleven miles away in Newbury – a large, glass-fronted shop with a red sign that sells leggings, cheap jeans, sweatshirts, and sequinned dresses. The shop is always busy. So are the other 4,371 branches of this chain that encircle the planet.

Stefan Persson inherited H&M from his father. The budget clothing chain has made him the richest person in Sweden, even after he stepped down as chairperson in May 2020 after 22 years in the role. Forbes.com has a 'Real Time Billionaires' calculator. Refreshing itself every five minutes, it calculates which of the world's billionaires have just become even richer, based on the cost of a single share. It makes for compulsive viewing and, the last time I checked in 2021, Persson's fortune stood at $22.5 billion. No one I met in Linkenholt shopped at H&M. They were, however, all aware that they paid rent

23

to one of the world's richest people and wryly acknowledged that he had probably bought Linkenholt with the 'change from his back pocket'. That is not to say that anyone spoke badly of him – the village narrative was one of gratitude that Persson had, so far, preserved Linkenholt's way of life.

There is a tension in Persson's ownership of Linkenholt – the romanticised preservation of English village life by a man made as rich as Croesus from selling disposable fashion. H&M clothes are made in factories from Tunisia to China. They are mass-produced, using valuable water and crop resources and cause appalling pollution. In January 2021, a 21-year-old garment worker named Jeyasri Kathiravel disappeared and was later discovered to have been raped and murdered by her supervisor at H&M supplier factory Natchi Apparels, owned by the fourth largest clothing exporter in India. In the aftermath of the murder, 25 more women came forward to state that sexual violence and harassment were widespread at the factory.[1]

It seems that nothing could link the peaceful lanes of Linkenholt with this globalised violence, but it does. Both are part of a business plan, devised within a capitalist system that allows vast resources to be concentrated in the hands of one person. This concentration of wealth and power recurs throughout the fashion world. The creativity and beauty of fashion is time and again channelled into the pockets of billionaire shareholders. But just how did selling T-shirts and hair clips make so many Forbes top-20 billionaires?

The New Mrs Jones

Mass-market fashion is a new concept. While clothes have long been the playthings of the rich, the working classes lived for centuries with only the bare minimum on their backs. In 1844, Friedrich Engels, co-author of *The Communist Mani-*

festo, observed at first hand the poverty in Britain's slums: 'the prevailing clothing consists of perfect rags often beyond all mending, or so patched that the original colour can no longer be detected. They wear ... a suit of tatters.'[2] The Industrial Revolution introduced the factory production of materials such as cotton. Yet clothes continued to be made in unsanitary cottage industry workshops, characterised by very low wages and unsafe working conditions which resulted in high accident and death rates. By 1900 the clothing industry in Britain employed 1.25 million people and was the second-largest employer of women and the fifth-largest employer of men.[3]

A pioneer of moving clothing production from home workshops to large, purpose-built factories was Meshe David Osinsky, a 'not quite penniless' Russian Jew who emigrated to Leeds in 1900 to escape the anti-Semitism of Tsarist Russia. Starting out as a door-to-door pedlar of shoe laces, Meshe David Osinsky became Montague Burton, owner of a shop selling ready-to-wear men's suits for a just about affordable 11s. 9d. By 1909, Burton had four shops and owned a factory – Progress Mill in Leeds.

Five years later, at the outbreak of the First World War, Burton owned 14 shops. Men's clothing production had been geared towards the mass production of limited styles and colours, which amounted to uniforms for working-class men.[4] This converged with the need for actual uniforms when 5.5 million men were called up to fight.

Women were also put in uniform for the war effort and the women's branch of the Board of Agriculture sold cheap clothes such as dungarees to women agricultural workers. In 1918, four million demobilised troops were given either a 'demob' suit or a small clothing allowance. As a result, by 1925 Burton owned the largest clothing factory in Europe. In the 1920s, working-class women could save up and buy ready-made clothes from chain stores, but most made their dresses from cheap materials using Paris-inspired patterns found in magazines like *Mabs Fashions*.

The Great Depression of the 1930s saw two million people out of work. The poor of Britain survived without coats and with holes in their shoes. Having just one set of clothing was commonplace. 'How amazing', wrote the journalist H. V. Morton in 1933, 'that in an age of electricity, of chromium, of trans-Atlantic flight and worldwide radio, the poor were still living like Saxon peasants.'[5] At the same time, Hollywood was in its influential Golden Age and the resulting fashions caused J. B. Priestley to tut that among the better-off urban populations there were 'factory girls looking like actresses'.[6]

By 1939, Montague Burton owned 595 shops, including five on Oxford Street.[7] The Second World War demanded more uniforms, but like a 'giant tapeworm'[8] it also brought rationing, sent factory workers off to fight on the front line, and reduced clothing consumption. The clothing trade was given a wartime boost (and Burton's was saved) by the government's Utility scheme between 1941 and 1952.

A drop in living standards and news of the 1917 Russian Revolution had caused a wave of agitation and dissent. Fear of an uprising was intensified by the Second World War. As Britain's allies fell one by one to the German army, the need to inspire people to fight for their country meant they had to be given a stake in society – in the Tory politician Quintin Hogg's words: 'We must give them reforms or they will give us revolution.' The government, led by Neville Chamberlain, hoped the Utility scheme's provision of good-quality, cheap clothing would keep up morale. The reluctant Chamberlain, a believer in leaving markets to themselves, set out to control raw materials. By May 1940, the government was the sole importer of nearly 90 per cent of all raw materials, including wool.[9]

Measures included the introduction of minimum production standards but also limited material use by restricting skirt lengths, sleeve widths, trouser turn-ups, and the use of elastic.[10] The Board of Trade insisted it was not looking to become a 'fashion dictator' but only wanted to ensure that the best possible use was made of supplies.[11] *British Vogue* approved and called Utility a mode of dressing 'well suited to these times'.[12]

In war-torn countries women were once again employed as munitions workers, bus conductors, front-line medical staff, and labourers. They wore trousers and jumpers and tied their hair up in scarves. At the Californian Radio Plane Company, David Conover, a photo-journalist, met a worker named Norma Jean Baker. The resulting photographs for *Yank Magazine* were Marilyn Monroe's first step towards stardom.

The war ended in 1945, but the hard times and rationing rumbled on. Central planning of cloth production ended, but price and quality controls continued. Utility clothing led commentators to write that the workers looked well dressed.[13] One writer declared that 'for the first time in history fashion (such as it was) derived from the proletariat, not from the privileged'.[14]

This was a big change. Paris had traditionally been the fashion centre of the world. Styles started there and then trickled down. The war had caused the loss of this sartorial guidance.[15] When the Nazis occupied France, their plan was to move the entire Parisian fashion industry to Berlin or Vienna. Although they decided against this, they did almost completely destroy the ready-to-wear sector, which had been a largely Jewish industry. The loss of French exports had given manufactures in New York a window to establish themselves as an alternative centre for fashion creation. For much of the fashion industry, the war's levelling of both the creation and wearing of fashion was disastrous. Where was the money in fashions that could not quickly be made unfashionable? How were the rich to be superior if egalitarianism eclipsed exclusivity?

The economic importance of the Paris fashion industry was summed up by Jean-Baptiste Colbert, an advisor to Louis XIV, who said: 'Fashion is to Paris what the gold mines of Peru are to Spain.' Determined to keep their gold mine open, in 1945 the Chambre Syndicale de la Couture Parisienne organised a tour of the latest Paris-designed fashions through Copenhagen, Barcelona, London, and New York entitled Le Théâtre de la Mode. To avoid causing offence to war-ravaged cities by showing off the luxurious designs, they were sold as a form of resistance – beautiful clothes made 'with frozen fingers in their famished city'.[16]

The endeavours of Paris to regain its dominance were embodied by a man who had spent the war designing clothes for the wives of Nazi officers and French collaborators – Christian Dior.[17] He now turned his talent towards reinserting rigid hierarchies into fashion. In February 1947, Dior presented a collection which the media dubbed the 'New Look'. In Dior's words: 'We were emerging from a period of war, of uniforms, of women soldiers built like boxers. I drew women-flowers, soft shoulders, flowering busts, fine waists like liana and wide skirts like corolla.'[18] Essentially, the New Look replaced ease of movement and physical strength with an ultra-conservative vision of femininity complete with corsets. The look matched the political agenda of returning women to home and hearth, the style's forward thrust of the hips a sign that women were designed for child-bearing.[19] As 1.25 million women left industry,[20] the message was clear: women no longer needed workwear.

Dozens of books and articles have been written on how this was what women wanted and how ultimately the women of the world *chose* to adopt the New Look.[21] But to claim this is to ignore both the political climate of the era and the role of the powerful fashion system. In the tradition of fashion promotion, the styles received heavy coverage through a sophisticated network of media, including magazines like *Vogue* and *Harper's Bazaar*, *Mademoiselle*, *Seventeen*, and *Women's Wear Daily*. The New Look had its own newspaper advertisements, publicists sent free clothes to influential women to wear and be photographed in, and department stores and shops promoted the style to encourage women to buy entire new wardrobes.

Dior and the New Look were funded by France's richest and most influential industrialist, Marcel Boussac. Known as the 'King of Cotton', Boussac backed Dior with an unprecedented 60 million French francs. It is no coincidence that the skirts of the New Look required 16 yards of fabric, a huge amount compared to the resourceful styles of the early 1940s. Boussac was determined that the fabric-heavy skirts of Dior's New Look would revitalise not just the Paris fashion industry but also the textile market.[22]

After a decade of death and deprivation, the desire to go from Cinders to Cinderella was real.[23] Among people without food, jobs, or housing, however, the New Look was not popular. '40,000 francs for a dress, and our children have no milk', was one shout that went up when Dior's creations made their debut in French shops.[24] It was not just that the style depended on reams of luxurious, expensive fabrics; there was also an emphasis on ornate accessories and jewellery which aimed at marking out the haves from the have-nots. There were organised protests against the style across North America, and in Britain the Labour government was asked to legislate against the long, wasteful skirts. 'I don't know whether to try to scrounge a lot of [clothing] coupons and sell off my clothes or just appear dowdy', wrote one working-class woman in 1947.[25]

In Britain, the New Look and Utility clothing coexisted for several years, with the Paris style pared down to fit rationing requirements. After the war, British retailers and manufactures lobbied for the abolition of the Utility scheme, while trade unions campaigned for its retention. This difference of opinion over the provision of cheap, good-quality clothing showed the disintegration of the wartime alliance between government, capital, and labour. With the war over, society was once again polarising.[26] Crudely put, Utility versus the New Look represented a political crossroads: For whose benefit should society be run? It is a return to our thought experiment, which asks what is fashion for: to clothe society in well-made, well-designed durable apparel or to make profits for businesses?

In 1937, George Orwell had written of the mass production of clothing toning down the surface differences between classes.[27] But while rationing had reduced the worst ravages of poverty, the New Look reversed this trend and put working-class women back at the bottom of the fashion pile. As the New Look took over, sartorial post-war class lines were firmly redrawn. Big business and the rich benefited while women and working people lost out.

By the 1950s, Britain's Apparel and Fashion Industry Association was monitoring an industry transformed. Planned mass production worked at maximum speed using minimum labour; it was scientific, mechanised, and employed trained managers and technicians.[28] The capability now existed to mass-produce fashion not just for men but also for women. All that was needed was for women to have the money to shop and the possibilities would be endless.

The post-war capitalist boom, which lasted from 1948 to 1970, was the result of continuing Cold War arms expenditure and consensus among governments that the state must play a firm economic role in industry and social welfare.[29] As the unemployment rate fell to 3 per cent in the United States and 1.5 per cent in Britain, women were drawn back into work.[30] The number of married working women rose dramatically and overtook the number of working single women. This figure rose steadily until, by the 1980s, more than half of married women were in paid work.[31]

From the start of the twentieth century, Britain saw the advent of an independent 'teenage culture'. In the 1950s this had developed into distinct youth cultures in Britain and the United States but not in France. As a result, the 1960s 'Youth Quake' (a term coined by *Vogue*'s editor, Diana Vreeland) saw the centre of fashion gravity shift temporarily from Paris to London. Brigitte Bardot told Chanel that couture was 'for grannies'[32] and the mini-skirt arrived. Although the 'Swinging Sixties' challenged the old guard, the infamous decade did not bring about fashion democracy. Rather than becoming egalitarian, fashion changed its currency. Previously the *grandes dames* with their money and social standing had been the focus of the fashion industry, now it was the turn of the mass youth.[33]

It was a case of fashion following the wealth line. This was the opinion of the influential fashion commentator Tobé Coller Davis. She pointed out that in 1929 the top 1 per cent of families in the United States had controlled 20 per cent of the country's wealth, but by 1953 this had dropped to fewer than 8 per cent.[34] Other senior figures in American department stores took the same view: 'I'd rather sell 5,000 units of something for $10 than one thing for $500', stated a buyer who left the high-end store Saks Fifth Avenue to work at the more down-market Sears. Stanley Marcus, owner of the Neiman Marcus department store, summed up the shift: 'We are geared to sell to the oilman, but even more, to the oilman's secretary.'[35]

The realisation that there was money to be made by selling clothes to more than just the top income bracket changed the industry's game plan. Manufacturing had been transformed, people had more disposable income than ever before, and women were working in unprecedented numbers. Coller Davis called this challenge the New Mrs Jones: 'a flock numbering over 30 million women; she doesn't command one income of, say, $4,000, but a Niagara of incomes of nearly one hundred billion dollars. If ever there were was a market, this is it.'[36]

Owning the Mass Market

In 1966, Paco Rabanne designed a paper dress as a publicity stunt for the Scott Paper Company. In a prophetic statement, Rabanne said: 'It's very cheap and the woman will only wear it once or twice. For me it's the future of fashion.'[37] Fifty-five years later the fashion market has accelerated into high-pressured, mass-produced overproduction driven by aggressive cost cutting. Replacing the traditional model of season-based collections, Zara brings out 24 new clothing collections each year while H&M offers 12 to 16 but refreshes them every single week.[38]

High-end fashion brands have also pushed the end of traditional seasonal collections with Burberry spearheading a 'see now, buy now' model that allowed shopping straight from the catwalk. Challenging both of these models is the ultra-fast 'slash fashion' method of digital fashion brands, typified by brands like Boohoo, SHEIN, Pretty Little Thing, and Fashion Nova. In February 2020, *Vice* found that Boohoo uploaded 772 garment options to its website over the course of a single week – a daily average of 116 individual garments.[39] The explosion of online fashion has also seen the rise of resale sites like Depop (owned by Etsy), eBay, and Vinted. One thing has remained the same however: large international corporations owning clusters of brands and operating them internationally.

In December 2020, as millions of garment workers lost their jobs and went hungry, the total wealth of billionaires worldwide reached $11.95 trillion. The ten richest of these billionaires had seen their fortunes rise by $540 billion since the start of the pandemic. Oxfam reported that one billion-aire in particular now had so much money that he could have given each of his 876,000 employers a bonus of $105,000 and still have been just as rich as he was before the pandemic.[40] This man is Jeff Bezos, founder of Amazon, and undisputed warlord of online shopping. It has been estimated that Amazon will be responsible for more than 40 per cent of e-commerce in the USA in 2021. In second place is Walmart, at about 7 per cent.[41] Amazon (as we'll see in Chapter 4) is under perma-nent scrutiny for its labour practices, from Covid outbreaks at factories, to aggressive union busting, to workers in its ware-houses experiencing rock-bottom wages and high injury rates.

Seemingly undeterred, however, Amazon is in the process of devouring fashion retail, with one expert claiming the site poses an existential threat to the entire traditional fashion trade.[42] While Amazon does not report specific fashion sales data, analysts place it as the leading fashion retailer in the USA, topping $30 billion in sales.[43] In yet more proof that there is a false distinction made between high-street and high-end fashion, Amazon's reach and clients include expensive brands and boutique labels. Another company capi-talising on internet sales is ASOS, which ships to 239 countries without having any shops of its own. In 2020, ASOS reported 2.7 billion visitors to its online shop with £1.98 billion spent in six months during 2020–1.[44]

In 2006, two employees of a company that supplied both ASOS and Primark decided to ditch the middleman and strike out on their own as an online shop. They were Mahmud Kamani and Carol Kane, founders of Boohoo. Boohoo rep-resent an ultra-fast online method of producing exceptionally short runs of clothing items (sometime as little as a few dozen) – Boohoo puts these on its website and reproduces only what sells. Items can go from design to sale in two weeks. This slash fashion method is also characterised by extreme sales where stock is reduced to a few pence.

Just as with other forms of fashion production it comes at a high price for workers and the environment. Forty per cent of Boohoo's merchandise is made in the UK, and investigations in the summer of 2020 found that workers at factories in Leicester making clothes sold by Boohoo were paid as little as £3.50 an hour, when the minimum wage was £8.72 an hour. Mahmud Kamani's net worth currently stands at £1.4 billion.[45] Along with their original brands, Boohoo PLC own Karen Millen, Nasty Girl, Pretty Little Thing, Coast, Miss Pap, Oasis, Warehouse, Wallis, Dorothy Perkins, Burton, and Debenhams. Many of which were hoovered up after they went bankrupt, in part due to pandemic trading conditions. In China, slash fashion brand SHEIN brings in revenues that Boohoo can only dream of. Founded by Chris Xu (formally known as Yangtian Xu), and with the USA as its biggest market, Forbes reports the online business as being valued at $15 billion.[46] In November 2021, researchers in Guangzhou found SHEIN factory workers working 75-hour weeks for a pittance.[47]

While the importance of e-commerce should not be underestimated, in March 2021 online sales only accounted for $14 out of every $100 spent on goods in the USA.[48] Bricks-and-mortar stores (or businesses who do both) still account for hundreds of billions of dollars' worth of fashion retail.

The eleventh richest person on the Forbes 2021 Rich List is Amancio Ortega, purveyor of cheap shirts, dresses, shoes, and blazers via the company Inditex. Ortega founded Inditex in 1963 in Spain with his former-wife Rosalia Mera (who died in 2013 with a personal fortune of $6.1 billion). Inditex is best known for the Zara brand but also owns Pull&Bear, Massimo Dutti, Bershka, Stradivarius, Oysho, Zara Home, and Uterqüe. By Inditex's own figures, it sold 1,597,260,495 bits of clothing in 2018.[49] When my earlier book *Stitched Up* was published in 2014, Ortega's personal fortune was $57 billion – rising by tens of billions over the course of the financial crisis.[50] By 2021 it stood at $77 billion. After her mother's death, Sandra Ortega Mera became the richest woman in Spain. Ortega and, of course, Stefan Persson at H&M, who has a personal fortune of $16.6 billion, are far from the only billionaires in mass-market fashion. The Spanish company Mango made billions for its founders, the Andic family. Bringing in $2.5 billion in 2017, Mango operates 2,100 stores in countries as diverse as Belarus and Iraq.

In Japan, Uniqlo founder Tadashi Yanai has a portfolio of brands including Helmut Lang. His net worth in 2021 was $38.5 billion, compared with $15.5 billion in 2014, making him one of the richest people in Japan. Danish billionaire Anders Holch Povlsen, who is now the biggest individual private landowner in Scotland, has a significant stake in ASOS and also owns retailer Bestseller along with Vero Moda and several others. In April 2019, his family was struck by tragedy when three of Povlsen's four young children were among the 290 people killed in the Easter Sunday bombings in Sri Lanka.

The field of sports apparel billionaires includes the founder of Lululemon and executives at Chinese company Anta Sports Products. Despite retiring in 2016, Phil Knight, founder of Nike, has a colossal $40.4 billion fortune. Also in footwear, Heinrich Deichmann, CEO of Deichmann, Europe's largest shoe retailer, has a fortune of $7.12 billion. In Britain, Mike Ashley's Fraser Group owns multiple brands including Sports Direct, Jack Wills, and Slazenger, as well as a 12.5 per cent stake in Mulberry. Supermarkets also account for a large chunk of clothing sales. One of the UK's biggest clothing brands is George from supermarket ASDA, which says its clothing website gets 800,000 customers per week.

No round-up of mass-market fashion would be complete without mentioning Primark, a company which for many has come to signify the evils of fast-fashion. In the first ten days of trading, Primark's Oxford Street store sold one million garments.[51] Primark is owned by Associated British Foods, a publicly traded company that is 54 per cent controlled by Wittington Investments, which in turn is controlled by the Weston family and which has a stake in or owns Sweaty Betty, Fortnum & Mason, and Heals. The 2021 Sunday Times Rich List placed the Weston family, long-term Conservative Party donors, at number ten in Britain with a fortune of $11 billion.[52] Shoppers who consider Primark too down-at-heel can cross Oxford Street to hand over their money at Selfridges – which, since 2003, has also been owned and operated by the Weston family,[53] though at the time of writing they were hoping to auction Selfridges off for £4 billion after having 'a difficult year'.[54]

Fashion is adept at giving an appearance of choice when supposedly competing brands are actually owned by the same corporation. In the United States, for example, in the casual clothes sector VF – 'We power movements of sustainable and active lifestyles for the betterment of people and our planet' – owns dozens of brands, including Supreme, Vans, Timberland, Dickies, Eastpak, Jansport, and The North Face. Similarly, Gap Inc. – 'We grow purpose-led, billion-dollar brands that shape peoples' way of life' – owns Gap, Banana Republic, Old Navy, and Athleta.

Another North American giant is PVH, which owns Tommy Hilfiger and Calvin Klein. Calvin Klein's retail sales reached $9.4 billion in 2019, up from $6.7 billion in 2010. Much of this profit came from licensing agreements. Licensing involves a designer selling the rights to their name so that a third party can produce and sell named products. Calvin Klein's licensing arrangements include fragrance, women's clothing, footwear, eyewear, watches, and jewellery. Another heavily licensed company is the publicly listed brand Ralph Lauren. The corporation includes multiple Ralph Lauren brands as well as Club Monaco.

Burton did not die with its founder in 1952. By 1987, the Burton Group had expanded to include 15 retail brands including Topshop. Sales of women's and children's clothes were higher than men's and it had a turnover of £1,338,600,000.[55] The Burton Group was renamed the Arcadia Group in 1997, and in 2002 Arcadia was acquired by Taveta Investments, which delisted it from the London Stock Exchange. Taveta Investments is controlled by the British billionaire Philip Green, who in 2005 received the biggest ever British corporate pay cheque: $1.2 billion. Conveniently, the company was registered with Tina Green, Philip's wife and a resident of Monaco.

Monaco is a principality of 35,000 people and 350,000 bank accounts.[56] You can walk across its entirety in less than an hour, a three mile stroll that will take you past handbags that cost as much as cars and cars that cost as much as houses. The coastline is a picture postcard snippet of the French Rivera where beach volleyball tournaments run in the shadow of hotels and casinos. Another thing to note about Monaco is that there is a lot of dog shit, due it seems to all the toy dog owners who wouldn't dream of lowering themselves to pick it up. In the old town, narrow winding streets of apartment blocks, chemists, and boutiques service elderly residents and their pets. A bus from the French city of Nice drops tourists off at Monaco harbour and the selfies begin almost immediately. People pose by yachts called things like *C'est La Vie* – an easy thing for a multi-millionaire to say. Couples stroll through the marina where each glistening white boat is bigger than the next – glistening because they have been well scrubbed by kneeling deck hands.

At the time of the Arcadia pay out one of these yachts, one so gigantic it had to have the word 'super' attached to it, belonged to the Greens. It was named *Lionheart* and prompted a notable satirical film moment. In Michael Winterbottom's film *Greed*, the film's central character, Sir Richard McCreadie (played by Steve Coogan and loosely modelled on Philip Green), ends up being mauled to death by a lion.

The yacht and the Monaco residency meant the Greens did not pay tax on the corporate handout. The *New York Times* has questioned why Monaco is even a country, labelling it 'a relic of Medieval Europe', but the Greens illustrate why Monaco exists. It is this kind of behaviour that got Monaco blockaded in 1962 by French President Charles de Galle who objected to his tiny neighbour allowing French residents to live there and avoid paying tax. But no one today is blockading the super-yachts.

Philip Green then went on to face heavy criticism for extracting over £500 million from the now defunct department store chain BHS and sparking a process that left the company bankrupt and its 11,000 employees with a shattered pension fund. In 2015, Green sold BHS for £1. The buyer was a Dominic Chappell, a 'former bankrupt businessman and racing driver who had no retail experience'.[57] BHS went bust in April 2016, leaving a £571 million pensions deficit. Green was accused of having sold the company to Mr Chappell to avoid the retirement plan liability, a claim he vigorously denied, and two years later he agreed a £363 million cash settlement with the Pensions Regulator to plug the gap in the pension scheme.[58] In 2020, Dominic Chappell was sentenced to six years in jail for evading £584,000 in taxes, having failed to pay the tax on £2.2 million in income he received after buying BHS.[59] The Pandora Papers leak in 2021 revealed that as BHS headed for collapse, Tina Green secretly bought four multimillion-pound properties worth £37.5 million using offshore companies.[60]

Green's troubles had, however, just begun. In 2018, the *Daily Telegraph* ran a front page that had a silhouette of a man under the headline: 'The British #MeToo scandal that cannot be revealed'. The newspaper was under an injunction from a 'leading businessman' who was attempting to prevent publication of an investigation into his personal conduct. Into this stalemate stepped Lord Peter Hain, a Labour member of the House of Lords. Hain used his parliamentary privilege (which grants legal immunity from repercussions like libel claims) to name the businessman in question: Philip Green. Hain stated: 'What concerned me about this case was wealth, and power that comes with it, and abuse.'[61] When the injunction was subsequently lifted, the *Telegraph* published a raft of allegations of racial, sexual, and physical abuse from former employees plus the cover-up of these abuses. Green denies any unlawful behaviour.[62]

In 2019, Philip Green was dropped from the Sunday Times Rich List as he was no longer a billionaire. The compilers of the list described the Arcadia Group, once a retail jewel, as 'worthless' due to its huge debts. In 2020, the Arcadia Group fell into administration – with its brands carved up between online retailers Boohoo (Burton, Wallis, Dorothy Perkins) and ASOS (Topshop, Topman, Miss Selfridge).

The Arcadia Group had employed 13,000 people, only a fraction of whom retained their jobs. In March 2021, *Retail Gazette* reported that the Arcadia Group was attempting to sell off furniture and fittings, including computers, cameras, desks, and office chairs to try and pay off creditors. One auction included black lacquer desks and a glass-fronted cocktail cabinet created by Green & Mingarelli Design, an interior design business set up by Tina Green. At the time of writing, Philip Green still retains the knighthood granted to him by Tony Blair.

Tax Justice

Despite clothing being a physical object, which should be easy to count and tax, the authorities, particularly in Italy, have investigated the tax affairs of multiple luxury brands. Bloomberg have highlighted Inditex, which owns Zara, for avoiding tax by putting $2 billion into a tiny subsidiary company that operates in Switzerland and the Netherlands.[63] A classic case of profits being put where they will attract as little tax as possible. The use of tax havens is rife in the fashion industry. According to accounts filed with Companies House, New Look is owned by a parent company based in the tax haven of Jersey. The same goes for Boohoo. The majority of the fashion industry is complicit in this practice. The Panama Papers, a huge cache of documents from Panamanian law firm Mossack Fonseca, revealed fashion power players with offshore accounts: London-based designer Roksanda Ilincic; the founder of Mexx; the owner of Jordache Jeans; and Valentino Garavani – namesake of the luxury brand Valentino.[64]

Tax revenue gives us what we need for society to function – schools, hospitals, roads, and so on. It also redistributes wealth and resources in a system that makes life an unequal playing field. If corporations do not pay taxes then a bigger tax burden is placed on working people and valuable public services get cut. This has a particularly adverse effect on women, who are often the lowest-paid workers in society and who most often work for free as caregivers.

'The fashion business provides a great illustration of something that affects the worldwide distribution of wealth and taxable profits', explains tax expert Clair Quentin. 'What people value more and more is the ideas that the clothes represent – the designs, and the labels and the brands. In other words, fashion is an industry based around intellectual property rather than production. Intellectual property makes it easy for companies to hide their profits offshore and not pay tax on them.'

While branding and design take place in wealthy countries, the manufacture of clothing takes place in very poor countries: 'So even if the profitability inherent in the fashion business were being taxed in full rather than flowing into secrecy jurisdictions, the profits would be arising where the design and the management and the retail take place, and not in the low income countries where the production takes place', Quentin explains.

What this means is that even if Bangladesh produces $20 billion worth of clothing for export, the profits made on those clothes by each factory after they have been squeezed by the brands is relatively small. This leaves Bangladesh with very little taxable profits – further denying an impoverished country urgently needed public infrastructure. 'While we in the so-called developed world congratulate ourselves on our sophisticated taste in clothes, when the system is viewed through a tax lens, that very sophistication, reflected in the apparent value of intellectual property, is doing ongoing damage to the material conditions of life for women worldwide', Quentin concludes.

Think for a moment of one seriously underfunded public service in Bangladesh: a proper inspectorate for the policing of building regulations. Such a health and safety service could have prevented tragedies like Rana Plaza.

The Treasure of Indigo Island

Mass-market fashion is an industry awash with billionaires. This is also true for mass market's older and more glamorous sibling, high fashion. Bernard Arnault is the CEO of LVMH (Moët Hennessy Louis Vuitton) and its major shareholder. In 2012, Arnault was Europe's richest man and the fourth richest person on the planet, with a net worth of $41 billion.[65] In 2021, his fortune stood at $190 billion, and when the share price of his brands is right he sometimes edges ahead of Jeff Bezos to become the richest person in the world. His wealth comes from alcohol, property, and fashion brands. Arnault is the chair and majority shareholder of the luxury goods group Christian Dior, which is the main holding company of LVMH. Above all other companies, LVMH dominates luxury fashion. A monopoly of 70 brands, LVMH's key brand is its namesake, Louis Vuitton. Louis Vuitton has been called the 'luxury Microsoft'[66] and also the McDonald's of the luxury industry: 'It's far and away the leader, brags of millions sold, has stores at all the top tourist sites – usually a step away from McD's – and has a logo as recognisable as the Golden Arches.'[67]

A French businessman, Arnault made his money in property development and then spent two decades vacuuming up vast quantities of luxury companies. A close friend of former French President Nicolas Sarkozy, Arnault became the butt of anti-rich sentiment in France, with one newspaper running the headline 'Get Lost Rich Idiot'.[68] At the same time, he received a knighthood in the United Kingdom for services to business and the wider community.[69] Arnault's acquisition tactics have been infamously ruthless. They heralded a new era for the world of fashion, ending the old boys' club. LVMH caused outrage and legal disputes by secretly buying up 22 per cent of Hermès in 2011. The Dumas family who own Hermès has now locked its 50 per cent share into a protected holding company. Bloomberg put the Dumas family fortune at $49.2 billion, making it one of the richest families in the world.[70] Hermès, along with Chanel (privately owned by Alain and Gerard Wertheimer, whose net worth was $19.2 billion in

42

2013 and £33 billion in 2021), are hoped to be 'better guarded than Fort Knox'[71] against acquisition. In January 2021, LVMH completed a deal for American jeweller Tiffany & Co. for $15.8 billion, believed to be the biggest luxury brand acquisition ever.

Among LVMH's main rivals is another conglomerate run by another multi-billionaire, François-Henri Pinault. The Kering corporation owns a raft of brands including Gucci, Bottega Veneta, Saint Laurent, Alexander McQueen, Balenciaga, Brioni, Christopher Kane, McQ, Stella McCartney, Tomas Maier, Sergio Rossi, and Puma. Kering was originally known as PPR, and before that Pinault-Printemps-Redoute, a company founded in 1963 to deal in woodcraft and building supplies. It was valued at $95 billion in 2021.[72]

The Spanish conglomerate Puig owns five luxury fashion brands, including Jean Paul Gaultier, Carolina Herrera, and Paco Rabanne, and controls a large chunk of the world's premium perfume market. Richemont own another swathe of the luxury market including Chloé and Alaïa as well as sales platforms Net-a-Porter and Yoox.

A number of brands remain independent. Historically there has been a trend among Italian luxury fashion houses for remaining independent, family-owned businesses. Family capitalism is a trademark of the Italian economy and the patterns in fashion are repeated in other sectors like manufacturing and engineering. By 2013, however, this had begun to shift. The Prada Group was floated on the stock market in 2012.[73] Versace is now owned by Capri Holdings Limited along with Jimmy Choo and Michael Kors. Similarly, Marni is now owned by the OTB Group along with Viktor&Rolf and Diesel. For now the Chanel, Hermès, and Max Mara Group remain privately owned as does Dolce & Gabbana. After a protracted court battle, Domenico Dolce and Stefano Gabbana were cleared of tax irregularities relating to the sale of the Dolce & Gabbana and D&G brands to their Luxem-bourg-based holding company, Gado Srl. Giorgio Armani remains the sole shareholder for Giorgio Armani S.p.A. Since 1978, Armani has been backed by GFT (Gruppo Finanziario Tessile), Italy's largest textile manufacturer. With no heir, he is thought to be establishing a trust that will take control of his company after his death.

One household name has been less fortunate. Despite critical acclaim and celebrity status, the French designer Christian Lacroix presided over a brand that never made a profit in 22 years of business. The company finally went bankrupt in 2009 and was bought by the North American conglomerate Falic Fashion Group. When he left, Lacroix lost the rights to his own name. He now designs interiors and uniforms for train com-panies and collaborates with high-street chains. This Faustian name loss has also happened to Halston, Martin Margiela, Jil Sander (three times), Karen Millen, and Jimmy Choo.[74]

Inside Luxury

Conglomerates spend millions on their brands. When Puig bought Jean Paul Gaultier, it fought off competition to take on €14 million worth of debt. These vast sums of money are con-sidered good investments because neither the financial crisis nor the Covid-19 pandemic has stopped the luxury sector making huge profits – profits that come from owning designs, labels, and brands.

The continuing sales of luxury goods are best taken as proof of the unequal impact of crises. In updating this book, one thing that stands out is the astronomical rise in the fortunes of fashion's billionaires. Fashion is the perfect example of the rich getting richer while the poor get poorer. Luxury billion-aires continue to make so much money because even in times of global crisis and hardship, the wealthy are still able to buy what they have always bought. They buy luxury brands to assure their status and to demarcate their position in society. This habit of conspicuous consumption was first pointed out by Thorstein Veblen, who argued that the wealthy leisure class used consumption as evidence of their wealth and power. It is a simple process: attach expensive items to your body, or the bodies of your spouse and children, then parade around where people can see you.

Another reason profits remain high is because the luxury fashion sector does not rely exclusively on the sale of very expensive clothes to make its profits. Instead, it employs a strategy known as the pyramid model: a small number of luxury products like luggage and couture are sold to extremely wealthy customers, but the biggest profits are generated through the sale of 'mass-market' goods (which are still very much overpriced).

As celebrity stylist Maeve Reilly told *Fashionista*: 'Most people aren't going to a store to buy a hundred-thousand-dollar ball gown. They're going to the store to buy the blazer or the bag or the crop top or the shoe from the brand that made the gown.' It is this emphasis on lightweight products that 'moves the needle' for sales.[75] Certain brands are expert at this differentiation. 'Chanel is a master of category segregation', described one analyst. 'This strategy involves confining iconic, core category products to high-end price ranges, while deftly positioning other product categories – lipsticks, for example – at lower price points to address aspirational customers.'[76] Cosmetics and perfumes are estimated to generate around a third of Chanel's annual sales.[77]

Going back to the 1950s, licences have been a huge source of income for the luxury sector. While Cristóbal Balenciaga refused to allow his name to be put on licensed goods,[78] Christian Dior licensed everything from handbags to hats. Perfume remains a heavily licensed, mass-produced commodity without which the luxury sector would not survive. Most perfumes are not created by design houses but by licensed multinational corporations like Procter & Gamble and Coty. There are huge profits to be made from perfume. Laboratories sell the liquid for two and a half times more than the cost to the licensee, who retails it for between two and four times the cost again, making a 30–40 per cent profit.[79] Pharmaceutical giant Coty, which is 60 per cent owned by German conglomerate JAB Holding Company, produces perfume for dozens of brands ranging from Miu Miu, Burberry, and Calvin Klein to Katy Perry and Adidas.

The mass-produced It Bag is typical of this pyramid strategy. The 'It' in It Bag seemingly comes from Miuccia Prada's comment on the subject: 'It's so easy to make money.'[80] The It Bag phenomenon of must-have bags seemed to reach the height of absurdity in 2006 when Louis Vuitton released a laminated chequered bag of the sort bought on market stalls and used to carry laundry, except the Vuitton bag retailed for £1,200. Jil Sander once produced a brown paper bag purse made of brown paper which retailed at $290, while Balenciaga sold a bag eerily similar to a blue Ikea bag for £1,705.

The creative director at Bottega Veneta called the It Bag process 'totally marketed bullshit crap. You make a bag, you send it out to a couple of celebrities, you get the paparazzi to shoot just as they walk out of their house. You sell that to the tabloids, and you say in a magazine that there is a waiting list.'[81] Even during the Covid-19 pandemic, the global market for 'luxury goods' was estimated to be worth $349.1 billion in 2020 and is projected to grow to $403.2 billion by 2027.[82] There is a huge mark-up on luxury goods with bags sold for over ten times their cost of production and destroyed before they are ever marked down to a sale price.[83]

Some luxury items are made by artisans who labour for weeks on a single pair of shoes. Yet one of the reasons why the mark-up on bags is so high is that many 'Made in Italy' goods, for example, are definitely not made in Italy. When I researched my second book, *Foot Work: What Your Shoes Tell You About Globalisation*, I went to a shoe factory in North Macedonia where there were piles of shoes and shoe boxes all stating 'Made in Italy'. We were, however, a long way from Milan. This is the result of something called the Outward Processing Trade (OPT) scheme, a specially designed blip in European Union legislation that allows manufacturers to export raw materials or semi-processed goods to non-EU countries and then reimport them when they have been worked on.

This system was developed by the European Union in the 1970s at the instigation of the governments of Germany and Italy, who wanted to outsource labour-intensive garment and shoe production to low-cost satellites while safeguarding their own industries. As one factory owner I spoke with stated: '"Made In Italy" just means finished in Italy.' Sometimes the final stage can be as slight as polishing or placing shoes in a box.[84] The shoes could not be correctly labelled as 'Made in Macedonia' because then customers would want a cheaper price because of the ingrained prejudice that 'Made in Italy' means superiority. In this way, the OPT system denies credit to the countries and people who actually make items like 'luxury' shoes all while keeping wages low and leaving countries like Macedonia less able to elevate their own brands or national status.

Along with bags, companies market items like belts, key rings, scarves, and wallets to people who dream of buying 'luxury'. For the TV series *Secrets of the Superbrands*, the BBC visited the Luxottica sunglasses factory in Italy where 55 million pairs of sunglasses are made each year for brands like Chanel, Prada, Bulgari, Ralph Lauren, and Paul Smith. Not only are the 'designer' sunglasses made in this factory but many are also designed there too. A pair of sunglasses from one of these brands retails for several hundred pounds, yet they are trifles light as air, nothing more than a few grams of plastic and glass shrouded in an illusion of luxury. Along with his family, Leonardo Del Vecchio, founder of Luxottica, had a fortune of $34.1 billion in 2021.[85]

Designer China

The Covid-19 pandemic hit China hard, but even this was not enough to dull the country's luxury market. In a report titled *China's Unstoppable 2020 Luxury Market*, management consultancy Bain stated that some brands saw double- and even triple-digit growth rates. Early lockdowns slowed sales, which climbed again in April 2020. Unable to travel to shopping destinations like Paris or New York, Chinese consumers shopped locally. The luxury goods market in mainland China now stands at approximately RMB 346 billion – $54 billion.[86]

This signifies a historic change in the geography of luxury consumption. The great capitalist boom in what was known as 'the West' came to a shuddering halt in 1973. After the Second World War, those countries with high levels of arms expenditure sacrificed their competitiveness. In contrast, the 'losers', Germany and Japan, boomed in terms of economic development.[87] By spending just 1 per cent of its gross domestic product (GDP), on armaments, Japan mastered new technologies and experienced an economic surge, laying the foundations for Japan to become a prosperous and avid consumer of luxury goods. China, however has surpassed these markers to the extent that, '[i]f China has a cold, luxury goods get pneumonia'.[88] The precarious nature of the Chinese market and the sense that many brands are now overexposed to China led the CEO of Richemont to once state: 'I feel like I'm having a black tie dinner on top of a volcano. In the morning we put on our ties and our watches, and the food's better, and the wine's better, and the weather is great, but let's not kid ourselves. There is a volcano somewhere, whether it's this year, in ten years' time, or in twenty years' time. We are exposed to China.'[89]

With the global luxury market declining at an expected rate of 23 per cent in 2020, mainland China's share of that market nearly doubled, growing from about 11 per cent to 20 per cent in 2020. Bain state that this puts China on track to claim the biggest share of the luxury market by 2025 – regardless of the world luxury market returning to pre-Covid-19 levels.[90] The scramble to attract and retain Chinese consumers continues, though executives at luxury brands keep being caught using racist language and actions. As I write, self-styled Instagram fashion watchdog *Diet Prada* faces a defamation lawsuit of $665 million from Dolce & Gabbana. This relates to *Diet Prada*'s publication of alleged messages from Stefano Gabbana which were so racist they sank D&G's Chinese market.[91]

It is not just luxury brands that are scrambling for China. In the world of mass-market fashion, brands like H&M, Uniqlo, Nike, and Zara are established in China. But China unsurprisingly has dozens of its own mass-market powerhouses, not just SHEIN but the HLA Corporation, Septwolves, Belle footwear, Metersbonwe, MJ Style Li Ning, and Anta to name a few.

Hong Kong-based Li & Fung might not be a household name, but no discussion of fashion supply chains is complete without them. The company was first founded in Canton in 1906 to trade in antiques and handicrafts. From the 1950s it diversified into other commodities, including garments which accounted for 80 per cent of all its business by 1997.[92] As a giant middleman in the garment industry, Li & Fung has two specialities: managing supply chains for brands and procuring low-cost clothing from manufacturers. One academic paper described Li & Fung as becoming 'a "one-stop shop" for Western retailers' by delivering 'product design and development, raw material and factory sourcing, production planning and management, quality assurance, and shipping consolidation'.[93] Li & Fung has, however, been besieged by the expansion of brands like Inditex who have their own supply chain management systems and speak directly to factories, and by Donald Trump's US trade restrictions on Chinese imports in mid-2018, announcing in March 2019 that it would source less than half of its goods from China that year as a result of the trade restrictions.[94] Li & Fung remains one of the world's biggest supply chain management organisations and came under heavy criticism for cancelling orders with factories during the Covid-19 pandemic.

Fashion's centre of gravity – both luxury and mass market – has shifted eastwards, yet on a global scale, the majority of the wealth and power as represented by the richest billionaires in the world remains in the hands of a few European and American billionaires.

* * *

In 2013, when I had just finished writing my earlier book *Stitched Up*, the *Business of Fashion* website stated that the global fashion industry was worth $1.5 trillion. Eight years later, McKinsey and the *Business of Fashion* put this figure at $2.5 trillion.[95] An extra trillion dollars (give or take) that has swelled the pockets of billionaires, bought dozens of superyachts, and paid for private islands, helicopters, and hilltop mansions. The amounts of money involved might have changed but the ownership principles have not. Monopolised ownership along with an illusion of choice for customers is king. The rich have become human dragons while the poor have starved. Trends and crises have come and gone but one thing remains: whether as workers or consumers – fashion is just an excuse for exploitation and inequality. To ensure that this illusion continues, the fashion industry needs a showcase to elevate their products to the stuff of legend. This shopfront – the fashion media – is the subject of Chapter 2.

CHAPTER TWO
The Fashion Media

Both in art and literature, the function of the frame is fundamental ... It allows the picture to exist, isolating it from the
rest; but at the same time, it recalls – and somehow stands
for – everything that remains out of the picture.

Italo Calvino[1]

Introduction

From 300-year-old magazines to celebrity influencers, the
purpose of the fashion media is to act as an intermediary
between brands and consumers by showcasing clothes that
most people will never come into contact with and elevat-
ing clothes to 'fashion'. With the transition to digital media,
including virtual dresses that cannot be worn being sold for
£8,000,[2] this chapter has needed an almost total overhaul.
It now includes the role of influencers, online activism, the
impact of social media on our brains, data mining and privacy,
and the links between fashion news sites and surveillance
capitalism.

Magazines

Let's start with magazines, an industry that has come a long
way since the publication of the first women's journal, *The
Ladies' Mercury*, in 1693.[3] It is now a multi-billion pound web
of media brands monopolised by a few giant multinational
corporations. Today's fashion magazine caters to two sets of
customers who bring in two streams of revenue. The first are
its readers; the second, its advertisers.[4]

Condé Montrose Nast worked his way up the American
publishing industry in the early 1900s before identifying
an elitist women's journal with a small circulation that he
decided to make the vessel for his theory for getting maximum
profits from magazines. The Nast strategy was to drop any

pretence of mass-market appeal and focus instead on attracting a wealthy minority who would attract advertisers. In his words: 'If you had a tray with 2,000,000 needles on it, and only 150,000 of these had gold tips, the 1,850,000 which were not gold-tipped would be no use to you. But if you could get a magnet that would draw out only the gold ones, what a saving!'[5] Nast acquired *Vogue* in 1909 and instructed his staff not only to 'get all their readers from the one particular class to which the magazine is dedicated, <u>but rigorously to exclude all others</u>'.[6]

A British edition of *Vogue* was launched in 1916, at the height of the First World War, when imports of magazines from the United States ceased. A French version was launched four years later. As a result of the Wall Street Crash of 1929, Nast lost control of his company and incurred business debts of $5 million. His namesake publishing empire, however, grew to formidable heights and became the hallmark of luxury chic. In 1959, the company was bought by the media mogul S. I. Newhouse's Advance Publications. Advance is still owned by the billionaire Newhouse family. The Condé Nast portfolio of media brands also includes *The New Yorker*, *Teen Vogue*, *Glamour*, *GQ*, *Condé Nast Traveller*, *Allure*, *Vanity Fair*, *Them*, *LOVE*, *Wired*, and *Tatler*.

Condé Nast's contemporary and rival was William Hearst, the businessman who inspired *Citizen Kane*. Hearst regularly used his media ownership to support his various campaigns for public office, including an abortive run for the US presidency.[7] Today Hearst owns *Cosmopolitan*, *Elle*, *Red*, and *Bazaar* among many others. *Grazia* and *Closer* are owned by the Bauer Media Group, while the now digital only *Marie Claire* is owned by Future PLC. Other than a handful of brands, like the privately owned *Business of Fashion*, the entire traditional fashion media are owned by just a few companies. This is publishing in the broadest sense of the word – not just websites and digital editions of magazines but e-commerce and pro-filing readers to drive sales. The component parts of these companies also work in unison using vast sums of capital. For example, AOL Time Warner can publish a book, turn it into a TV show followed by a film, and produce every conceivable type of themed merchandise. Meanwhile, these products can be publicised in their media outlets and promoted at branded festivals and even universities. One editor described this cross-platform collaboration in the following terms: 'We use everything that we do to promote everything that we do.'[8]

Big business monopolies dominate other sectors of the economy such as tobacco, oil, and computer technology, and these unhealthy concentrations of ownership leave industries vulnerable to the failure of big firms, market fluctuations, and unfair domination by a single corporation. But what we see with the fashion media is that the ownership of our received ideas, culture, and information are dominated by just a few companies.[9] Fashion is an industry that sells itself as providing choice and variety, yet its press follows the pattern of being controlled by a few huge companies. There appears to be a choice between *Glamour* and *Vogue* or *Elle* and *Bazaar* but it is merely a choice between two media brands espousing the same profit-driven values and owned by the same giant corporations.

Complimentary Copy

In 1893, Frank A. Munsey cut the price of *Munsey's Magazine* from $3 a year to $1. Choosing to sell the magazine for less than the cost of production, he nevertheless made vast profits by growing his audience and making his profits from advertising.[10] Magazines are still sold at far less than the cost of their production, with advertising making up the difference and providing the profits, with one estimate being that if adverts were removed, magazines would have to double in price.[11] Dallas Smythe developed the theory that the purpose of the mass media is to produce an audience that can be sold to advertisers, something that is done through the provision of a 'free lunch' of editorial content.[12]

The job of a fashion journalist is, therefore, to deliver readers so that advertisers will buy space,[13] while editors take care to cultivate an environment which advertisers want to be associated with.[14] Studies show a direct correlation between advertising and the exclusion of certain issues from magazines, with lung cancer from smoking and skin cancer from sunbathing just two of the issues magazines notably avoided talking about to avoid upsetting advertisers.[15] Which issues are now being excluded? As Dallas Smythe noted, the media do not just affirm the status quo, they actively prevent the raising of serious questions about our society.[16]

As well as creating a supportive editorial atmosphere, editors must also maintain what former editor Gloria Steinem called 'complimentary copy'[17] – writing articles about 'beauty secrets', for example, in order to attract adverts for cosmetics. 'Complimentary copy' is guilty of spawning endless articles describing perfumes, which are usually reduced to describing the bottle and its packaging once journalists run out of adjectives for fragrance.

Between pure editorial and pure display advertising is 'advertorial', the practice of magazines using the template of their design style to create an advert for a brand. These are supposed to be clearly flagged as promotions, but more often than not they blend in with editorial content. It might be more accurate to describe everything in fashion magazines as advertorial. As one former *Vogue* publisher stated: 'The cold hard facts of magazine publishing mean that those who advertise get editorial coverage.'[18] This was reinforced when former *British Vogue* Fashion Director Lucinda Chambers gave an explosive interview to *Vestoj* which included the line: 'The June cover with Alexa Chung in a stupid Michael Kors T-shirt *is* crap. He's a big advertiser so I knew why I had to do it.'[19]

Don't Upset the Emperor

Unlike other cultural publications, fashion magazines are utterly obsequious about the products they display. Fashion is such a messed-up industry, yet where is the rigorous press criticism? In the past, there was a realised fear that critiquing designers might result in not being invited to their shows. As a result, criticism has tended to come from newspapers, which are less reliant upon fashion's advertising revenue.

But this has tended to be about design rather than systemic analysis or calling brands out for labour and environmental abuses. In the last ten years, the media have gotten slightly better at covering these issues – but it is still the case that the odd condemnatory article is vastly outnumbered by the same obsequious sales pitches and tedious ramblings about how people need to buy more stuff.

What passes for fashion journalism is 99 per cent not journalism. It does not 'comfort the afflicted and afflict the comfortable'. It is unable to shepherd people through the enormous structural change that will come either via climate breakdown or through the active steps required to avoid it.[20] Above all, the fashion media are unable to move beyond boiling everything down to the question of consumption – what to buy or not to buy. Instead, it aggressively sells products that people do not need by intensifying a sense of insecurity. There are some excellent journalists who investigate fashion, but so little is expected of 'fashion journalists' that most of what is delivered is the uncritical reproduction of press releases and shopping lists.

To understand this requires getting to grips with two concepts – complacency and myth making. It could be argued that the poor state of the fashion media is not the result of a conspiracy of deliberately evil editors who want to obstruct truth but rather the result of complacent editors and journalists who do not have the lived experience, do not feel affected, and do not care enough to report properly on the Global South. Therefore, major supply chain issues are ignored (until they become so big they warrant commissioning a token article or two) and the same boring content is recycled, in many cases for an elitist audience that is just as complacent.[21]

In addition, the fashion media do not criticise because they have a vested interest in maintaining the myth and glitz of the fashion industry. To do damage by criticising would be to damage themselves – not just because the fashion weeks and parties would disappear, along with the Insta followings, but because proper criticism would expose the *entire* industry. If the emperor is naked, then so is the fashion press. After all, once a commitment to rigorous investigating and critiquing started, where would it stop?

Instead, all parts of the fashion industry must perpetuate the myth that the industry is the sole source of beautiful clothing and that everything is fine and can continue as it is forever. Rather than just being the victims of advertisers, the fashion media are a complicit and integral myth-maker.

Blog Your Way to the Top

In the 2010s, fashion blogs disrupted magazines in an explosion of unauthorised reportage whose ingredients appeared horrifyingly simple: 'a blog, a camera, and a healthy dose of personal style'.[22] For proponents of blogging, this was the long-awaited democratisation of fashion. Gone were the class barriers of attending the right school, wearing expensive clothes, and working for free at internships secured by influential relatives. Instead, you could be from anywhere and have a distinctly unmodel-like appearance – it was the American Dream come true in a blaze of digital glory. Or was it?

A closer look at the basic requirements for creating a successful fashion blog sheds light on the demographic of people who are really able to make a living from their blog or website. The basics are: a camera, a computer, the ability to write and read English, access to lots and lots of clothes, a network that includes contacts interested in the fashion and popular culture industries, a great deal of spare time, start-up money, the ability to travel, a studied personal appearance that conforms to accepted beauty standards, no objections to selling products for multinationals, and no objections to creating an editorial environment that is attractive to multinational corporations. The blogging industry swiftly corporatised, with the fashion industry picking its favourites. They became front-row guests, had bags named after them, got magazine jobs and book deals, charged tens of thousands of dollars for appearances, sold advertising space on their pages, and got modelling contracts and Hollywood agents.

None of this signalled a fashion democracy. Bloggers can influence what styles of clothing are produced for sale by corporations – having drawn inspiration from society, they feed into the industry as an often unpaid 'look book'. Bloggers can also increase the sales of clothes they promote. But this is not the same as saying that bloggers have power over the industry. The power to influence the industry is not the same as the power to control the industry.

The Influencer Market

Dictionaries now carry duel definitions of the word 'influencer' – 'someone who affects or changes the way that other people behave' and 'a person who is paid by a company to show and describe its products and services on social media, encouraging other people to buy them'.[23] While there are influencers for every market, this practice has become synonymous with fashion. Influencer marketing is now a core strategy for brands to communicate with consumers – with influencers providing a veneer of trust and authenticity. The most 'successful' fashion influencers have become wildly rich by commodifying their appearance and their lives to sell as advertising space to corporations. It is a much maligned profession, with people paid to promote everything from clothes and make-up to voter registration, weight-loss products, and plastic surgery.

There is a particularly reactionary intersection of influencer culture and the fashion industry. The following section might seem harsh, but it is not is not aimed at any one individual but at a practice which repeatedly inflicts damage on social justice campaigns. Recent history has seen a repeat pattern of celebrities, minor celebrities, or influencers being paid by fashion brands to advertise their 'sustainability merits'. These spokespeople are selected for several reasons: the first is their huge follower count, the second is because there is something about their appearance or identity that the fashion industry wants to commodify (the sector is overwhelmingly made up of bland white women). The third reason people get picked as the public face of 'sustainability' is unfortunately because brands think they are useful idiots who will do anything for money. The chosen spokespeople are not climate scientists, climate justice researchers, or labour rights campaigners, they are people who will say anything they are told for a pay cheque. And I mean *anything* – saying a leading fashion brand is sustainable is the equivalent of saying smoking is good for children or the fossil fuel industry has done wonders for human rights in Nigeria.

The fourth reason unscrupulous celebrities and influencers are given lucrative contracts is because of the very movements they undermine with their words and actions. Brands pay influencers to say they are sustainable because the climate justice movement has these brands on the run. For the first time we are seeing strong global opposition to fossil fuel, tobacco, mining, and fashion companies – all of which are climate arsonists. These industries know they are finally being seen as the problem and so hiring corrupt and unprincipled influencers and celebrities to undermine the movement for change is a deliberate tactic.

Commodifying Personhood

This is not to say that all people who work as influencers are unscrupulous. There are many people around the world who use large social media followings to support social justice movements. The unappealing upper echelons of this profession also hide vast ranks of lesser influencers, many of whom are badly exploited by corporations. With smaller followings (10,000–100,000) having greater engagement rates than larger ones (10,000,000), brands are turning more and more to micro-influencers.[24] Among the overnight sensations on TikTok or Twitch are people who toil away for years earning far less than the profits they generate for brands.

This style of business model has been characterised by Professor Jodi Dean as being based upon expanding the field and then monetising the few people who make it to the top. In a 'winner takes all' society, everyone is promised that they can 'make it' but very few actually do. This competition between people is, she says, a particular form of exploitation under neoliberal capitalism: 'Rather than having a right to the proceeds of ones labour by virtue of a contract, ever more of us win or lose such that remuneration is treated like a prize ... people work for a chance at pay.'[25] While it is easy to say that no one forces people to enter the competition economy – whether that is to attempt to be an influencer, a writer, or an artist – as this form of 'prize-logic' exploitation increases even those who do not enter the competition find themselves with fewer opportunities to enter into contract-based work because the overall field has changed.[26] Like the traditional modelling industry, minor influencers face pressure to say yes to whatever pay and conditions are presented to them. Part of the knack of influencer marketing is to make it look effortless, but it is a real job and hard work – something that is often dismissed given that the profession's demographic is characterised by young women.

An interesting article in *Dismantle Magazine* discussed how the all-encompassing labour of social media turns influencers into 'products themselves'. This leaves limited ability to separate oneself from productive work – a situation which can intensify feelings of alienation. Brands seek 'authenticity' from influencers to drive audience engagement, but 'this is also the aspect that capitalism measures, divides, and turns into profit'. Living out life on social media places people's whole being 'under the microscopic view of a shifting market economy'. An influencer is, therefore, both product and labourer – 'living in the body as a grid of monetization'. This unenviable state exemplifies the constant search for new horizons of commodification that takes place under capitalism.[27]

Behind the appearance of independence and authenticity is big business. When companies pay money or give freebies in exchange for posts, stories, videos, photos, or testimonies then the content is compromised. The defence that 'they didn't tell me how to write it' is simply naïve. The required opinion is implicit in the acceptance of the pay cheque or gift. This is also the case for blogs or influencers who claim they only collaborate with brands whose 'aesthetic aligns with our aesthetic'.[28] It is corporate PR disguised as fresh young opinions, with as many rewrites or reshoots as the brand requires.[29] This industry is the result of an overarching system where, without an internet tax on advertising revenue or state funds for cultural producers like bloggers and influencers,[30] subsistence means selling out and selling advertising space. The sums they make, however, pale in comparison to the profits made by the platforms that dominate the digital landscape.

Behaviour Modification Empires

When last I checked, 2.89 billion people had Facebook accounts, while 3.51 billion people were using at least one of Meta's core products – Facebook, WhatsApp, Instagram, or Messenger – every month.[31] Instagram and TikTok both had a billion users, 2.29 billion people used Google-owned YouTube, and 330 million people were on Twitter. These tech giants control mountains of money. Facebook/Meta founder Mark Zuckerberg is one of the five wealthiest people in the world with a personal fortune reaching $140 billion. But where does this money come from? On the surface, these companies offer connectivity, information, and entertainment. But scratch the surface and it gets very sinister, very quickly. Never forget that if you don't pay for the product, you are the product and in this case 'specific changes in our behaviour is the product.'[32]

In his book, *Ten Arguments for Deleting Your Social Media Accounts Right Now*, Jaron Lanier describes social media corporations as 'behaviour modification empires' – and with good reason. To paraphrase Lanier's argument, every day we carry around smartphones, devices that are suitable for algorithmic behaviour modification – meaning repeated techniques used to create behaviours and cure or *create* addictions in animals and humans. A key behaviour modification is making you shop. Whereas old-fashioned advertising measured the success of an advert based on how many products were sold, now companies measure why and how individuals – you and I – change our behaviours. We are continuously submitted to algorithms and social media feeds that prompt us to change. This behaviour tracking is deeply intimate: where your eyes flick to on a page and how long they stay there, where you are in the menstrual cycle, whether you are sad or on medication, whether an advert played for 5 or 4.5 seconds after a joyful cat video makes you more likely to buy something. The ability to modify our behaviour has collided with tech companies seeking customers who will pay to modify our behaviour.[33] You only have to read the Cambridge Analytica reports of election manipulation to see just how bad this can get.

Surveillance Capitalism and the Fashion Press

Professor Shoshana Zuboff has termed this state of affairs *surveillance capitalism*. She defines this as 'the unilateral claiming of private human experience as free raw material for translation into behavioural data. These data are then computed and packaged as prediction products and sold into behavioural futures markets – business customers with a commercial interest in knowing what we will do now, soon, and later.'[34]

Websites have changed from being static pages to a collection of dynamic content from a multitude of places. They include tools for placing adverts, running analytics, and 'fingerprinting' to know who each user is and how they're interacting with a website. These tools can be harmless ways for people running websites to gather information to improve what they are doing, or they can allow things like taking payments via other companies. But often these tools are built and used to undermine the privacy of users and to secretly follow us from site to site as we make our way around the web.[35] There are hundreds of different companies now specialising in tracking and recording our browsing habits by placing tiny images or invisible JavaScript on websites. Each of these tracking companies tracks you without your consent over multiple different websites – effectively they are stalking you.

I set a timer for 45 minutes and spent the time browsing eight commonly used fashion news sites – *Refinery 29* and *i-D* (both owned by Vice), *Stylist*, *BoF*, *Dazed*, *Fashionista*, *British Vogue*, and *WWD*. I also switched on *Light Beams* – a browser extension originally developed by Mozilla Firefox to let people view the third-party trackers embedded in each website. *Light Beams* uses a small white triangle to represent each tracker and they began to bombard my screen like sharp little bullets. When I went onto a new site, many of the trackers would join up.

These third-party companies take all the information they collect about you from one site (what articles you clicked on), then add it to the next site (what was in your weekly shop), and the next one (train tickets or perhaps a new pair of shoes). The more data they gather the more valuable it becomes. If this was not bad enough, this data is combined with our social media accounts so that these companies can build extensive, identified profiles – not just of random data but details about exactly who we are, what we like to do online, and what people in our social networks like to do as well.

This non-consensual invasion of people's privacy is completely wrong and it is inextricably linked to fashion news sites. Within 45 minutes I had 629 third-party trackers on my browser. When I tested these sites individually, by far the worst offenders were *Refinery 29* and *WWD* with 259 and 213 third-party trackers respectively. It is important to be aware that you do not need to browse these sites for these trackers to start stalking you – 151 got added to my browser the second I opened *WWD*. Next were *Fashionista* with 159, *The Cut* with

129, and *British Vogue* with 123. Then came *i-D* with 103, *Dazed* with 95, *Stylist* with 83, and *Business of Fashion* with 55 third-party trackers. Fashion sites within newspapers were no better – when I looked at the *New York Times* Style section I got hit with 74 trackers, *Guardian Fashion* was another 113, and *Telegraph Fashion* 148. Trying to find a site not so intent on stalking, I looked at BBC News, which placed 19 third-party trackers, most of which were BBC analytics. *The Fashion Law*, *Fashion United*, and *Now Fashion* all had fewer than 20. These numbers can change from day to day and user to user but they are still very high.

'With fashion sites, advertisers probably see readers of these sites as more open to shopping than people reading general news, so they make a more inviting target to have their data gathered, analysed and resold', says Eliot Bendinelli at Privacy International. 'Big publishers of news sites might also feel greater public pressure to guard privacy and avoid problematic ads meaning they curate their ads and trackers more, whereas fashion sites likely feel less pressure or scrutiny and instead may believe the more the better.'

Fashion news sites also keep us hooked by offering themselves as 'informed best friend' sources of information. This means it is not just fashion data being gathered as people browse. You might hope that when you search for things online (for example, advice on medication, sex, drugs, alcohol, pregnancy, or debt) your personal business is not being broadcast to dozens of companies you've never heard of – but that is precisely what is happening.[36]

As a control, I browsed eight news outlets – *The Guardian*, *BBC*, *i News*, *The Times*, *New York Times*, *Houston Chronicle*, *Huffington Post*, and *The Atlantic*, and by the end had 434 third-party trackers on my browser. What this experiment shows is that there is a serious problem with third-party trackers across the media and that people who enjoy reading about fashion are punished for doing so. By reading fashion news, 200 extra third-party trackers stalk you around the internet – a gendered exploitation aimed at young people who may have no idea what is happening to them.

Under pressure, Google announced in 2021 that they will ban third-party trackers, but this does not mean that Google intend to stop collecting your data or using your data to target ads.[37] A key reason our personalities are packaged up and sold as data is so brands can try and sell us stuff we do not need. Fashion consumption is something people are continually told they must 'just stop doing', but this simplistic approach fails to take account of the systemic issue of internet privacy and non-consensual data collection. As we will see, consumption is a social act and any attempt to reduce it must tackle the structural compulsion of psychological targeting which drives an unhealthy, warped relationship with fashion consumption.

A New Dependence

It is not just everyday online browsing that subjects people to surveillance and a warped sense of self. Marx wrote about capitalism contriving to make us subservient 'to inhuman, refined, unnatural and imaginary appetites'. He could have been writing about Silicon Valley and social media: 'every person speculates on creating a new need in another, so as to drive him to a fresh sacrifice, to place him in a new dependence'.[38]

Billions of people have signed up for social media accounts because of the need for human connectivity in an alienated world. Particularly in urbanised consumer societies, people seek escape from lonely, unfulfilling, overworked lives, with social media promising emotional fulfilment.[39] A state that brings to mind Marx's phrase that 'every real and possible need is a weakness which will lead the fly to the glue-pot'.[40] Indeed, the abyss of a window into an array of seemingly perfect lives is far more likely to prompt feelings of unhappiness than contentment. Medical studies have repeatedly found social media, and in particular fashion-synonymous app Instagram, to be detrimental to mental health.[41]

In 2021, the *Wall Street Journal* exposed secret Facebook documents that it said showed the corporation knew Instagram presents a significant mental health risk to a sizeable percentage of users, most notably teenage girls. Among Facebook's own research were statements including: 'We make body image issues worse for one in three teen girls', and 'Thirty-two percent of teen girls said that when they felt bad about their bodies, Instagram made them feel worse.' Facebook found that 'comparisons on Instagram can change how young women view and describe themselves', and that teenagers specifically identified Instagram as the cause of their anxiety and depression. Alarmingly, the *Wall Street Journal* reported that among teens who reported suicidal thoughts, 13 per cent of British users and 6 per cent of American users traced the desire to kill themselves to Instagram.[42] While other apps focus on performance or opinion, Instagram's core purpose is on presenting 'perfect' bodies and lifestyles. With people following not just their peer group but an endless feed of celebrities, 'fitness instructors', and influencers, it is little wonder the site is linked to eating disorders, body dysmorphia, and depression. And yet Facebook continues to preach that 'using social apps to connect with other people can have positive mental-health benefits'.[43]

Marx argued that human needs can only be gratified to the extent to which they contribute to the accumulation of wealth.[44] So, while we seek connectivity and community within social media, we are not only a product but also unpaid labour – we are turning our lives into optimised content so Zuckerberg and co. can gain another few billion dollars. Marx also stated that humans are not fixed in their nature but are made through their repeated activities.[45] The bad news is that we are caught in a loop that is making us into unhappy lab rats; the good news is that we can change this.

If reading this makes you feel defensive about social media, this is something worth exploring. Corporations like Instagram and Twitter have poured billions into making social media accounts seem like extensions of the self, so an attack on the company or the system feels like a threat. Jaron Lanier actively promotes total disengagement from all social media while stating: 'If you have good experiences with social media, nothing in this book invalidates those experiences.' Instead, he hopes society will find a way to keep and improve what we love about social media by being precise about what must be rejected.[46]

Social media has brought a sea change in connectivity. Young Black people in Britain have talked about the importance of the diversity social media has created: 'Growing up in the UK it was a struggle to find people who looked like me on TV but social media changed that.'[47] Other marginalised people, for example people with disabilities, have found a space to pursue activism and have a voice. LGBTQ+ (lesbian, gay, bisexual, transgender and queer or questioning) youth have been able to find communities and resources which would previously have been much harder to find. But while this connectivity is to be celebrated and encouraged, why, as Lanier argues, should drastic third-party manipulation be the price of that connection?[48] Or as Professor Zuboff says: 'It's impossible to imagine surveillance capitalism without the digital, but it's easy to imagine the digital without surveillance capitalism.'[49] You can love the good parts of the internet without accepting the surveillance, manipulation, and attacks on our collective mental well-being. Let us return to the recurring question in this book: What kind of society do we want to live in and what is the role of the fashion press in that society?

Surely we do not want our social networks and news sites to mine our intimate human experiences for profit at the expense of our mental health.

As we will see in Chapter 6 on body image, it is no insult to suggest that capitalism – in this case thousands of algorithms based on behavioural psychology and directed straight at your brain – can have an effect on you. My personal story is that Instagram hit me really hard. I found myself being reduced to two sets of numbers – the number of followers I had and the number of likes I got – and this was destructive, addictive, and alienating for my brain. I constantly felt like I was 'not good enough'. When I watched *The Social Dilemma* I finally understood my place in the machine: That even were I to be 'successful' at Instagram, that success was a form of pyramid sales – making other people spend longer on an app medically proven to be bad for mental health. So I quit for good. For now, I have other social media accounts but no apps on my phone. No regrets, more space, more time to write, and a happier brain.

Don't Make Art for Algorithms

When I left Instagram I got a mixed response. Some people applauded and said they wanted to leave too. Some people felt Instagram was benign. On the other side were people who were affronted at my decision to leave. Mostly it seemed to be because they felt too trapped to quit. This level of feeling trapped, especially among creatives, needs further investigation. Instagram has become synonymous with fashion. Among designers, photographers, students, and even journalists and activists, it has become unusual not to have an account – as if the badge of being one of these things is the account instead of the production of designs, photographs, campaigns, articles, and so on. Not that being on social media makes creatives happy. An informal survey of illustrators found that 'while everyone saw [Instagram] as a valid and necessary marketing tool, it mostly left them feeling negative and unhappy with their work',[50] with people constantly comparing themselves to other accounts and judging their work based on whether it was a 'success' on Instagram rather than its creative meaning.

There is a need for what Lanier has called 'deleter pioneers': people who will create ways of existing without all these apps, which for some people have now been an insidious presence since birth. This means redefining how to conduct our social and work lives; how to share personal and political information with networks; how to build inclusion and communication across borders;[51] how to push back against the madness that artists or writers can be judged on their 'following' – 'as if the real point of connection weren't the work itself';[52] how to take back our time and energy from the Zuckerbergs of this world; and how to build supportive, real-life artistic communities where people are not judged or ranked by accounts and do not feel that the purpose of their life is to optimise. It's an open field, with creatives and creative thought being vital for getting us out of the glue pot. The more creatives who are stuck, however, the harder it will be.

Communicative Capitalism

Beyond the emotional pain of individuals is an even larger problem concerning the internet's effect upon resistance and our collective ability to bring about social change. Professor Jodi Dean developed the theory of *communicative capitalism* – where the values heralded as central to democracy take material form in networked communications technologies. These values are access, transparency, participation, discussion, having a voice, and so on – everything democracy and the internet are both supposed to represent.

The catch, however, is that instead of all of this communication and connectivity leading to freedom, democracy, and an equal sharing of wealth, in reality political change is undermined in 'a deluge of screens'.[53] Communicative capitalism can be understood through the question Dean poses: 'Why, at a time when the means of communication have been revolutionised, when people can contribute their opinions and access those of others rapidly and immediately, has democracy failed?'[54]

Think of this through the prism of fashion activism. Never before have we known so much about how and where our clothes are produced, never before has there been such sustained anger over labour rights and environmental destruction. At the same time, never before have we been connected at the touch of a button to not just thousands of our peers around the world but to governments, politicians, and global institutions. We are told we can talk directly to brands and let them – and the world – know our thoughts on their actions. And yet, by every measure things are worse. Factory wages are worse, planetary systems are on the verge of collapse, the pandemic made the rich richer and the poor poorer. There is no democracy whatsoever in the fashion industry.

So what is going on? By Dean's measure, this is not a problem of people not being involved or not caring, it's that 'the forms of our involvement are captured in ways that reinforce the system rather than undermine it'.[55] While the internet upholds democratic rhetoric, this rhetoric actually serves to strengthen the hold of capitalism on networked societies. Not only does this infrastructure that we find ourselves in fail to deliver a democracy that tackles issues like inequality, factory safety, climate change, and war, but even worse, it makes us worship the technology that is supposedly making things happen (even while things get worse). At the same time, communicative capitalism replaces traditional forms of resistance that bring about massive social change – physical demonstrations, strikes, class-based organising, and action.[56] The theory of communicative capitalism does not argue that networked communications never facilitate political resistance, nor that all web-based activities are trivial. As the case study of Jeyasre Kathiravel shows (see below), the internet is very useful for connectivity, but the question remains: 'why in an age celebrated for its communications there is no response'?[57]

Fashion campaigns have a tendency to fetishise both technology and consumer power. In the Global North, passive online campaigns are favoured over and above physical collective activities like protests, shop blockades, marches, and strikes or labour solidarity work. The main exception to this is XR (Extinction Rebellion), with their series of demonstrations outside London Fashion Week which had such an impact, partly because they had become unusual. The centring of online consumer campaigning slows the rate of progress and sidelines and takes resources away from workers' struggles in the Global South. When I interviewed Nandita Shivakuma, India coordinator for the Asia Floor Wage Alliance, she spoke of the imbalance between worker power and consumer power which can only go so far in terms of change: 'Consumer power cannot be the forefront of a campaign, it cannot be the forefront of the movement. Too much space is being occupied by consumer campaigns, too much money is flowing into consumer campaigns, but not enough money and not enough power is being built into the worker movement in the Global South.'

This power imbalance is up to each of us to push back on: to not accept campaigns that start and end with online consumer activity and have no link to workers organisations in the Global South; to not accept the dampening of our political will because we have signed an online petition or shared a post; to not disavow tried and tested forms of active political struggle or as Dean outlines, fetishising technology as being political and doing our job *for us*.[18] It is vital here also to keep a sense of perspective and not conflate effective activism with follower counts. Categorically, the people and organisations on the front line of making actual change happen in the fashion industry (most of whom are in the Global South) either have no online following or a very small one.

As Dean writes, technology is inherently political and should not be separated from other political struggles. Every form of technology emerged from 'within the brutalities of global capital' and exists because of 'racialised violence and division'. Sites, apps, and devices are not going to save us, rather they must be held in a political space that recognises both their origins, beneficiaries, and true purposes while we maintain the hard work of organising and struggle. As Lola Olufemi wrote in *Feminism Interrupted*: 'Activist work is tireless, but it is important that we do it anyway because it is one of the few methods that provide us with a chance of transforming the way we live.'[59]

Justice For Jeyasre

Jeyasre Kathiravel was a 21-year-old Dalit woman from Tamil Nadu, India. She was the first person in her village to go to college. She got a job as a garment worker at a factory called Natchi Apparel in a rural part of Tamil Nadu. Natchi Apparel is owned by Eastman Exports Global Clothing, India's fourth biggest apparel exporter, and is a supplier factory for multinational fashion brand H&M. It was a job Jeyasre intended to leave as soon as she could find other employment. On 1 January 2021, Jeyasre did not return home from work. After an extensive search by her family and community that lasted four days, she was discovered dead in a patch of wasteland, having been raped and murdered. Her supervisor at Natchi Apparel confessed and was charged with this horrific crime.

Jeyasre Kathiravel's death could have and should have been prevented. She had been repeatedly harassed at work by the man who eventually attacked and killed her. In the aftermath of her murder, more than 25 women came forward to report harassment and sexual abuse at Natchi Apparel, making it clear that gender-based violence at the factory was widespread. Workers have also described being forced to make more than 1,000 items of clothing a day under relentless pressure.[60]

Jeyasre Kathiravel was a member of the only Dalit-women-led trade union in India, the Tamil Nadu Textile and Common Labour Union (TTCU). The TTCU, supported by the Asia Floor Wage Alliance in India and Global Labour Justice in the USA, began a campaign with three aims: (1) compensation for Jeyasre's family; (2) an end to all coercion and retaliation against Jeyasre's family, colleagues and union; and (3) an enforceable agreement with brands, Eastman Exports, and the TTCU to end gender-based violence and barriers to freedom of association.

A global day of action calling for Justice For Jeyasre was set for 1 April 2021. This was in the midst of a pandemic, and here in London there was both a risk of contagion in crowds and £10,000 fines for organising a protest.[61] The campaign group UK Justice For Jeyasre asked people to make #JusticeFor-Jeyasre placards and take a photo outside their local branch of H&M, to make banners and hang them from their windows, to hold die-ins outside branches of H&M, and to invade H&M's own feeds and disrupt them with messages. Everything was to be shared across all social media accounts with H&M tagged in every post. The campaign gave people as many digital tools as possible – producing sample tweets in English and Swedish, sample letters to send, sample posts and infographics – all of which were checked with the TTCU and Jeyasre's family via the Asia Floor Wage Alliance so that the messaging was in line with what workers and the family wanted.

On the morning of the day of action H&M announced it would pay compensation. Despite this attempt at appeasement, hundreds of people took part in activities to push for fulfilment of the last two demands. In London people risked fines by holding small protests outside branches of H&M. At H&M's flagship store on Oxford Street the protest included the laying of flowers in Jeyasre's memory. In Manchester, a group of volunteers at the Manchester not-for-profit Stitched Up sewed a Justice For Jeyasre banner. The protests spread to mainland Europe, with activists holding small protests in Germany and XR activists in the Netherlands letting off smoke bombs and holding a protest outside H&M. Throughout the day, across social media, people crafted signs, graphics, and embroidery.

The *Oh So Ethical* blog is run by a 26-year-old British Bangladeshi activist who wishes to remain anonymous. She played a central role in organising UK Justice For Jeyasre, along with War on Want and Fashion Act Now (full disclosure, I also co-organised the UK campaign). 'This was the best campaign I've been a part of', says Oh So Ethical:

> Being so in contact with the TTCU and AFWA and Jeyasre's family made me feel so at ease in terms of having the blessing of her family and union. It's really important that your activism is grounded in knowledge about what is wanted by workers and unions so being able to check what we were doing and publishing was so important. It is such a sensitive topic but we were instilled with determination because we'd got that blessing and we knew it was right.

Three weeks later, Indonesian unions and women's rights organisations held an in-person vigil using the 'blood-splattered' H&M logo designed by activists in London. An online vigil was then attended by over 1,000 people from 33 countries who gathered in solidarity with the Kathiravel family and the TTCU. We heard from Thivya Rakini, the state president of TTCU and from Muthulakshmi Kathiravel, Jeyasre's mother: 'As a mother, I don't want this to happen to any daughter, any worker', she said. 'I lost a beautiful daughter I can no longer get back. I consider all the workers present in the textile sector [to be] my daughter, so the incident that happened to my daughter should never ever happen to any young workers.'[62]

This level of connectivity, especially in the precarious days of a global pandemic, would not have been possible without the internet. It was not, however, the internet that caused the fight against gender-based violence, nor was it the internet or apps that gave this event its potency. (In fact, if we weigh up the role of the internet and apps like Instagram in this struggle, might we not find they have mostly provided H&M and its peers with the ability to make everything look just fine?)

The potency on 1 April 2021 came from the physical risks and energy that people took by engaging in the day. This is something that can been seen to a greater extent with bigger struggles like the so-called Arab Uprisings, the Gezi Park protests in Turkey, Occupy Wall Street, and the Black Lives Matter movement – all of which it is said resulted in large part from social media.[63] These movements count for so much precisely because, as Dean argues, rather than sitting at home behind their laptops and phones, people actually went outside. They flooded onto the streets to work arm in arm with strangers for a political purpose, often in the face of lethally violent state repression. In each of these instances posting on Instagram or circulating online petitions was seen as an inadequate political practice to challenge injustice.[64]

As this chapter closes, it is fitting that we now turn to the endgame of the fashion media, not to critique, inform, guide, and entertain but to encourage the consumption of billions upon billions of bits of apparel.

CHAPTER THREE
Buyology

Dresses are like political opinion. There's always a newer, more exciting idea on the horizon especially when conflicting parties are involved.

Anne Fogarty, *The Art of Being a Well Dressed Wife*[1]

It's my flimsy for the evening – Jackrabbit designed it ... A flimsy is a once-garment for festivals. Made out of algae, natural dyes. We throw them in the compost afterward. Not like costumes. Costumes you sign out of the library for once or for a month, then they go back for someone else. But flimsies are fancies for once only.

Marge Piercy, *Woman on the Edge of Time*

The year 2020 was one of dramatically reduced physical and social orbits. Across the UK it was often illegal to have visitors to your home, while social gatherings, work commutes, and school runs all but disappeared for months on end. Much was made of a global pause and of people rediscovering what really counts when the bustle of normal life drifts away. But one thing that did not pause was shopping for non-essential items.

In April 2020, I spoke with Jak, a stressed-out delivery driver contracted to ASOS. Orders had reduced, but they had not stopped. Within his postcode patch he found himself repeatedly delivering packages to the same customers. People would open their doors without giving him time to safely step back two metres, he had to press lift buttons and touch door handles without knowing if they were infected. He lacked proper PPE (personal protective equipment) and only one person had ever bothered to acknowledge his role in their life and say thank you. He was not happy to be risking his life so people could have a new T-shirt.

When toilet paper mania hit the UK at the start of the pandemic, judging other people's shopping habits became something of a national pastime. The temptation is to dismiss those ASOS customers as merely hopelessly selfish beings who lack the willpower and the moral fortitude needed to cope with a global crisis. The same goes for the Primark customers who enraged people by forming queues outside the budget store once lockdown eased. But to treat them in this way would be to lose critical insights about consumption. If we dismiss shoppers and shopping we will never truly understand how we have collectively become so lost.

There are many reasons to challenge overconsumption and its driving force of overproduction, not least because we are in an extreme climate crisis and must radically overhaul how we distribute and consume resources. But this must be done in a way that critiques and moves to overthrow capitalism rather than attacking the people caught in the maelstrom.

While 'isolated in our own crude solitariness', as Engels put it,[2] we scroll though shop websites, mediating our existence and our connection to the world via our relationship to things rather than other people or the planet. By most metrics – and by the evidence of planetary turmoil – this is not a healthy way to live. The commodities that surround us, from clothes to electronics, are steeped in violence. From the violence of colonial trade routes to present-day workers trapped in burning factories. At the other end of supply chains, life bubbles with dissatisfaction – bullshit jobs, an acute loss of control, and a system that presents shopping as salvation, identity, community, and entertainment all rolled into one.

Is it any wonder that under neoliberalism, having endured decades of propaganda that says community is dead and the 'consumer is king', that people wanted to shop to deal with Covid's sadness and uncertainty? And that we sometimes feel more of a sense of connectivity with the things we buy than with the human beings, like Jak, who deliver them to our doors? We have been sold a nightmare, one in which the communal question of 'What do we need?' is less important than the consumerist question of 'What do I want?'[3] Yet the paucity of this strategy is here for all to see. We are interconnected and we cannot make it alone, we deserve more than a life of doom-scrolling and competitively hoarding toilet roll because we feel convinced no one will help us if the worst happens.

This is a chapter about what fashion is currently for. The way it functions as a system of exploitation at both ends of the industry, and the way it serves as an excuse for exploitation, which is inexplicably linked to the economic system we live under. As we dive into the knotty question of consumption, I once again invite you to return to a central question in this book: What kind of society do you want to live in and what is the role of fashion in that society? As you read, think about how, not just the clothes, but the world could be different.

Covet

A dark, rainy Paris street. A woman driven to criminality by desire. 'There it was. Staring at me. I had to have it.' Sarah Jessica Parker kicks in a shop window and tries to grab a bottle of perfume before being handcuffed and led away. Begging a police officer for just one little spritz of the scent, she is last seen wild-eyed and unrepentant behind prison bars repeating the mantra: 'I had to have it.'

The advertisement for Sarah Jessica Parker's fragrance Covet is exceptionally similar to an earlier one for Dior's Addict perfume, in which Liberty Ross is on the run from the police through rainy Paris streets having smashed a shop window to steal perfume. Playing on the themes of the power of desire for objects and the irrationality of female shoppers, the advert's message is that criminality in pursuit of fashion is understandable, sexy, and humorous.

During the summer of 2011, riots swept across Britain. Sparked by the police killing of Mark Duggan in Tottenham, the rioters smashed town centres and torched buildings across the country. The causes of the riots – police violence, social exclusion, poverty – have been hotly debated ever since, but one recurrent feature was the looting of clothing and shoe shops. Amid the chaos, one particular image was seized on by the media – that of 22-year-old Shereka Leigh, filmed trying on shoes from a looted store before stealing them. She later received an eight-month prison sentence having been found with just a few hundred pounds' worth of goods.

The riots, and the harsh sentencing that followed, illustrate the tense disconnect between society's messages. People are taught: 'I shop therefore I am' – that shopping equals success and that they should go to any length to consume. Our ability to shop, discard, and replace has become the prime indicator of our social standing and personal success.[4] Even as adverts like those for Covet and Addict make light of criminality, they fail to mention that theft is acceptable only if the perpetrator is a beautiful, rich, white woman. Otherwise you can expect to serve 16 months for stealing ice cream or 6 months for the theft of £3.50 worth of water.[5] The causes of the unrest have not been dealt with; in fact, they have intensified. Calls for change are often dismissed for fear that they mean a lifestyle downgrade or protracted scarcity. However, the problem we face is not scarcity but inequality. If we pause to look around us, the Covid-19 pandemic was a giant neon sign screaming that capitalism fails humanity. How is it right that online shopping has turned Amazon founder Jeff Bezos into the richest person on the planet while over 9 per cent of the world's population fell into an extreme poverty existence of £1.50 per day? To transform how we consume we must end inequality.

As riots and uprisings show, this system brings people to the boil through a combination of poverty on the one hand and the bombardment of images of things they will never have on the other. Expecting them not to boil over is foolish. As the eminent sociologist Zygmunt Bauman reasoned:

> Objects of desire, whose absence is most violently resented, are nowadays many and varied – and their numbers, as well as the temptation to have them, grow by the day. And so grows the wrath, humiliation, spite and grudge aroused by not having them – as well as the urge to destroy what you can't have. Looting shops and setting them on fire derive from the same impulsion and gratify the same longing.[6]

An Unequal Fashion

Oxford Street in London's West End is Europe's busiest street. Navigating through the crowds takes a shopper past several branches of H&M, with its turnover of up to 50 collections per year; Nike Town, where lines of fanatical shoe fans queue overnight; Primark, where fights break out during the sales; and Uniqlo, the Japanese clothing company that boasts of making 613 different varieties of sock.

All of this is possible only because of the existence of a surplus in society. Whereas animals produce only what they need, humans go beyond their immediate physical needs to produce a surplus of food, shelter, clothing, and other commodities. There is more than enough wealth in society to support everybody, but a walk down Oxford Street clearly shows that socially produced surplus wealth is not evenly distributed. Despite the Covid-19 crisis, the 2020 'luxury goods' market was estimated to be worth $349.1 billion,[7] while outside Bond Street underground station the homeless beg for spare change. Despite these glaring inequalities, some still argue that fashion is now egalitarian.

It is true that following fashion trends and owning vast quantities of clothing is no longer the preserve of the wealthy. Slash fashion outlets like Boohoo and SHEIN flood the market with endless cheap options, as do Primark and Peacocks, all while H&M and Target release 'designer' collections. The second-hand market has also enjoyed a renaissance of cool with charity shops, vintage stores, kilo sales, eBay, Depop, Vinted, and more offering second-hand trade in clothing. This widespread availability of relatively cheap clothing (of dubious quality and options) is not, however, the same as fashion democracy. There is no democracy when it comes to controlling the major issues in this industry.

Fashion consumption is deeply unequal, and generalisations about fashion consumers are misleading. The activist academic Juliet Schor says that instead of simply asking *why do* we consume so much it is important to clarify *who* is doing all the consuming.[8] A statistic such as the fact that in one year North Americans discarded 300 million pairs of shoes[9] seems straightforward, but it obscures the fact that some 50 million Americans live below the poverty line and another 100 million subsist on a low income.[10] Legitimate concerns, particularly about the environmental impact of fashion, are not helped by blanket calls for everyone to 'shop less'. These calls are irrelevant to families forced to choose between a pair of shoes without holes and putting hot food on the table for their children.[11]

Back in the summer of 2020, lockdown had just eased and temperatures were rising. When Primark reopened, it sparked a wave of condemnation across social media regarding people who had queued up to shop. Some posts were blaming Primark shoppers for climate change and factory conditions, some said they should save their money and buy something they 'really wanted', others said people in the queues were automatically racist for buying fast-fashion, others that people should shop second hand – seemingly forgetting that when charity shops eventually reopened, at least half of their stock would be from Primark or its competitors. It made for endless scrolling, and photographs of the queues adding to the sense that 'those people' should feel shame.

What was lacking on that June day, and what continues to be absent from so much of the debate around fashion consumption, was the ability to criticise capitalism as a system of oppression rather than to attack the people it oppresses. In particular, fashion must be seen as a corporate drive for profit and not the fault of people in queues.

There are structural issues that make the fashion industry exploitative of people and planet. It has never been, and never will be, something that can be changed within a vacuum. Four key elements are so inextricably linked that fashion would not exist without the exploitation of: (1) women, (2) people of colour, (3) the global working class, and (4) the planet (the biosphere and animals). Any action, any post, any campaign must have these four intersectional issues at its heart. Otherwise it does more harm than good.

It is also important to note that consumption critiques must encompass high-end as well as high-street fashion and not just fall into the trap of focusing solely on 'fast-fashion'. Post-lockdown, customers spent US$2.7 million at the Hermès flagship store in Guangzhou – believed to be the highest ever daily takings for a luxury boutique in China. In the same vein, Louis Vuitton started selling a face shield for $1,000, yet, despite the epically offensive nature of such an object (how much PPE could have been made instead?), there was no outpouring of angry photos, posts, and hand-wringing over rich shoppers. Displays of excess wealth are as much a product of poverty as a £2 bikini, there is no luxury without blinding inequality and exploitation. Nor is there any evidence that shopping for expensive clothes is better, or that wealthy 'good' shoppers have smaller carbon footprints. Rich people in the USA create more carbon driving their car than an entire household of poorer people do in eight months.

Style as Humanity?

As well as inviting a false sense of equality, ignoring the link between fashion consumption and class ignores material circumstances in favour of theories of identity. The street fashion blog *The Sartorialist* published a photograph of a homeless man with the caption: 'Not Giving Up Hope'. Scott Schuman and his fans expressed astonished delight that the homeless man had matched blue boots with blue glasses and gloves. This, they concluded, meant he was dignified and had 'Not Given Up'. Comments included, 'Powerful. He doesn't even look homeless. Blue is great on him', and, 'I often look at homeless folks for inspiration on what to wear. There is a certain softness to the clothes after being worn day in, day out.'[12]

At the time, academic fashion blog *Threadbared* argued that this approach summed up the problems inherent in reading clothes and style as expressions of identity. While people express themselves through commodities such as clothes, this does not mean that making a judgement about someone's clothes and their identity should bleed into evaluating them as a person.[13] If style is taken for humanity, then the reverse can also be true. Presumably, had the unnamed man been 'badly' dressed he would not have merited time or attention. This 'no style, no humanity' approach grades people's right to be treated as human beings based on their appearance, something that history, from the trade in enslaved people to Nazi ideology, has shown to be abhorrent. Ignoring class also implies that the wearing of 'bad' clothes is something people *consent* to because they have 'Given Up'. This approach neglects to mention the maelstrom of class, race, gender, and economic crises that contributes to poverty and prevents people having control over their lives. As Engels pointed out in 1844, economic circumstance cannot be offset by a willingness to work, thrift, perseverance – or being well dressed.[14]

Without class there would be no fashion industry as we know it. Clothing is a key way for the rich to signal and reproduce their power.[15] Once the masses gain access to elite fashions (or close approximations of them) the rich move on in order to leave everyone else behind. In the late 1990s and early 2000s, Burberry's elite position suffered a temporary downfall when it became a working-class favourite. Corporate greed had led Burberry to sell hundreds of licences for its plaid print which led to the mass production of a once exclusive product. At one point even Burberry-print dog nappies were being manufactured. As one eighteenth-century commentator wryly noted: 'Nothing makes noble persons despise the gilded costume so much as to see it on the bodies of the lowliest men in the world.'[16]

King Consumer?

In the foreword to *Green Is the New Black*, model and actor Lily Cole wrote that consumers need to take responsibility for their purchases because 'capitalism is only as ruthless as its consumers. After all the consumer is king, right?'[17] Arguing that consumers are more powerful than corporations is indicative of a shift of responsibility, of blaming customers for the ills of the fashion industry. The previous chapters have shown fashion corporations to be more powerful than ever, yet, as Juliet Schor writes, growing corporate power has been accompanied by the dominance of an ideology that insists that the opposite is true and that the consumer is king.[18] One way to determine whether the corporation or the customer wears the crown is to examine why fashion is produced.

I originally wrote this on a day when most of the United Kingdom was blanketed in snow and I was wearing 18 pieces of clothing in an attempt to keep warm. Then and now, it seems obvious that humans need clothes. Indeed, 40,000-year-old sewing needles have been found on Palaeolithic sites.[19] Yet I still cannot argue that I need all the clothes that are hanging in my wardrobe. So why are they there? Because fashion is not about answering human need but about producing corporate profit. In *The Poverty of Philosophy*, Marx writes: 'World trade turns almost entirely around the needs, not of individual consumption, but of production.'[20] Corporations must produce fashion in order to make money. If everyone bought only the clothes they needed it would spell disaster for corporations, so instead 'false needs' are created to keep everyone shopping. These needs are false because they are the manufacturers' needs not those of the consumer.[21]

In 1690, the economist Nicholas Barbon called fashion 'the spirit and life of trade' because 'it occasions the expense of cloth before the old ones have worn out'. Barbon praised fashion's ability to 'dress a man as if he lived in a perpetual spring – he never sees the autumn of his cloth'.[22] 'Autumn cloth' – threadbare cloth that needs replacing – is never reached thanks to the cycle of fashion that replaces clothes long before it is necessary. Fashion is more than just clothes; it is a commodity cycle of newness that makes clothes go out of date and keeps retailers in business. This makes consumption the final stage in the production of fashion: 'A product becomes a real product only by being consumed', wrote Marx. 'A garment becomes a real garment only in the act of being worn.'[23]

There is thus a symbiotic relationship between people and the fashion industry. Fashion should not be simplified as something that is merely imposed on people from on high. There is cross-pollination, with many trends originating at street level before being quickly co-opted, commodified, and marketed.

People are a vital component of fashion. If *le mode* is clothing and *la mode* is fashion, then as the fashion academic Ingrid Loschek explains: '*Le mode* becomes *la mode* when *le mode* reaches the streets.'[24] This was Gabrielle ('Coco') Chanel's point when she remarked: 'A fashion that does not reach the streets is not a fashion.'

Value Chain

Fashion involves clothing being valued for something other than its use-value – the value of a commodity based on its ability to meet a human need. Instead of use-value, symbolic values, like love, wealth, and power, are attributed to commodities.[25] Capitalism has changed what we value as a society. Value is now associated with market-based value alone – that which can be traded or sold. Real value, that of love, solidarity, truth, connection, and nature, has been reduced to existing in a haunted form.[26]

Because of this, it is possible to come home with the results of a long day of clothes shopping and immediately want more. As a young teenager I remember going out with my best friend Tamar to buy coordinated clothes and shoes on the local high street and then waking up the next morning in a clothes-messy bedroom feeling a black hole inside of me that could never really be filled. If we had been looking for things based only on their use-value we would be sated (and probably overwhelmed), but because we were looking for symbolism, we face a search based on empty belief which the ancient Greek philosopher Epicurus said 'plunges out to infinity'.[27]

Shopping is continually proffered as the way out of emotional pain. Yet shopping to repair the emotional pain of a broken heart, a lost job, or boredom is like trying to fill a hole with air – the black hole of wanting does not go away no matter how many clothes you buy. The unfulfilling nature of modern society means that a lot of shopping gets done and a lot of commodities fruitlessly consumed. In her book *Plenitude*, Schor has called this 'the materiality paradox'. As items like clothing become more and more valued for their symbolic value, their production, consumption, and disposal increases rapidly. The paradox means that while we consume far more items in an attempt to find meaning, we value them less.

In modern society, the times when your need for non-material meaning is greatest are the times when you are mostly likely to maximise your consumption of material resources.[28] Magazines abound with advice about cheering yourself up using consumption, but if a job interview went badly, or a break-up is causing emotional pain, it's not more objects that are needed but social connection and support systems – for example, fulfilling company and probably a hug.

Isolation, lockdown, and quarantine showed what is vital – community, other people, public services, shared well-being, purpose and culture, travelling, outdoor space, and working collectively to make the world a fair and just place. The precious immaterial world of human connection that is so often hidden gained rightful recognition. But this state of renewed awareness could not be allowed to last or gain traction. Globally, fashion is a $2.5 trillion dollar industry.[29] Because stagnation would spell disaster for capitalism, governments and institutions sometimes intervene to ensure that what is produced is also consumed.[30]

Christmas 2020 saw Mayor of London Sadiq Khan encourage shopping even during the pandemic: 'I'm encouraging people to shop safely and shop in London.'[31] This echoed the days following the 2001 attacks on the World Trade Center when, because the US economy could not afford for people not to shop, President Bush announced that retail sales were strong: 'I encourage you all to go shopping more.' Similarly, in the late 1990s, when the Adbusters Media Foundation tried to buy airtime for its Buy Nothing Day campaign, it was turned down by CBS on the grounds that it was contrary to the country's current economic policy.[32] These are examples of the subordination of human needs to the imperative of corporations to accumulate wealth. Imaginary appetites and false needs are created without regard to whether they are real or dehumanising,[33] and without regard for what they have done, and continue to do, to the biosphere, the animal kingdom, and the planet. While fashion can provide an outlet for aesthetic creativity and enjoyment, this is subject to the demands of the markets that control fashion production. In this way, the human need for clothing and creativity has been commodified into the production of fashion for profit.

Shop to Live

The 'king consumer' ideology obscures fashion as a compelling economic need. Because it is constantly changing, fashion has become synonymous with being modern and competent. Keeping up with fashion can determine whether or not people find and keep employment, housing, and their standing in society. The concept of aesthetic labour – of a person's job depending on their appearance – is generally applied to those working in the modelling, acting, or music industries.[34] But maintaining a certain appearance is a prerequisite for people throughout the workforce. This makes fashion an economic necessity that people must consume to remain current. As *Vogue* once described it: 'Just when you thought you had nailed your autumn/winter wardrobe – tunic (check), sheath dress (check), fuzzy knit (check), midi skirt (check), lace blouse (check – so many compliments) – a whole new set of options arrive in store.'[35]

One of the most enduring trends of the economic crisis that began in 2008 was that of workwear. As unemployment and job insecurity rose, people were told to transform themselves with some well-tailored clothes. *The Times* reported that 'looking like someone who actually works for a living seem to be coming back into vogue'.[36] Another commentator summed up recession fashion by stating: 'It's OK to be redundant. It's not OK to look redundant.'[37] An extreme example was a magazine editorial that encouraged readers to buy an inordinately expensive necklace: 'Sure it's a recession but you're not dead yet!'[38]

Similarly, during the pandemic, unemployment and job insecurity rose again with furlough schemes, redundancies, and companies shutting down. Of the people who clung on to their jobs, millions ended up working from home. People were no longer in an office environment, no longer meeting people face to face. They were now at home, on their sofa or at a quickly assembled desk. While this could and should have signalled the end of workwear, at least for a while, what happened instead was a hyperconcentration on the top half of the body. As the *Wall Street Journal* put it: 'In the Zoom era, eye-catching, above-the-waist attire is key.'[39] Rather than give people a break, fashion articles sprouted up recommending the best shirts, blouses, make-up products, and lighting to enhance a video call. Plastic surgeons also began to report a 'Zoom boom' as people grew disheartened by staring at their on-screen appearance all day. Nobody was allowed to relax.

This is the promise–threat model of fashion. Keeping up appearances by buying will keep you safe from harm, while not buying courts disaster.[40] Such is the importance of clothes for finding work that numerous charities exist to help people dress for interviews. Dress for Success 'solves the Catch-22 that confronts disadvantaged women trying to enter the workforce: Without a job, how can you afford a suit? But without a suit, how can you get a job?'[41]

The need to maintain an appearance to secure work is not new. A factory worker's letter published in a newspaper in

1954 complained about the need to wear make-up: 'You can't go out hunting even a factory job looking as tired as you might feel. Cosmetics brighten up a weary face and give the illusion of the necessary vigour and youth.'[42] In the same series of letters another woman wrote: 'Personally, I would be greatly relieved if I could forgo the trouble and expense of make-up, but capitalism won't let me. I'm no sucker for beauty-aid ads, but economic pressure – I have to earn my living – forces me to buy and use the darned stuff.'[43] How many people today would happily give up make-up or fashion in its entirety if it were not for the need to earn a living? The radical Evelyn Reed explained in 1954 that there is a difference between criticising people for enjoying buying and wearing fashion and criticising capitalism for compelling people constantly to buy new clothes. The freedom to wear and enjoy fashionable clothes must also be accompanied by the freedom not to do so. If we do not critique capitalist compulsions, then statements from make-up magnates like Helena Rubenstein ('There are no ugly women, just lazy ones') become truisms rather than merely grasping attempts to make billions by exploiting people's insecurities.

The late feminist academic Sandra Lee Bartky wrote that while no one is marched off for electrolysis at rifle point, women are still compelled to conform to certain beauty ideals.[44] If make-up is a creative pursuit allowing women to express their individuality, why is the same picture painted day after day with little room for novelty or imagination? The woman who does not paint her face encounters sanctions that would never be applied to someone who 'chooses not to paint a watercolour'.[45]

Think of Me as Evil?

G. K. Chesterton declared that 'it is really not so repulsive to see the poor asking for money as to see the rich asking for more money. And advertisement is the rich asking for more money.'[46] Advertising is a bridge corporations use to reach consumers. Its purpose is to sell products to gain maximum profits. As such, the advertising industry is merely a symptom of the system that we live in and not the main problem itself. It represents massive waste, however, with experts expecting worldwide spending on advertising to surpass US$630 billion in 2024. North America is the region that invests most in the sector, followed by Asia and western Europe.[47]

Adverts are everywhere. Not just on billboards but covering newspapers, magazines, radio, public transport, inside schools, colleges, and universities, hospitals, museums, and, as we have seen, every inch of the internet and social media. One clothing company stuck raised metal plates on park benches to imprint adverts onto people's bare skin when they sat down. A train company used sheep as living billboards. People have even sold sections of their bodies as tattooed advertising space. Advertising has become inescapable, and 'if anything is following you around that doggedly, you're better off knowing what it's up to'.[48]

When accused of increasing pollution and poverty, advertising agencies argue that they merely redistribute existing desires rather than increase people's desire for 'stuff'. This premise is extremely important to cigarette advertisers, who argue that they do not cause more people to smoke, they just steal existing smokers from other brands. Similarly, fashion corporations claim that they are simply responding to human needs and use advertising to compete for existing markets, relieving them of responsibility for the millions of tonnes of textiles found in landfill. Yet the evidence suggests the opposite. The more people are exposed to advertisements, the more they consume. *Think of Me as Evil? Opening the Ethical Debates in Advertising*, a report produced for the World Wide Fund for Nature and the Public Interest Research Centre, stated that the implication that advertising increases aggregate material consumption means it can be pinpointed as an engine of the least sustainable aspects of an economy.[49]

For some liberal economists, seeing thousands of adverts a day is a sign of healthy competition and choice. Competing companies, however, are already part of the monopoly of private property.[50] Working people have been dispossessed of any kind of ownership of productive property. Instead, corporations own everything from factories to farms to offices.[51] The fashion industry is particularly monopolised, with the majority of brands owned by a few multinational corporations, as discussed in Chapter 1.

Advertisements also act collectively to pump out the same message. The message is that we should shop – we should shop for clothes that will make us richer even though we've just spent all our money.[52] Real choice has been eroded and replaced by consumption choices.[53] While a consumer cannot choose whether their taxes go towards cancer treatments or F-16 fighter jets, or whether the firm they work for builds social housing or speculates on the cost of wheat causing famine in Africa, they *can* choose between 'island bohemia' and 'polo lounge' trends for their summer wardrobe.

Nor can we choose when we encounter adverts. The television can be switched off, adverts on billboards, public transport, and social media cannot. The authors of *Think of Me as Evil?* were so convinced by the impact of advertising that they recommended a disclaimer should be placed on every billboard:

This advertisement may influence you in ways of which you are not consciously aware. Buying consumer goods is unlikely to improve your well-being and borrowing to buy consumer goods may be unwise; debt can enslave.

Buy Now, Pain Later

In 1966, a fashion commentator in the United States made the following prophetic statement: 'The credit card has become a badge of belonging. It began as a zephyr. It's a strong wind now. It may be the hurricane that blows up our economy.'[54] Total consumer debt in the USA stands at $14.9 trillion – a figure that includes credit cards, student debt, car loans, and mortgages.[55] While debtors' prisons were abolished there in the nineteenth century, in 2011 the *Wall Street Journal* identified over 5,000 debt prisoners as wages dropped and homes fell into negative equity.[56] In 2020, the *Clarion Ledger* in Jackson, Mississippi worked on an award-winning investigation into people being locked up *indefinitely* while they work to pay off court-ordered debts.[57]

Outside of incarceration, multiple studies have linked household debt with increased depression and stress, a decline in relationships, parenting behaviour, and positive child outcomes.[58] This is not a problem of irresponsible consumers: people are actively and officially encouraged to get into high levels of debt for systemic reasons. Interest rates are kept low to keep people shopping for goods that are becoming more expensive even as real wages drop. Debt offsets the drop in living standards that would otherwise occur.[59] Without debt the economy would shudder to a halt.[60] Fashion is inexplicably linked to debt. This was characterised by an episode of the TV series *Sex and the City* where the lead character, Carrie Bradshaw, discovers that she has spent $40,000, the then equivalent of the downpayment on her apartment, on shoes alone. Facing homelessness she realises that she 'will literally be the old woman who lived in her shoes'.[61]

Fashion is one of the biggest industries in the world; its corporations represent the global trend for brands to function as a label and a distribution system but not much else. With a few exceptions, fashion giants do not own factories, and everything they sell has been subcontracted many times over. Determined to retain its plastic crown as 'capitalism's favourite child', the fashion industry is a neoliberal icon of what economist David Harvey described as an increasing reliance on fictitious capital and debt creation.[62] The pandemic has spot-lit the role of personal debt in keeping this industry going. Under the guise of Lady Gaga endorsements, pink posters, catchy slogans, and hordes of influencers, debt has allowed a new generation of shoppers to consume fashion even during a crisis.

Founded in Sweden, Klarna is a bank that has spread like a pink rash over the fashion industry. Along with a slew of other payment providers, Klarna pops up on websites, offering the chance to 'buy now, pay later'. By the summer of 2020, Klarna had 85 million global customers with 200,000 retailers, including ASOS, Boohoo, H&M, Hugo Boss, Bulgari, Nike, and Urban Outfitters, adding Klarna and its offer of instalment payments to their checkouts. The pink branding hides the reality of financialisation behind a facade of respectability or luxury.

Debt's role in fashion is not new, but Klarna has attracted the attention of campaigners for its unscrupulous targeting of young people. As MoneySavingExpert.com founder Martin Lewis commented: 'It's even been talked about in some ways as a lifestyle choice – but it is not. It is a debt, and it should be treated as a debt.'[63] The British government has promised to finally consult on how to regulate buy now, pay later, a move welcomed by debt advice charity StepChange, who say they are worried by the 'disproportionately high' number of young people seeking advice in recent years. 'Among StepChange clients, those who have buy now, pay later (BNPL) debts frequently have eight or nine other debts, and they are typically young, with more than a third aged under 25', explains Sue

Anderson, Head of Media at StepChange, the UK's leading debt advice organisation. 'BNPL services are often marketed as a source of convenience but the financial commitment should not be underestimated – it's important to remember that the main benefit to retailers of offering these services is to sell more goods.'[64]

The financial crisis led to StepChange reporting a 21 per cent increase in people asking for help between 2008 and 2010. Similarly, in 2021 they reported that since the start of the pandemic, 11.3 million people in the UK had suffered a fall in income that affected their ability to meet day-to-day costs. Twenty-nine per cent of those who experienced a fall in income had endured hardships, including skipping meals, rationing utilities, or going without clothing or footwear appropriate for the weather.[65] In the chaos of the pandemic, buy now, pay later schemes were ideally placed to capitalise not just on the shift to online shopping but on this rise in financial vulnerability and inequality.

'One central feature of the way capital accumulation works now is that it has to be based on debt', explained Marxist historian Neil Faulkner. 'This is debt at both ends of supply chains because the working class – both as a class of producers and as a class of consumers – goes into debt both to afford the bare necessities, but also stuff they don't need but have been persuaded to buy to sustain levels of demand.' This incurred debt then also becomes a tradeable commodity and an additional means of making the rich richer and the poor poorer.

Fashion during Covid-19 has been a depressing example of what Marx described as the superfluous being easier to produce than the necessary. Modern slavery factories, including in Britain, churned out short-life fashion items while medics wore bin bags due to chronic PPE shortages. Companies like Klarna are symptoms of dysfunction. The company was valued at $10.6 billion in September 2020, which rose to $31 billion in

March 2021 and then to over $40 billion in June 2021.[66] The fashion industry is pivoting ever further away from production or creativity and more towards financial speculation.

Mirrored Debt

Young people in Britain taking on debt to buy clothes is mirrored by people in the Global South being forced into debt in order to produce fashion. This is not, however, to simplistically divide the world into producers and consumers. As we have seen, young people targeted by finance capital while browsing on their phones are also experiencing a crisis of low wages and insecure employment. Likewise, people stuck working in garment factories are similarly subjected to all the powers of advertising and alienation that cut off their creative impulses and push them to shop.

In this bone-crushingly unequal system, corporations compete for profits not just through sales but by driving down the costs of production. This has been viscerally illustrated by the treatment of factory workers during the pandemic. Khalid Mahmood is the director of the Labour Education Foundation in Lahore, Pakistan, and spent 2020 fighting the fires of exploitation fanned even higher by Covid-19. Debt is a constant reality for garment workers in Pakistan – even before the pandemic, workers had to borrow money to subsidise poverty wages. But during the pandemic, as brands cancelled orders and abandoned factories, wages fell even further. 'Some of the workers had to sell household items, for example, mobile phones or washing machines', Khalid explains. 'Most of them have borrowed money from family or friends, and had to get food from shopkeepers on credit, plus they are in debt for their children's school fees and house rent.'

In Lahore, families have taken their children out of school, and many have had to move to smaller, cheaper homes

– sometimes leaving behind their possessions as a guarantee they will pay rent arrears. This crisis is replicated across the fashion industry – one survey found that 75 per cent of garment workers have taken out loans during the pandemic.[67] Hardship at the bottom of the fashion system is inseparable from the vast accumulated wealth at the top. While capitalism creates intergalactic wealth for a tiny percentage of people, billions of others are left in poverty. In one sense this inequality is not good for business. If accumulated wealth makes too many people poor, how are they going to keep buying commodities like jeans, bandeaux tops, and trainers? This is where the catchy slogans and pink posters of Klarna come in. 'The system is on life support, and that life support is debt', says Neil Faulkner. 'Were you to cancel debt and remove the possibility of people getting into debt in order to buy things, not just the fashion industry, but the entire global financial system would collapse.'

Fetishes, Snake Oil, and Alienation

An anonymous executive at Louis Vuitton has been quoted as describing the company's success as 'the biggest sleight of hand since snake oil. Can you imagine that this is all based on canvas toile with a plastic coating and a bit of leather trim?'[68] How is it possible for scraps of stitched canvas and leather to be given so much meaning? Why do they sell for thousands of pounds? Marx termed this anomaly 'commodity fetishism'. The term was taken from early Portuguese anthropological writings in which amulets or charms were known as *feitiço*. The amulets were described as magically artful; possessing one was believed to give the owner special powers.[69] It is this same imbuing of objects with powers beyond their composition that still occurs today. While the term 'commodity fetishism' is extremely useful and applicable to today's society, it is worth noting that the anthropological writings it is based upon often took a disparaging stance towards the non-European societies being scrutinised.

Each winter brings advertising copy implying that handbags can cure seasonal affected disorder (SAD). Advertisements promise, 'Escape those January blues with Jeremy Scott's collaboration with accessories giant Longchamp. It's a ray of sunshine!', or, 'This highlighter yellow satchel is the perfect pick-me-up for right now.' The only purchase that the NHS recommends as treatment for SAD is a light box. The fashion industry not only ignores this but hints that it can also cure other ailments – Wonderbra: 'Your Not So Secret Weapon'; Adidas: 'Impossible Is Nothing'; Diesel: 'For Successful Living'; and French Connection: 'FCUK Advertising'.

Engels observed that under capitalism, competition and private property 'isolates everyone in their own crude solitariness'.[70] In a marketised society, people are judged by their material worth. A designer handbag gives its owner status by signifying the amount spent. This speaks to the fundamental importance of viewing fashion consumption as a social act. While some consumption theories present shopping as a lonely act or something done purely as a result of unhappiness (think of the cliché of the lonely suburban housewife mindlessly shopping), this does not get to the root of why we shop. For Dr Schor, shopping is overwhelmingly an innately social activity. Even suburban housewives consume in groups, remaining hyperconscious of their peer group and their place in it. 'The primary forces that drive consumption', Dr Schor says, 'are social forces, social dynamics, dynamics of inequality and social competition, and the role of goods in giving status.'[71]

None of this, however, can be separated from alienation. Under capitalism people are locked into a mindset where having is more important than being. We learn to value things only when we directly possess them rather than looking for happiness in ourselves, in labour, in society, or in nature.[72] Commodities acquire meaning because people are alienated. The Marxist John Berger described people balancing endless stretches of meaningless working hours with a dreamed future of exciting, enviable consumption: 'The more monotonous the present, the more the imagination must seize upon the future.'[73] Arthur Miller also noted how shopping is offered as a cure for emptiness in his 1968 play *The Price*: 'Years ago, a person, if he was unhappy, didn't know what to do with himself – he'd go to church, start a revolution – something. Today you're unhappy? Can't figure it out? What is the solution? Go shopping.'

Life as a 'servant of the wage'[74] is a familiar monotony for most people. The novelist Patrick Hamilton called London a 'crouching monster' that breathed commuters: 'Every morning [they] are sucked up through an infinitely complicated respiratory apparatus of trains and termini into mighty congested lungs, held there for a number of hours, and then in the evening, exhaled violently through the same channels.'[75] Under this system, people are forced to sell their labour without any control over what they produce or how they produce it. Few people ever have the chance even to imagine their full potential, let alone reach it, because they too are turned into commodities. Rather than being an end in themselves, people become a means for someone else's profit.

Take this description from *Foot Work*:

Through a set of double doors is a shoe factory staffed by workers in matching red T-shirts. All but a few are women. They are bent over workstations around a green conveyor belt. The workers take pieces of shoes out of green baskets attached to the conveyor belt. Completing their task, they return the pieces to the basket as it moves on to the next station. The conveyor belt moves slowly but never stops. Everyone must work in tandem.[76]

This is what Marx called the reduction of people to an abstract activity and a stomach.[77]

It is not only factory workers who experience alienation. Work in non-manufacturing industries is also carried out according to management edicts rather than personal creativity or judgement. This trend is predicted to intensify in the future, with the spread of what David Graeber termed 'Bullshit Jobs' and the electronic revolution chopping up, codifying, and digitalising skills. In Marx's words, alienation means that a person only 'feels himself outside his work and in his work feels outside himself'.[78] This devastating alienation means that people become alienated not just from themselves but from products. It is this distance that provides space for the idea that commodities can have special powers. Consumers are far removed from the production of goods like shoes, handbags, or clothes. Items appear in shops without revealing a trace of the manufacturing process, which is seemingly independent of people. This gives the illusion that there is a source of wealth separate from human labour. We can admire a beaded evening gown or a solid pair of work boots without connecting them with the workers that produced them. This mystification of products means our society is arguably not materialistic enough.[79] Being materialistic in this sense does not mean doing more shopping; rather, it is a call for people to recognise that products such as shoes and handbags are dependent on nature and labour and have a physical, material reality independent of thought.[80] It calls for use-values to take precedence over endless symbolic values.

The fashion industry is adept at hiding human labour behind a glitzy facade. To create even a T-shirt requires a chain of designers, cotton pickers, sweatshop workers, dye technicians, and freight drivers. Advertisements similarly conceal their means of production. Model agencies, photographers, stylists, make-up artists, cleaners and caterers, infighting, cellulite, boredom, starvation, and Photoshop are all hidden because consumers are not allowed to look behind the scenes.[81]

This imperative comes from the need to generate surplus value. An inherent part of capitalism, surplus value arises from the difference between the value of labour-power and the value of the commodities that the labour-power produces. A study by Swiss labour rights group Public Eye estimated that the financial details of a black Zara hoodie with the word Respect printed on it were as follows. The total for wages paid throughout the entire supply chain from cotton field to printing factory were just €2.08. When the hoodie retailed for €26.66, Zara made €4.20 – double what had been split between workers toiling in cotton fields and factories.[82]

As we have seen, luxury goods also come with their true labour costs hidden from sight. By hiding the real labour costs and the methods used to manufacture a 'luxury' handbag or pair of shoes, corporations can charge more than if it was common knowledge that it was made in the same factory as regular items. This mystifying process makes commodities appear independent of the labour that made them and thus capable of possessing independent powers. In an ideal world it would be the people who made the commodities who would be valued and respected rather than just the commodities, but this is not the world we presently live in.

Despite the pain and violence that makes fashion production possible, shopping for the resulting objects is still proffered as a cure for everything from heartbreak to low self-esteem. Zygmunt Bauman describes how, '[f]rom cradle to coffin we are trained and drilled to treat shops as pharmacies filled with drugs to cure or at least mitigate all illnesses and afflictions of our lives'.[83] In reality, a new dress cannot mend a broken heart; a new bag can only metaphorically and not literally satisfy hunger.[84] Because we live in a marketised society, it is little wonder that the 'visible divinities' of money and commodities are purported to cure heartache. Our real needs are ignored and what we experience instead are the artificial needs created by capitalist society.[85] In this way we lose out twice.

The artist Rob Montgomery 'space-jacked' a billboard with the message: 'The spectacle of advertising creates images of false beauty so suave and so impossible to attain that you will hurt inside and never even know where the hurt came from ... '[86]

Far from being 'kings' who control the market, consumers of fashion are used to generate vast profits for corporations who create false needs. Our lives are inescapably linked to class and economic circumstances. There is no fashion democracy and no level playing field. Instead, there is an ever-turning wheel on which we must all run.

CHAPTER FOUR
Stitching It

The concrete room at the end of the narrow walkway behind the Ansar Ali supermarket is in darkness thanks to another power cut. Faded posters line the walls of the small, sparsely furnished trade union office. Sat on a plastic chair in the middle of the room, sunlight filtering in through the open door, Shahorbanu relives the story of losing a son to Rana Plaza. Siddique was a 24-year-old garment worker, a tall man who was affectionate with his mother and his little son, Parvez. When, on 24 April 2013, the eight-storey factory complex collapsed, Siddique became trapped under thousands of tonnes of rubble. He managed to take his mobile phone out of his pocket and call his mother. Shahorbanu describes his terrified voice pleading: 'Ma, please save me. Somehow, just please save me.'

As Shahorbanu tells her story, Rafiqul Islam, a senior union worker in the Greater Dhaka city suburb of Savar, walks through the door. Tall with curly black hair, the sight of him brings Shahorbanu to tears. 'My son was just like him. I miss when he would come back home and call me Ma – "*Umma*". It is a great suffering to bury the body of a son.' It was Siddique's 19-year-old brother Bijan who eventually found his body, five days after the collapse. Working as a rescuer digging bodies out of the rubble left Bijan traumatised. Shahorbanu says he's 'unable to tolerate any loud sounds – even loud talking'.[1]

The Path to Rana Plaza/the Road to Savar

The horror of Rana Plaza speaks to a long history of violent exploitation. In a shocking photomontage by London-based artist Amneet Johal, a photo of the Bengal famine is superimposed over an image of the Rana Plaza tragedy. Johal created this image 'to draw parallels and make visible the postcolonial infrastructures that exist and are built on colonial foundations'.[2]

The 1943 Bengal Famine, engineered by Churchill and colonial British attitudes towards India, caused the deaths of three million people. The British Empire exerted its reach around the world through colonialism, slavery, military force, terror, and financial weight, and its rule allowed for a colossal extraction of wealth. Renowned Indian Marxist, Professor Utsa Patnaik, calculated that between 1765 and 1938, Britain drained $45 trillion from India.[3] To attempt to put this staggering figure into perspective, Britain's entire GDP for 2018 was approximately $3 trillion. The looting of this wealth over centuries caused incalculable damage even while it built British infrastructure.

What we see today in the garment industry are the latest iterations of this colonial exploitation. We still live in a world where life and dignity are repeatedly sacrificed to a system that values profit over people. Never forget that fashion brands make their sourcing decisions deliberately – following colonial pathways to industrial sites where they can evade the standards that keep people safe and where they think any resistance to their crimes can, and will, be crushed.

This colonial exploitation is backed by deeply unequal global financial systems. The reason over four million Bangladeshis work in fashion production is because Bangladesh was steered into treacherous overdependence on clothing exports by the neocolonial polices of the International Monetary Fund (IMF) and World Bank.[4] These institutions pushed for Bangladesh to abandon dreams of self-sufficiency and instead enter a dead end in the global economy as a source of intensive, extremely low-paid labour. Forty years later, Bangladesh remains in this precarious trap, creating vast profits for some of the most powerful multinational corporations in the world while being unable to achieve financial stability. In today's world 'fashion' is just a word the robbers wrap their spoils in.[5] It is just an excuse for the rich to exploit the poor.

A strong trade union might have been able to evacuate Rana Plaza, but Bangladesh's labour laws are skewed in favour of factory owners. Rafiqul Islam, the tall, curly haired union organiser whose appearance reminded Shahorbanu of her lost son, has long experience of the kind of violence meted out by factory owners. When I met him in 2014, he rolled up his trouser legs to reveal shins covered in scars from being beaten with sticks by factory management thugs. He explained that when factories want to terminate a worker's contract, one tactic is to place a gun or a knife in full view of the resignation forms they want signed.[6] Labour movement figureheads face kidnapping, violence, and even murder. In 2012, Aminul Islam, the chief organiser of the Bangladesh Centre for Worker Solidarity, disappeared. He was found two days later tortured and murdered.[7]

In the aftermath of Rana Plaza, strikes numbering 200,000 workers took to the streets in September 2013 demanding justice for Rana Plaza and for better pay and conditions across the industry. The striking workers were accused of treason, of bringing Bangladesh into international disrepute, and of threatening the country's ability to attract foreign contracts. When a wave of strikes and protests broke out in Christmas 2017, garment trade unions described becoming targets for the police and thugs hired by factories: 'more than 50 local goons came and attacked our office ... they burned our documents, such as membership forms, receipt books, leaflets, and banners. They also took our office equipment, such as chairs and tables.'[8]

In December 2018 and January 2019, another huge wave of wildcat strikes saw over 50,000 garment workers protest in Dhaka, Ashulia, Narayanganj, Savar, and Gazipur districts. They were angry that the increase of the minimum wage to 8,000 Taka (US$94) would not benefit all workers or meet the rapidly rising cost of living. The crackdown saw an estimated 5,000–7,500 workers fired and thousands more facing criminal charges. Hundreds of people were beaten and shot with rubber bullets. Twenty-two-year-old Sumon Mia, a garment worker who was not involved in the protests, was shot dead.[9] In June 2021, 32-year-old Jesmin Begum was killed after police attacked a garment worker protest. The workers had blocked a highway in protest at the loss of months of unpaid factory wages, but instead of receiving their payment they were attacked with tear gas shells, rubber bullets, water cannons, and baton charges.

The Bangladesh Accord

Bangladesh's export-oriented, modern garment industry began in the late 1970s with fewer than twelve garment factories. By 1985, there were 450 factories – a figure that skyrocketed to almost 7,000 by 2015. By the 1990s the factory workforce was 90 per cent women and Bangladesh was being hailed as an economic success.[10]

But the women stitching hems, snipping threads, and folding and pressing garments were paying a high price, both physical and emotional. Between 2005 and 2012, more than 500 people died in factory fires and collapses in Bangladesh.[11] Even before Rana Plaza, the roll call of death was a long one – the Spectrum factory, the Tazreen factory, the Smart factory, to mention but a few. Each of these disasters prompted an outcry and campaigns of their own from both the local and international labour movement. Then came Rana Plaza – proving once and for all that voluntary agreements and 'business as usual' had failed utterly.

But, even with its scale, Rana Plaza might have been one more horror in the news cycle were it not for unions and campaigners in Bangladesh and around the world. Sick of their warnings going unheeded, campaigners capitalised on the outpouring of global anger by creating the groundbreaking building inspection programme, the Accord on Fire and

Building Safety in Bangladesh. The Accord was different than anything that had come before – it was legally binding and brands committed to arbitration if they broke the terms. Brands also committed to sourcing from Bangladeshi factories at the same capacity for five years.

Giving brands an ultimatum was a risky strategy. On 13 May, three weeks after the disaster, the proposed agreement had attracted just two 'maybes'. Media, and social media, pressure in Sweden quickly put H&M in a corner and brought them to the table. But many companies remained unmoved. Trade union solidarity from around the world was crucial in getting brands to sign the Accord. In the UK, the Union of Shop, Distributive and Allied Workers (USDAW) lobbied companies like Marks & Spencer and Next. 'Our members are the ones that sell these clothes', an USDAW representative said at the time. 'They are linked with workers in Bangladesh; they care about what happens to these people and their families.'[12] The campaign was a success: 190 brands signed the agreement which covered 1,600 factories staffed by two million workers.[13] The Accord was established to run for five years before being extended for three years in 2018 in a transitional agreement. The Accord had powerful opponents. Rogue retailers Walmart and Gap formed a rival, voluntary, corporate-led initiative called the Alliance for Bangladesh Worker Safety, which shunned union involvement. Other brands clung to the model of self-inspection, ignoring the fact that Rana Plaza had twice been audited by Primark, which, shockingly, did not identify any risks with the eight-storey building.

Catastrophic Failure

In 2014, I visited the Accord offices on the twelfth floor of a Dhaka tower block. From the window, Dhaka looked like an infinite web of pale buildings in a haze of smog. Roughly

4,000 of those buildings were garment factories. 'During a catastrophic failure it's columns that fail', explained Brad Loewen, who was working as the chief inspector for the Accord. 'A building such as the Rana Plaza complex should have been built to withstand twice its anticipated load, but in Dhaka, with its lack of construction watchdogs, buildings commonly get "under-built".'

Rana Plaza had numerous illegal floors built on a hopelessly weak structure. Its construction materials were of extremely poor quality, and giant vibrating generators were keeping the sewing machines running during the city's regular power cuts. More and more people, machines, and fabric bales were crammed inside until the load-bearing columns cracked apart. 'No one's watching them', Loewen said at the time of Dhaka's contractors. 'There's no government regulator, there's no overall project management. They're just building whatever they want.' In the years since the Rana Plaza tragedy, Loewen's team of 70 Bangladeshi engineers evacuated or closed dozens of critically unsafe buildings. Fifty buildings were evacuated for structural integrity standards which placed them at imminent risk of structural failure.[14]

Violent Pathways

The physical bricks-and-mortar facts of why Rana Plaza collapsed do not tell the full story of Bangladesh's garment industry. As ongoing waves of strikes and unrest show, there is more to ethical production in Bangladesh than safer factories. Those trying to organise for workers' rights face a hostile state apparatus that routinely uses lethal violence to disperse protesters.

Critics of the Accord argue that its remit was too narrow, and that its top-down approach emphasised building safety rather than workers' rights and did not represent the interests of workers.[15] Certainly neither the Rana Plaza watershed, nor the Accord, were revolutionary moments in the fashion industry. The horror did not convert into equal rights for garment workers. In 2018, one study found that brands were paying Bangladeshi factories 13 per cent less since Rana Plaza. The same study also found that lead times had declined by 8.14 per cent between 2011 and 2015. Both of these things spell disaster for garment workers – wages drop while hours and pressure increase.[16]

As we saw in Chapter 1, brands have continued to steal hundreds of billions of dollars from workers' pockets. During the Covid-19 pandemic the #PayUp campaign was launched to try and retrieve billions in stolen wages.[17] This maximisation of profits by squeezing costs is inextricably linked to poor building safety. To save money, factory owners seek out cheap, substandard buildings. These cheap 'under-built' structures with their dangerous wiring and lack of ventilation and fire exits are directly traceable to the cost-cutting decisions made in brand boardrooms.[18] The spike in union organising that followed Rana Plaza was also swiftly met by a backlash of union rejections by the government.[19] While the problems of the fashion industry cannot be solved in a vacuum, the Accord has fulfilled its most 'crucial mandate' – the prevention of another Rana Plaza.[20] The Bangladesh Accord was due to expire at the end of August 2021, but after a concerted campaign, a new version, the International Accord for Health and Safety in the Textile and Garment Industry, came into force with the intention that the factory safety programme can spread beyond Bangladesh.

Violence *a la Mode*

The fashion industry's relationship with violence is such that there would be no fashion without constant violence and its threat. Guns placed on tables, workers and organisers attacked, state-sanctioned live ammunition used, land-based colonial violence, and endemic sexual violence. All of these form part of the systemic violence that allow for 'the smooth functioning of our economic and political systems'.[21]

Thinzar, a garment worker whose name has been changed, got her first job as a machinist aged 16. She started work at 7.30 am and worked until 6.00 pm unless overtime meant a 9.00 pm finish. This is her description of a factory making clothes for two of the biggest European brands in the world: 'They shouted at us when we could not produce the required quota, or when we made sewing errors. Some even swear, it is worse when they swear. Some people get slapped. There are so many humiliations.' When was the last time your boss slapped you at work? For most people this is not a normal part of daily wage labour, but in the garment industry Thinzar's account is typical. It is this humiliating violence, both verbal and physical, that keeps control of 60 million workers across the Global South – many of them teenagers, the majority of them women, all just trying to keep their heads above water.[22] Violence is a means of subjugating freedom and preventing the growth of labour rights, women's rights, and self-expression. It is designed to crush the spirit and make change seem hopeless so the profits keep rolling in. Because of its impact on people and society, Marx once described capital as 'dripping from head to foot, from every pore, with blood and dirt'.[23]

In his book *Violence*, Slavoj Žižek describes how life for a wealthy minority depends on a systemic violence that resembles 'the notorious "dark matter" of physics'. It is everywhere and constant. What needs to be recognised with the fashion industry is, as Žižek says, not only the direct physical violence like the slaps 'but also the more subtle forms of coercion that sustain relations of domination and exploitation, including the threat of violence'.[24] A report on conditions inside cotton-spinning mills in Tamil Nadu, India, which interviewed 725 workers, found that '[w]orkers internalise the threats they receive, and think that whatever their employers and superiors are threatening them with will actually happen'.[25] This violence is at the heart of every question in the fashion industry – why did workers eventually go inside Rana Plaza? Because the threat felt greater than the risk. What is awe-inspiring is that time after time people's spirits are not crushed. For example, the minute she turned 21 Thinzar joined the leadership of the trade union at her factory. She was punished for peaceful organising of course – facing the despicable accusation that it is the people pushing for an alternative who are violent rather than the system and capitalism itself. But she did not give up. Thinzar is from Myanmar, a country we now turn to in examining factory violence a little longer.

Jail Time

Even before the coup and the pandemic, Myanmar was described as the worst place in South East Asia to be a garment worker.[26] A country long under the boot of military dictatorship, Myanmar seemed to have turned a corner with the election of Aung San Suu Kyi in 2015. But the promise of freedom turned out to be a false one, certainly for Myanmar's Rohinga Muslim population who faced genocide but also for wider society. Unions and civil society began to agitate for freedom amid anger at the slow pace of change regarding the minimum wage and workers' rights. The Covid-19 pandemic struck Myanmar hard, and a wave of strikes and protests began as garment workers feared for their safety in overcrowded factories but were often denied wages when factories shut down.

On the morning of 4 May 2020, garment workers Zar Zar Tun and Lay Lay Mar led one such strike at a factory in the city of Yangon. Within 24 hours the two women were inmates in

Myanmar's notorious Insein prison. Arrested, charged, tried, and convicted within a day, they were first placed in a prison quarantine hall where they spent 21 days chained together. Zar Zar Tun described how, while shackled, 'we had to empty buckets of faeces and urine, and sweep and mop the floor'.

The two garment workers spent three months in prison. Zar Zar Tun slept next to a stinking toilet with other inmates climbing over her through the night. During the day they were put to work cleaning the prison. At home, the two women's families struggled without them. Zar Zar Tun's wages had supported her elderly parents as well as her two-year-old daughter, and while she was imprisoned her husband lost his construction job. Their 'crime' had been blocking a public area, gathering people together during a pandemic, and – because they camped out at the factory before the protest – violating a night-time curfew introduced in April to curb Covid-19. This case is a chilling insight into the rise of authoritarianism in the garment industry and the use of Covid-19 legislation to silence labour activists. In 2020, thousands of unionised garment workers were fired across Myanmar, most of them women. 'Only workers are sent to prison', says Zar Zar Tun. 'For employers, even if they violate the laws, nothing happens to them.'

Not all factory owners rely on the judicial system to intimidate workers; some take measures into their own hands. At a different factory, workers were hospitalised after the owner hired thugs to attack union leaders. 'We were being followed when we worked. They followed us when we went to the toilet. When we were sewing, they would come and sit on the plastic chairs beside our sewing machine', explained one worker. Eventually, because the workers refused to close down their union, the factory sacked over 50 per cent of the workforce, including all the union leaders and members.

Like much of the garment industry, factories in Myanmar also have a blacklisting system, whereby the names and photographs of 'troublemaking' garment workers are shared among factories to stop them from being hired. One labour organiser described visiting a factory and seeing the photos of union leaders from nearby factories pinned to the wall of the clinic where all new workers underwent a health exam.[27]

On 1 February 2021, Myanmar's crisis was intensified by a military coup. Very quickly the entire labour movement was outlawed and union leaders, journalists, and activists were rounded up and sent to prison. Before, the coup workers had been able to express themselves through strikes and protests – even in a limited form. Afterwards, the military junta began shooting people in the streets. Bent Gehrt is the South East Asia field director at the Worker Rights Consortium; he says that even in a harsh region, Myanmar's military is the most hostile to the labour sector. 'If the Generals succeed in keeping power, they will not accept any form of expression of labour rights in the country. If you don't have unions then workers can't voice grievances, which would mean the employers could act with total impunity.' Within months of the coup, the Association for Political Prisoners monitoring group, whose figures are being used by the United Nations, estimates that 1,652 people had been killed and over 12,617 more had been detained. Manufacturing in Myanmar connects leading international clothing and shoe brands to harsh and even deadly repression of worker rights through the murder of civilians, military tribunals, and inhumane imprisonment.

On 15 March 2021, 3 people were shot dead and 17 more arrested after a military truck opened fire on a protest outside a shoe factory in the Hlaing Tharyar industrial zone. The workers had been making cowboy boots for export to Texas, and they had gathered outside the Xing Jia factory to ask for 15 days' wages to be paid when a military truck arrived and opened fire.[28] Despite this violence, garment workers have been at the forefront of the pro-democracy movement – marching, protesting, and organising dissent. At the time of writing, the risks of dissent remain high. Thiri May, whose name has also been changed, said soldiers were stationed outside her factory checking workers' phones. Anyone who tried to hide their phone or refused to show it was arrested. Night raids were also taking place on households suspected of dissent. 'Because of the coup, our human rights are lost', says Thiri May. 'I don't want to live our life this way. I want to go out and express myself freely. That's why we are fighting against them.' Brands with a recent history of manufacturing in Myanmar include Marks & Spencer, H&M, Primark, Bestseller, Aldi North, Lindex, Next, C&A, and Benetton.[29]

Authoritarianism

Myanmar's brutality points to a trend of increasing authoritarianism in the garment industry. From India to Cambodia to Ethiopia, governments are increasingly using punitive measures to intimidate labour movements. Even countries where the garment sector has a hard-won reputation for being more ethical, there are serious problems. 'Everybody accepts Myanmar is militarised, but they are not realising what is happening in Sri Lanka', says Dr Kanchana Ruwanpura, at the University of Gothenburg. 'The apparel sector needs to start thinking about what does [a militarised regime] mean for claims around ethicality.' Sri Lanka created a Covid-19 task force entirely made up of military officers, many of whom have internationally recognised brutal war records from the conflict against the Tamil Tigers in 2009, when up to 70,000 Tamil civilians were killed. Large sections of Sri Lanka's garment workforce are young women who migrated to factories in free trade zones from war-torn rural areas. As well as creating a dangerous atmosphere in which dissent over labour rights abuses leads to intimidation, the creation of an army-led Covid-19 response has seen garment workers forcibly moved hundreds of kilometres to quarantine centres.

One of the most dangerous places in the world to be a trade unionist is Guatemala, where 87 labour leaders were murdered between 2004 and 2017.[30] Violence is often carried out by inter-mediaries, from hired assassins to workers allied to bosses. In one factory, union organisers found that toilet walls had been graffitied with threats to kill them. As a result of this climate, of Guatemala's 173 garment factories, only two have unions.[31]

The fashion industry is like a beautiful cake. Its outward appearance is fancy in the extreme, multiple tiers, swirling icing, ribbons of cream and colourful sugar flowers. Yet if you take a knife and cut into this cake, beneath the crunch of white icing oozes a repulsive concoction of rubble, blood, fear-sweat, and petrochemicals. It is rotten to the core. The oven that baked this foul cake is capitalism. Where workers are killed either by bullets or fires, where strikes and protests exist, or where stones are thrown and the odd vehicle burned, what we are seeing is the result of an abhorrent political system. Bound up with capital accumulation and subjugation – fashion is violence.

Homeworkers

Homeworkers are the hidden pillar of globalisation and a central reason why the price of clothes and shoes remains so low. Before the pandemic an estimated 260 million women and men produced goods or provided services from in or around their homes, 224 million of them in the Global South.[32] They work out of sight, yet follow their supply chains and you will often find the biggest brands in the world. The work they do is subcontracted by factories who want to pass on the risks and costs of manufacturing. Today, people assemble clothes, shoes, footballs, jewellery, and even electronics in their homes. A major problem with homeworking is that it involves taking a living space and turning into a workplace – in the garment industry this means requiring people to store vast quantities of highly flammable and neurotoxic glue in their house, to stoop over unsuitable work stations in dim light, and to carry the burden of building costs like electricity. Home-workers also work on piece rates at the mercy of unscrupulous factory agents. It can also be particularly hard for homework-ers to find respite from violence – whether it is from husbands, in-laws, or factory agents it is simultaneously domestic and workplace violence.[33]

Far from being a small-time cottage industry, homework-ing is a vital part of the global economy, with homeworkers expertly attuned to its fluctuations. The Covid-19 pandemic hit homeworkers extremely hard – by January 2020, home-workers in India knew something was afoot because of slowing contracts and problems with raw materials from China. The city of Tirupur in Tamil Nadu is known as the knitting capital of India. Thousands of garment factories, which make clothes for the domestic market and for export, coexist with garment districts full of homeworkers. Some workshops just stitch on buttons, other households snip loose threads before pressing and packaging clothes ready for sale. With its sewing machines rattling through the day, textile agents going from house to house, rickshaw drivers blowing their horns, and children running underfoot, Tirupur is known as a busy industrial city. By March 2020, there was no work whatsoever. The once bustling streets of Tirupur fell silent. 'We saw the absolute shutting down of supply chains. No work. That's it. Period', says Janhavi Dave, International Co-ordinator of HomeNet South Asia. For families who subsist on poverty wages at the best of times, the Covid-19 global shutdown spelled disaster.

In Dharavi – a sprawling township embedded within the Indian city of Mumbai – communities of informal workers came together to support each other as almost all home-workers, domestic workers, street vendors, micro-factory workers, garment workers, and ragpickers found themselves out of work. Women homeworkers found themselves on the front line of the Covid-19 response, organising everything from dishing out food aid to negotiating access to Dharavi's communal toilets. Food rations arriving haphazardly in shops had to be fairly distributed, social distancing in queues had to be organised, migrant workers who did not qualify for rations had to be fed, and families in total crisis had to be found and nursed back to health.

On an international scale, homeworkers have also been fighting back against invisibility and isolation. HomeNet International, for example, is now a global federation of 36 organisations of homeworkers from 20 countries. Janhavi Dave lists things that need to change for the better: homeworkers must be made visible and recognised as workers by their employers – both domestic factories and global brands; they must be guaranteed regular work and a living wage; and they must have contracts and full social security. It's also vital that the culture and history of much of what is made is afforded full respect and value. 'A lot of what homebased workers make is art', Dave says. 'When homebased workers sell something, it is not just labour but labour art and tradition.' One example of this is garments and accessories made from allo (Himalayan nettle) in Nepal. Making allo thread to weave is a time-consuming community process that has been handed down from generation to generation.

Shaping the Map of the Industry

To understand why the fashion industry looks as it does today, we must examine its history through the prism of globalisation, colonial trade, industrialisation, and industrial struggle. We turn now to historic production sites in Britain and the USA as a means to chart the shift in industry that created the present-day map of fashion production.

In pre-industrial Britain, cloth was traditionally made by families spinning and weaving raw materials in their homes. Then came the Industrial Revolution. In 1764, James Hargreaves, a weaver in north Lancashire, invented the spinning jenny, which vastly increased the amount of spun yarn that one person could produce by enabling eight threads to be spun at once. Later improvements increased this to 80 threads.[34] This reduced the price of yarn, which in turn increased demand. Wealthy members of the ruling class established factories containing multiple water-powered spinning jennies. Automated machines required fewer workers, which in turn meant even cheaper yarn.

As advances in machinery accelerated, homeworkers were forced to replace outdated machinery more frequently in an attempt to keep up with production. It was an impossible race, and one by one workers with the least money were forced to give up self-employment and seek factory work. When Dr Cartwright launched the power loom in 1804, the outpacing of workers by machines was complete. Home workshops could no longer produce yarn or cloth at the volume or price of factories. As Engels noted, 'the history of the proletariat in England begins ... with the invention of the steam engine and of machinery for working cotton'.[35]

The wealthy family of Friedrich Engels owned a textile mill in Manchester where the 22-year-old German 'upstart' was sent to work in the hope that it would relieve him of his radical inclinations. Manchester had the opposite effect and led Engels to write his groundbreaking book, *The Condition of the Working Class in England*. The move to Manchester also introduced Engels to the two loves of his life – the radical factory worker Mary Burns and, after her death, her sister Lizzie. It was these two women who guided Engels round Manchester and stopped him being robbed and beaten up in the slums as a wealthy foreign interloper.[36]

Engels reported that the Industrial Revolution led to 'a rapid fall in the price of all manufactured commodities, prosperity of commerce and manufacture, the conquest of nearly all the unprotected foreign markets'.[37] The scale of the Industrial Revolution can be seen in the enormous leap in cotton imports that Engels recorded. In 1775, five million pounds of raw cotton were imported into the UK; by 1844 this had increased to 600 million.

This was cotton inextricably linked to colonialism and cruelty, much of it grown and picked by people who had been violently taken from Africa and enslaved. The origins of the fashion industry and the trade in enslaved people share several disturbing intersections. By 1750, mills in Manchester were producing cloth modified to meet African tastes in prints and patterns.[38] As outlined in Karen Tranberg Hansen's book *Salaula*, it was clothes, both new and second hand, which often filled the cargo holds of ships sailing to Africa from Britain. Once in Africa, clothes were traded for captive people with rulers like King Kazembe III of Luapula.[39] The West's Industrial Revolution abused Africa twice over, using the North Atlantic trade in enslaved people to gain both enslaved labour and markets for clothes.

Colonialism also destroyed many existing fabric industries. Two hundred years ago, the finest and most expensive material on the planet was Dhaka muslin. So fine it resembled 'woven air', it was made via an extravagant 16-step process from a rare cotton that only grew along the banks of the Meghna River in Bengal, now Bangladesh. This industry was purposefully destroyed by the British East India Company.[40]

As workers in Britain were forced to seek employment in the newly industrialised towns, urban populations grew faster than the infrastructure could cope with. The 'slumification' of Britain had begun, and by the end of the nineteenth century over a quarter of Britain's population was estimated to be living at or below subsistence level. The 1833 Factory Act illustrates how bad things had become. It was considered highly controversial to ban children under the age of 9 from working in textile factories and to restrict children aged between 9 and 13 to working 12 hours a day. Those aged 13–18 could legally work a 69-hour week. As well as running sweatshops, industry owners also portioned out work to unregulated, starving homeworkers in order to undercut factory wages.[41]

Uprising

Garment workers have always fought for self-determined freedom from oppression. Media narratives of sweatshops often impose stereotypes of victimhood on garment workers, reinforcing stereotypes of passive Asian or immigrant women.[42] Yet what is clear is that groups of predominantly female garment workers engaged in some of the bitterest and hardest fought battles of the international labour movement: from the half a million textile workers who went on strike in the Southern Textile Strikes of 1929 and 1934[43] to the 40,000 Chinese workers who went on strike at Yue Yuen, the biggest producer of sports shoes in the world in 2014.[44]

In November 1909, it was a young immigrant woman named Clara Lemlich who led what is known as the Uprising of the Twenty Thousand in New York. Around 15,000 garment workers fought a bitter, but ultimately successful, battle for better wages and working conditions which lasted for over two months and set off a wave of women's strikes that spread from New York to Philadelphia, Cleveland, Chicago, Iowa, and Michigan between 1909 and 1915.

Lemlich reached the United States in 1903, fleeing with her family from the pogroms of Tsarist Russia. She described garment workers as reduced 'to the status of machines' and joined the newly formed International Ladies' Garment Workers' Union. Being an active member of the executive was a dangerous role and Lemlich was beaten up by management thugs.[45]

Yet the dangers of *not* struggling for change were far worse. On 25 March 1911, disaster struck at the Triangle Shirtwaist Factory in New York. A fire swept through the building killing 146 workers, mostly young Jewish and Italian women. The death toll was greatly increased by a lack of fire safety precautions and locked fire escapes. It was alleged that locking the doors meant that employees could be searched for stolen goods; it is more likely that they were locked to keep out union organisers, as the factory had been a continual site of industrial action.[46]

One of the workers, Rosey Safran, who was interviewed in the days after the fire, said the union had demanded adequate fire precautions: 'The bosses defeated us, so our friends are dead.'[47] Aided by a corrupt judge, the factory owners, Max Blanck and Isaac Harris, escaped responsibility. The tragedy galvanised the fight for workers' rights and in time led to the gradual implementation of fire codes for homes and workplaces.

Epilogue for a Fire

Over a hundred years later, as I wrote the first edition of this book, the same avarice-fuelled fire that killed so many in New York struck again – this time with a death toll twice as high. When fire broke out at the Ali Enterprises factory in Karachi,

Pakistan, there was no way for workers to escape the flames – no firefighting equipment, no functioning fire alarms, no safety procedures in place – just steel bars on the windows and too few fire escapes, some of which were locked.

The fire, which took place on 11 September 2012, killed 259 people. Saeeda Khatoon, who lost her son that day, became a prominent member of the Ali Enterprises Factory Fire Affectees Association, which has been fighting for justice ever since. This is her description of that terrible time:

> That day was like the apocalypse. Every house in our neighbourhood seemed to have a dead body on their doorstep. There were 17 bodies in my immediate neighbourhood that day, then 24 more bodies arrived the next day. In total, our neighbourhood received 112 dead bodies. About 13 of these were women. It was a day from hell.[48]

Ali Enterprises was a death trap which broke multiple Pakistani building safety regulations, and yet it had been issued with a prestigious SA800 inspection certificate just weeks before the fire. The certificate was awarded by Italian auditors RINA Services who subcontracted the job to local firm RICA. RINA Services had been accredited by Social Accountability International who developed the SA8000 certification system.[49]

With so many dead, these certificates were once again shown to be worth less than the self-regulating paper they are printed on. When a monitoring system is corporate funded it cannot and will not protect workers. Pakistan's health and safety legislation has been swept aside at the behest of wealthy industrialists[50] and greedy multinational corporations and as a result, factory fires are common. On the same day as the Ali Enterprises fire, 25 people died in a shoe factory fire in Lahore. Pakistan's apparel industry accounts for 38 per cent of its workforce and more than half of the country's exports – Ali Enterprises' main client was German retailer KiK. Workers reported earning an average wage of about $80 a month.[51]

Subcontracting to the Global South

Back in 1920s Manhattan, trade union strength was improving pay and working conditions. Wary of shrinking profits, suppliers subcontracted work away from union strongholds to smaller contractors. Old-style competition between contractors returned and standards dropped through the floor.[52] If this sounds familiar it is because this is the pattern that has characterised the garment industry ever since. The apparel industry is the site of a perpetual struggle between labour and capital. Subcontracting complicates this conflict because, unlike in other industries, fashion retailers do not own the factories that produce their stock.

Retailers hire manufacturers, who hire subcontractors, who hire garment workers and homeworkers. This chain allows retailers to claim that they are not responsible for garment workers, when in fact they exercise almost total control over the pay and conditions of garment workers by forcing factories to accept rock-bottom prices.

In the 20 years between 1970 to 1990 there was a dramatic shift in where clothes were made and the conditions and wages of workers. Europe and North America suffered huge job losses while Asia and other parts of the Global South gained jobs. A 1996 report from the International Labour Organization (ILO) charted a 597 per cent increase in textile, clothing, and footwear (TCF) jobs in Malaysia, a 416 per cent increase in Bangladesh, and a 334 per cent increase in Sri Lanka. Meanwhile, the UK lost 55 per cent of TCF jobs, while Germany lost 58 per cent and the USA 31 per cent.[53] The term 'global scanning' was coined to describe corporations systematically seeking out the most profitable sites for production.[54]

Then came two more major upheavals. Fearful of domestic industry sinking under a flood of overseas clothing, in 1974 US and European governments developed a system of quota restrictions called the Multi-Fibre Arrangement (MFA). The quotas were intended to allow the TCF industry in places like Britain to adapt and survive. But, as Liesbeth Sluiter points out in her book *Clean Clothes*, the MFA actually propelled the globalisation of the garment industry.[55]

Economists have neatly divided the production of fashion into different processes.[56] The primary one is known as CMT, which stands for 'cut make trim'. This is the most basic form of apparel assembly and involves no design work. It generally involves countries importing consignments of fabric to be cut, sewn, trimmed, then exported. Typically, each worker focuses on one aspect of garment production, for example sewing on pockets or button loops or snipping loose threads. Prices are kept low because there are thousands of factories competing with each other. CMT is an extremely cheap production system which relies on millions of exploited workers.[57] Because of this, an apparel factory is easy to move, being basically rooms full of sewing machines and people ready to learn the required skills.

When the MFA was established, businesses scanned the globe for countries like Thailand, Cambodia, and Laos whose quotas had not yet been filled, or for countries where there was no quota. Saipan, for example, is one of 14 Northern Mariana Islands in the northern Pacific Ocean. As part of the United States Commonwealth, anything 'Made in Saipan' can be certified as 'Made in the USA' and is both duty- and quota-free. While the MFA was in force, Saipan became a giant compound housing tens of thousands of workers – predominantly young Chinese women.[58]

In the 1980s, Pakistan, Viet Nam, and China joined the fray, exporting as much clothing as they could before quotas clamped down on their success. In the 1990s, the fall of the Iron Curtain brought the industries of former communist countries into the mix, alongside Turkey which swiftly became an export powerhouse. Korean and Taiwanese corporations, meanwhile, upgraded to the most profitable, and intangible, areas of apparel production – design, branding, and marketing. They began to invest in factories across Asia, Africa, and Latin America – moving on once quotas were imposed. Unlike the first wave of relocation countries that profited from increased skills and industry, most of those that came next did not. To give a sense of just how much garment companies can hop about, Sluiter points out that between 2001 and 2006 the Sri Lankan company Tri-Star Apparel came and went from Botswana, Kenya, Tanzania, and Uganda.[59]

It is estimated that the MFA took millions of jobs and billions of dollars of exports away from the Global South, with the global welfare cost of the MFA reaching $7.3 billion a year in the mid-1980s.[60] When the MFA quotas came to an end in 2005, the loss of 30 years of restricted access caused a tremendous flux in the global geography of fashion.[61] In 2005, Saipan had 34 garment factories producing $1 billion worth of goods a year. By 2013 none were in operation – abandoned factories held bin bags full of labels that would have once been sewn into clothes. Young women workers without the means to return home turned to work in Saipan's sex tourism industry.[62]

The end of the MFA unleashed China's production capabilities. Even before the restrictions ended, China made over 20 billion pieces of clothing in 2002 – almost four for every person on the planet. In the months after the quotas ended, Chinese exports to the USA jumped by 75 per cent while exports to Europe increased by 46 per cent.[63]

After the MFA, textiles and apparel fell under the jurisdiction of the World Trade Organization. Then came the economic crisis of 2008, which had a devastating impact on apparel production. By 2009, imports into the United States had dropped by 15.7 per cent and every major garment supplier in the world was reporting a decline.[64] In China, ten million Chinese textiles and apparel workers, a third of the country's total of 30 million, lost their jobs as production slowed.[65] One million (1 in 35) Indian apparel workers also lost their jobs, as did approximately 20 per cent of the Cambodian apparel workforce (75,000 out of 352,000).[66]

Two Cheers for Sweatshops?

The *New York Times* once ran an article entitled 'Two Cheers for Sweatshops'. It begins with a description of Thai workers eating beetles – the premise being that sweatshops are acceptable in South East Asia because people there have a different 'mindset' and 'a different perspective from ours, not only when it came to food but also what constitutes desirable work'.[67]

An entire book could be written detailing everything that is wrong with suggesting 'a different Asian mindset'. But far from being an Asian phenomenon, sweatshops are as 'American as apple pie'.[68] Here is a social worker's description of working conditions in Philadelphia in 1905: 'The room is likely to be ill-smelling and badly ventilated. Consequently, an abnormally bad air is breathed which is difficult for the ordinary person to stand for long. Thus result tubercular and other diseases which the immigrant acquires in his endeavour to work out his economic existence.'[69]

Sweatshops continue to exist in both Leicester and Los Angeles. While these are typically staffed by new immigrant workers, this is not because immigrants are predisposed to being 'insect-eating drones' as the *New York Times* article implies but because they represent the most impoverished section of the workforce. They have the fewest opportunities due to their ethnicity, class, gender, and language barriers[70] – hardly something that should prompt cheering.

This argument also appears absurd in the light of the countless examples of industrial struggle in Asia in recent decades. Where there is oppression there is resistance, and wherever there are sweatshops there are struggles to improve them by the very people working in conditions the article describes as 'tantalizing to a Thai labourer getting by on beetles'. The article also misses the fundamental point of why people eat beetles in the first place: because they are poor. Beetles do not constitute the diets of wealthy Thais. The difference is not one of 'mindset' but of poverty versus life-threatening destitution. Superficial differences like diets or skin colour should not be used to justify exploitation.

Another pro-sweatshop argument is that sweatshops lift countries out of poverty. This has the bizarre effect of portraying multinational corporations and exploitative factory owners as benefactors. The reality is that this industry is often a step backward in terms of workers' rights. In Indonesia, Nike persuaded the government to let them flout the minimum wage and circumvent laws by paying workers 'apprentice wages'. In Haiti, factories making clothes for companies including Dockers, Nautica, Hanes, and Levi's actively prevented Haitian legislators from raising the minimum wage above $0.31 an hour. The Haitian parliament passed a law in 2009 raising the minimum wage to $0.62 an hour, but this was blocked by factory owners with the help of the US Agency for International Development.[71]

Where reductions in poverty happen at all, it takes place despite multinationals not because of them. Pro-sweatshop arguments also ignore the fact that the wealth created by the factories is extracted by corporations, leaving little behind in the host country. As Arundhati Roy has stated, 'trickledown' economics is a myth; what has happened instead is 'gush-up' economics whereby profits are sucked up to the top of societies with much of it being sucked out to overseas coffers.[72] Nor is this just about economic growth. As we have seen, civil society and trade unions are often the first victims of authoritarian regimes trying to appease corporations.

While 'well-meaning' pro-sweatshop arguments state that factory jobs are better than hod carrying, prostitution, or sewer cleaning, they tend to ignore the existence of structural poverty that drives people into sweatshops. This poverty is a recent phenomenon caused by colonial and neoliberal strategies.[73] Poverty wages were used by colonial powers to create mass destitution that forced people to take any work that was going at whatever cost to themselves. Neoliberalism followed this pattern, with the IMF and World Bank pushing structural adjustment programmes that destroyed local industries such as fishing and small-scale farming. This has created the hordes of people forced to migrate to cities in search of work.

Under capitalism there is a mass of unemployed, semi-employed, and casually or precariously employed people. Marx called them the 'reserve army of labour'. John Steinbeck's *Grapes of Wrath* recalls this mass as the means by which capitalist landowners are able to pit starving workers against each other and drive wages down. This reserve army of labour is now a global phenomenon, purposefully maintained to allow capitalists to play a global game of 'race to the bottom'.[74]

* * *

Garment factory jobs are characterised by being dull, dangerous, severely underpaid, and deeply exploitative. Yet these jobs form the basis of survival for an ILO estimated 60 million people around the globe. Recognising that these two truths exist simultaneously does not lessen the need for urgent action. It is vital that people do not just scrape by on a subsistence living but are able to find dignity, self-determination, and even joy from work.

Working for reform of the industry remains vital; every struggle for a wage rise or better conditions must be supported internationally. Those seeking change should support trade unions, pickets, boycotts, solidarity movements, and strikes on a global scale. Yet this should never distract from the fact that revolutionising labour rights in fashion supply chains requires a fundamental change in the structure of society to end violence and oppression. The fashion industry will not be changed in a vacuum; real, lasting change in the fashion labour system will take an internationalist struggle that builds workers' power to create a world based on the principles of equality, justice, and people and planet rather than capitalism's competition and profit.

CHAPTER FIVE

A Bitter Harvest

Have we fallen into a mesmerized state that makes us accept as inevitable that which is inferior or detrimental, as though having lost the will or the vision to demand that which is good?

Rachel Carson, *Silent Spring*

Picture a desert, a diseased salt-rock desert plagued by winds that blow carcinogenic dust into villages causing throat cancers and tuberculosis, a pesticide-infused desert that acts as a grave-yard for abandoned boats. The fishermen have gone, their children suffering from malnutrition and high infant mortality rates. The summers are hotter and the winters colder. Teaming schools of fish have been replaced by camels grazing on scrub-land and a few cows seeking shelter in the shade of a rusting hull. This desert was once the Aral Sea, the world's fourth largest lake, home to 24 species of fish and thriving fishing communities and surrounded by lush wetlands teaming with wildlife and rare forests. This has all gone. By 2014, there was just 15 per cent of the sea left, an inhospitable stretch of water whose saline levels have risen by 600 per cent. Roughly 25,000 square miles of sea bed lie exposed – the equivalent of six million football pitches[1] – a catastrophe that has reduced the stability of the climate of the entire region.

Two thousand miles to the east, picture a multitude of waste pipes that have pumped 2.5 billion tonnes of toxic waste water a year into the rivers and lakes of just one country.[2] Picture 300 million people without access to clean drinking water because 70 per cent of their rivers, lakes, and reservoirs are polluted.[3] Imagine 75 per cent of all disease and 100,000 deaths a year resulting from polluted water. Picture China's 'cancer villages' and the twelve million tonnes of grain polluted by heavy metals each year. Imagine the dead fish, the dead birds, the colourful sludge clogging the rivers as women struggle to find the least dirty bit of water to cook and clean with. All this is taking place in the shadow of giant factories whose owners wilfully commit violation after violation without fear of censure.[4]

Next, picture a hot, dusty farm in the outback of Australia, the sun beating down on a series of large concrete tanks filled with a writhing mass of crocodiles. The tanks stretch on and on, housing 70,000 factory-farmed reptiles,[5] which will get a bullet in the head once they have grown enough scales to satisfy European handbag manufacturers. Picture crocodiles that have lived in the wild for over 200 million years now in over-crowded tanks. Picture their wounds from fighting and their deformities from being unable to walk or swim. Picture filthy, overcrowded water with a distorted bacterial balance that leads to infected wounds.[6] In the wild, crocodiles can live to be 70 years old; on factory farms, they are shot at the age of three.

Finally, imagine a chemical so toxic that just one teaspoon can kill an adult human if it touches their skin. Picture gallons of this chemical being sprayed onto the cotton and citrus fields of the United States. Then picture the scene when 40 tonnes of this chemical exploded into the atmosphere of Bhopal, India, cloaking the city in poison and killing at least 15,000 people:

> The poison cloud was so dense and searing that people were reduced to near blindness. As they gasped for breath its effects grew ever more suffocating. The gases burned the tissues of their eyes and lungs and attacked their nervous systems. People lost control of their bodies. Urine and faeces ran down their legs. Women lost their unborn children as they ran, their wombs spontaneously opening in bloody abortion.[7]

* * *

There is nothing 'natural' about a single one of these environ-mental catastrophes. They are all the result of the workings of the fashion industry under capitalism. Earth, air, animals, water, and human health – all are subject to fashion's bitter harvest.[8] The draining of the Aral Sea is due to its waters having been appropriated to irrigate Uzbekistan's 1.47 million hectares of cotton, a practice which began under Soviet rule. Cotton is hugely water-intensive: a single cotton bud uses 3.4 litres of water, and a single cotton T-shirt consumes 2,000 litres. Uzbekistan is now the world's sixth largest exporter of cotton, making $1 billion from the sale of its annual cotton harvest.[9] Until his death in 2016, the crop provided Uzbekistan's brutal dictator, Islam Karimov, with the vast majority of his export earnings.[10] Under Karimov there were no civil liberties in Uzbekistan and journalists and protesters were regularly killed. Uzbek cotton became synonymous with slavery as each autumn, schools were closed and students and teachers forced to harvest cotton, with head teachers given cotton-picking quotas and students facing punishment and even expulsion for non-compliance.[11] Uzbekistan remains an authoritarian state. Since 2016, child and forced labour has been banned in the cotton sector but this has not stopped the practice.[12] Reporting in 2020, the Uzbek Forum for Human Rights, which has monitored the harvest for ten years, stated there were still widespread instances of child labour and forced labour in the cotton harvest.[13]

The rapid development of China's textile industry has led to extreme environmental stress with toxic wastewater being produced mainly by the printing and dyeing industry and the chemical fibre industry.[14] The Chinese textile industry has repeatedly ranked as the third worst water polluter out of the country's 41 surveyed industries.[15] Decades of discharge from textile factories has ruined many waterways in China. 'When not properly treated, it can destroy fragile river ecosystems, contaminate drinking water sources and render water too polluted for agricultural and industrial use', said Greenpeace East Asia toxics campaigner Deng Tingting in an interview

137

with *Newsweek*. 'Chemicals can accumulate in the same fish that end up on supermarket shelves and on dinner tables, creating health hazards for humans.'[16] This water often goes on to contaminate lakes and tributaries downstream of the spill as well as polluting groundwater.

In 2017, China decided to crack down on major polluters – increasing inspections, issuing fines, and moving factories into industrial parks. Problems persist, however, with experts saying the industrial parks sometimes cannot cope with the volume of wastewater produced and factories have been caught building secret pipes or discharging wastewater at night to avoid costly fines.[17] This pollution, both historic and current, is inextricably linked to large international brands who contract to factories committing serious environmental violations. One report that surveyed 62 major brands in 2019 found that less than a quarter had any kind of target set to reduce water pollution, and only 6 per cent were monitoring progress against these targets.[18] This pattern of 'hydrocide' is repeated throughout the industry.[19]

Crocodiles are kept in squalid captivity and then shot or bludgeoned to death to meet demand from fashion houses like Hermès. A crocodile typically has a brain the size of a finger encased in bone 2 cm thick. It is impossible to stun them for a humane killing. In Australia, farmed crocodiles are supposed to be shot through the head, but killing methods in the United States include severing the spinal cord with a chisel, which can take five to eight blows with a mallet and merely paralyses the animal. Other methods include beheading crocodiles with machetes and trying to smash their skulls with baseball bats or mallets. Speaking on the cruel methods he has witnessed as a farm inspector, reptile biologist Dr Clifford Warwick stated: 'Few people would realise that an alligator or crocodile with his head cut off will be alive for an hour before it loses consciousness.'[20]

The longer a crocodile is kept alive, the less money the farm makes, so as soon as it has grown to the required belly width it is killed.[21] Once a crocodile has been killed, its belly, throat, and leg skin is removed and blasted with water jets to remove excess flesh. The skin is then dipped in chemicals, drained, salted, and shipped in chilled freezers to tanneries in South East Asia. Hermès uses between three and four crocodiles to make one handbag. These bags can have $200,000 price tags and waiting lists are years long. This difference between the actual cost of a factory-farmed, but so-called 'luxury', material and the marked-up price of the handbag allowed Hermès to post total revenues of €6.389 billion in 2020.[22]

Aldicarb (known commercially as Temik) is one of the most toxic pesticides ever registered in the United States.[23] It was banned in the European Union in 2003. Aldicarb is made of methyl isocyanate mixed with aldicarb oxime and methylene chloride. Until 1987, Union Carbide (now Dow Chemicals) was the sole manufacturer of aldicarb. The company built a huge plant in Bhopal, believing India represented an enormous untapped market. But Union Carbide underestimated the poverty of Indian farmers, who were too poor to buy their pesticides. The Bhopal plant ceased production in the early 1980s and, still containing vast quantities of poisonous chemicals, was left to rot. Falling into disrepair, safety systems that should have prevented a leak were left unmaintained. Thus, in December 1984 an explosion released 40 tonnes of methyl isocyanate into the atmosphere of Bhopal. At least 8,000 people died in the immediate tragedy, a figure that could be as high as 15,000 people.[24] Up to 200,000 people have since experienced increased mortality or morbidity – premature death or partial or total disability.[25] There has been no justice for Bhopal from Union Carbide or Dow Chemicals.[26] In the decades since the disaster, survivors have been plagued with an epidemic of cancers, menstrual disorders, and what one doctor described as 'monstrous births'.[27]

The pesticide industry is a product of the Second World War, when insects were used to test chemicals as agents of death for people.[28] It should come as no surprise that such brutal carnage followed the explosion. What links the horror of aldicarb and Bhopal to fashion is its primary use as a pesticide for cotton (along with beans and peanuts). When my previous book *Stitched Up* came out, the United States was set to end worldwide production of aldicarb by 2015 and to end distribution by 2017. But in 2021, campaigners had to fight off then President Donald Trump's attempt to give aldicarb a new lease of life.[29] Aldicarb remains one of the most dangerous neurotoxic chemicals found anywhere in the world and is banned in 125 countries. 'It never should have been registered in the first place back in 1970', stated Pesticide Action Network North America. 'By the mid-1980s there was sufficient data to suggest it should have been taken off the market. The system is designed to leave things like this on the market as long as possible.'[30]

'We're in Deep Shit'

Drastic change is urgently needed. In a world of floods and wildfires, climate scientists are no longer mincing their words when it come to the breakdown of stable climate conditions: 'We are in deep, deep shit!'[31] Einstein's definition of insanity is doing the same thing over and over again and expecting different results. The fashion industry is taking a devastating toll on our world. Yet proffered solutions currently include trusting corporations to do the right thing, trying to get people to buy fewer clothes, recycling, renting, developing a circular economy, and the invention of wonder fabrics – all solutions that appear more concerned with keeping capitalism intact than with saving the planet. As a counterpoint, this chapter aims to expose the systemic issue of capitalism and show why it is so damaging. It is not a review of every fantastical idea that purports to reduce fashion's harm, and I urge you to be wary of 'solutions' that risk 'deferring radical change by instilling a false sense of progress'.[32] After 20 years of such 'solutions', how can it not be insanity to think that capitalism – the cause of the disasters we face – is the key to saving the planet?

As communities once dependent on the Aral Sea understand, nothing comes for free; there will always be someone or something that pays. There are only so many rivers, so much clean air, so much topsoil. We must act collectively and fast. Friday 13 September 2019 saw a different kind of start to London Fashion Week. Just before dawn, a group of five XR protesters glued themselves to the doorway of event space, 180 The Strand. Hand in hand they stood quietly in flimsy white clothes. As the cold sky lightened, more protesters arrived and soaked the pavement with buckets of fake blood. Police and security guards moved in as protesters lay down on the pavement, their 'Fuck Consumerism' and 'Beyond Fashion' T-shirts soaking up the red ink.

Two hours later the Fashion Week audience arrived in logoed Mercedes Benz and black cabs. Above the London pavement, plastic billboards promised beauty, glamour, and excitement with every purchase. Many of the protesters used to be part of the fashion system – until they woke up and smelled the burning. So now they were disrupting Fashion Week, as a living reminder that our society, led by the promises of retailers, has gone badly wrong. 'Why is this industry, one perceived as the definer of the zeitgeist, not acting on the warning signs and instead focusing on showing clothes for a season that marks the turning point we must adhere to, to avoid collapse?' asked former fashion designer Sara Arnold.

The next time the trade show returned to London, brands would be producing and showing clothes for the year 2021 – past the climate deadline set by the UN. All fashion is ghostly – once clothes reach the runway they are already dying, soon to be replaced by something else.[33] But to show fancy clothes that are to be worn in a time of stated ecological collapse takes a certain kind of cognitive dissonance. The fashion industry's relationship with the future is deeply disturbing – it is simultaneously obsessed with the future and unable to confront it. As an industry, it constantly looks ahead and yet it won't. Fashion wants to *be* the future, to construct it by defining what new things we should lust after, and yet it refuses to see the looming precipice this approach has created. All it can truly promise is a headlong rush into disaster.

Four days later XR staged a funeral procession which marched from Trafalgar Square to London Fashion Week, complete with marching band and thousands of 'mourners' dressed in black veiled costumes. 'Let's put the fashion system to rest and revison fashion … We will not stand by this parade of excess whilst the natural world is being taken from beneath our feet', read the call to action. Just as death signifies change and renewal as well as ending, the funeral procession was designed to be an awakening. The pandemic paused widespread environmental justice protests, but they sprang into life again with COP26 in Glasgow in October 2021, acting as a call for us all to redouble our efforts to physically challenge exploitation in its entirety.

Capitalism Hurts

XR described Fashion Week as 'wearing the manifestation of our denial'. Ultimately denial and indifference has one purpose – it makes exploitation easier. This exploitation – of the planet, of animals, and of people – is the beating heart of the fashion industry. But why does the fashion industry persist in inflicting such serious environmental devastation on the planet? The short answer is: because under capitalism it has to. Corporations need to maximise profits. To do this they must acquire the component parts of their products as cheaply as possible. Other than under a system of slavery, labour has to be paid for, whereas nature is seemingly available for free. The fashion industry rests on an economic model where resources like water, oil, and land are cheap – an easy but extremely short-termist existence.[34]

Crucially, the environmental crisis we are living in is not the result of bad corporations or bad executives but of a bad system. Capitalism's mantra is, in Marx's words: 'accumulate or die'.[35] Factories spew out toxic waste because they are bound by the logic of competition, of finding the cheapest way to produce a higher rate of profit than their competitors.[36] This is why costs are cut, safety measures ignored, and pollutants discharged into rivers. Because of this we are not faced merely with the challenge of persuading those at the top of society to change their ways. We are faced with crunch time. If the fashion industry, or capitalism in general, was forced to internalise all of the social and environmental costs for water, air, soil, and animals it generates, it would go out of business.[37] Capitalism should therefore be regarded as an economy of unpaid costs.[38] Humanity's ecological debt to nature is now huge, and if nothing changes, this may ultimately be repaid at a terrifying price. The world's leading climate scientists say we have less than a decade to keep global heating below 1.5 degrees centigrade and avoid major catastrophe.[39]

While the fashion industry functions according to the unavoidable imperatives of capitalism, it does seem to be particularly predisposed to high levels of pollution and waste. Adding together the millions of tonnes of textiles produced each year, the kilowatt hours of electricity, the millions of tonnes of coal, and the trillions of litres of water, plus the pesticides, acid dyes, animal skins zippers, and metal buttons, Lucy Siegle, author of *To Die For*, concluded that fashion's footprint resembles a scorched earth strategy.[40] Nor are the eco-claims of brands to be trusted. An investigation by the Changing Markets Foundation examined 12 brands and over 4,000 products and found that brands were 'routinely deceiving consumers with false green claims'. Fifty-nine per cent of green claims flouted the rules set by the UK Competition and Markets Authority guidelines. The worst offenders were H&M with 96 per cent false claims, ASOS with 89 per cent, and M&S with 88 per cent. Shockingly, H&M's 'Conscious Collection' contained a higher share of synthetics than its regular collections – 72 per cent compared to 61 per cent. Self-regulation has clearly failed, with the report predicting that the industry's addiction to synthetics will worsen as no brand had a plan to curtail plastic fibre overproduction. Rather, the report stated that fashion companies 'rely on delaying and distraction tactics, including greenwashing', concluding that 'it is more urgent than ever for policymakers to step up and find effective legislative solutions to put the fashion industry on a more sustainable track'.[41]

People can give their own testimony[42]

Recently there has been upset over inaccurate reporting of fashion's impact on the environment. 'Facts' have been recycled, misquoted, or misunderstood.[43] I would point people to a political understanding of data – the world doesn't count the people it doesn't think count. As with garment workers, there is scarce data on the impact of pollution on people, animals, and places that 'don't count'. How do we get around this? I think we keep drilling down to ground level – to the eyewitness accounts of people who have seen their rivers turn blood red, indigo blue, milky white, and jet black, to the labs of local doctors and scientists treating surges in cancer patients, to the asthma clinics, to the aerial photos of rainforest destruction and shrinking seas, to the floods and wildfires, and to the lived stories of fisherfolk, herders, farmers, and waste pickers. We crowdsource what we know is happening and make our own data.

I would also point people towards the work of the Environmental Data Justice Lab, an Indigenous-led, Indigenous-majority lab that focuses on the relationships between data, pollution, and colonialism. The lab is 'researching the history, operations and pollution activities of the Imperial Oil Refinery in Canada's Chemical Valley, the oldest refinery in North America. Chemical Valley is located on Anishinaabe land and surrounds Aamjiwnaang First Nation.'[44] In an interview, the lab's co-director Professor Michelle Murphy stated that a lot of data produced by the company and the state was inadequate for addressing environmental violence in Chemical Valley. 'One approach would be, let's make more data, let's extract more numbers from bodies in order to show this violence is happening', Professor Murphy stated:

Well, you don't need to do that. You can just stand anywhere in Aamjiwnaang and the smoke is thick and you feel it in your skin and it's every day, and there's an accident, a release of flare. So then what our lab tries to do is take this existing data that's produced by companies, the state mostly … and try to use it to show that pollution is colonialism, show the bad relations that are attached to data. And then can we attach data – about air pollution levels or health information – that's almost always treated in isolation of one another and reattach it to one another? Can we put it under the jurisdiction of Indigenous law and make that data work for people in a different way?[45]

When I asked Dr Murphy about this, she stated: 'We know that data has a kind of aura or charisma to it. It can be politically useful, but we also know that it's mostly used to create bad relations. It's mostly used to legitimate projects that put GDP and profit first. We've seen that over and over including in the garment industry.' While numbers are alluring, Dr Murphy explains, they do not necessarily tell the truth. With every set of numbers we must ask what are the social relations that made that data and how and why is it being used. What is being highlighted and what is being hidden, and how can that data be used to expose the power that maintains such a demonstrably problematic system?

What is it about fashion in particular that makes it so wasteful? In Chapter 3 we discussed the important link between use-value, symbolic value, and rampant consumerism. Fashion is a deregulated, subcontracted, trend-based industry that relies on selling billions of short-life units every season at a maximum profit. Brands sell clothes that are not of the highest quality, ensuring that they can make them cheaply, that they will wear out, and that you will be forced to buy new ones.

The throwaway culture of the fashion industry is hugely encouraged by the domination of exchange value over use-value.[46] Capital's sole aim is to expand by selling goods and accumulating surplus wealth.[47] It does not matter whether an item fulfils a need or will last a long time. All that matters is how much it can be sold for. This spells disaster for the environment and led Marx to describe capital as having a vampiric relationship with nature, 'a living death maintained by sucking the blood from the world'.[48] Fashion is not just based on exchange value, it is an active champion of forgetting about use-value altogether. Slash fashion brand Boohoo has come under fire for selling dresses at a 99 per cent discount, sometimes for as little as 12 pence – a deliberate strategy to shift old stock and create a large online buzz, followed by a secondary buzz of condemnation. But to 'discount' is also to decide that something – someone's word, a version of events – is unworthy of consideration. In this case the dress discounts both human labour and planetary resources. It is no coincidence that 'hyperbolic discounting' is also a term used to describe an extreme disregard for what might happen in the future,[49] reminding us once again of fashion's toxic relationship with our collective destiny.

Flight from Nature

The concept of alienation is also vital for understanding fashion's impact on nature. People are far removed from the production of the clothes that they wear. The average high-street shopper will never experience 20 years of picking cotton in sweltering heat or work in a polyester factory in Zhejiang. This gives the impression that clothes exist independently both of people and of nature. The fashion industry is adept at hiding the human labour behind its wealth and power; it is even better at hiding the materials that go into producing our clothes.

Take the use of living creatures in fashion production. As well as crocodile, mink, dog, fox, and snake all sell for exorbitant prices. While still alive, a python has a hose pipe inserted into its mouth. The water makes the snake swell and stretches its skin. Once swollen, the snake is impaled on a meat hook and skinned alive.[50] Foxes, minks, and dogs are mass-farmed across the world, mostly in China but also in places like Finland and the United States. Fur production has been banned in the United Kingdom due to its cruelty. In China, animal cruelty is not banned by a stand-alone law, though there is now animal rights legislation covering endangered species.[51]

There is, however, an explicit distinction to be made here between industrial fur farming and Indigenous fashion practices, which 'demands respect and reciprocity when engaging with plant and animal life'.[52] The use of fur and other animal products within localised Indigenous fashion and clothing production should be seen as vital for the survival and sovereignty of Indigenous cultures, land, and people.[53] As is conveyed by Alethea Arnaquq-Baril's film *Angry Inuk*, about the anti-sealing movement, a belief in animal rights should not impose harmful 'cultural prejudices' or conflate the practices of 'people who have been the guardians of this earth' for thousands of years with industrial capitalism.

In industrial fur farms, however, animals are crammed into tiny, filthy cages, and when it is their turn to die they are often electrocuted, hung, or bled to death – any method that protects their fur and increases factory profits. The idea that this fur is ethical or sustainable is a lie. The production of a farmed fur coat uses 20 times the amount of energy used to make a *faux* fur coat. Fur dressing, the application of chemicals to stop fur and skin from rotting in your wardrobe, is rated as one of the world's five worst industries for toxic metal pollution.[54]

Under capitalism we relate more to commodities than we do to nature itself. We no longer see ourselves as a *part* of nature; rather, nature is something to be gloriously conquered for profit.[55] Everything becomes property: land becomes real estate, animals become fur, the Lake District becomes a nuclear waste dump, and oceans become sources of fish. Everything must have a profit squeezed out of it.[56]

Rather than exist in harmony with each other and with the planet, humans are taught to measure themselves by their distance from the rest of the population and from nature itself.[57] Bertell Ollman described alienation as the 'splintering of human nature into a number of misbegotten parts'.[58] Ecologists now argue that losing sight of the fact that humans are part of nature means all exploitation becomes easier. Vociferously exploiting nature is one and the same as exploiting people. Environmental degradation is the degradation of human relationships.[59] The exploitation of the planet is produced by the same imperatives that result in the exploitation of people in sweatshops. They both result from alienation from nature. If we were not alienated, we would not even be able to *conceive* of abusing the planet. Losing sight of the fact that humans and the planet are utterly intertwined is the starting point for our destruction.

Marx is sometimes accused of Prometheanism, of being in favour of industrialisation at any cost. In fact, he believed deeply in the oneness of humanity and nature, saying that it was their separation, not their unity, that required explanation.[60] The flight from nature encourages the idea of the duality of humans and nature, including animals, rather than their oneness. It is no coincidence that under capitalism the things we are taught to aspire to are ruling-class symbols of cruelty and power over nature – furs and skins. What is a 'luxury' skin handbag in a Paris boutique other than a sign that you are rich and powerful enough to command and destroy nature? That you can have living things die for your decoration and pleasure?

Freedom Is Not about Shopping

Living in an era of unprecedented levels of clothing consumption, the question arises: Are consumers to blame for the state of the fashion industry? In the midst of yet another economic crisis, with many people living from pay cheque to pay cheque, there needs to be a more realistic analysis of the highly pressurised role that fashion plays in people's lives, as discussed in Chapter 3. 'The consumer is no freer than the producer', wrote Marx. 'His judgement depends on his means and his needs ... Both of these are determined by his social position, which itself depends on the whole social organisation. World trade turns almost entirely round the needs, not of individual consumption, but of production.'[61] This points us once again to the question this book poses: What kind of society do you want to live in? One whose primary function is to serve corporations? One where one of fashion's primary functions is the exploitation of the planet for corporate profit?

Fashion environmentalists are often accused of being elitist and of using fast-fashion to blame the poorest members of society for climate change. Should fast-fashion be left alone because it makes working-class life better in the same manner as cheap flights? The short answer is no. Fast-fashion is a false emancipation that is disastrous for the global working class. It is the working class that are held captive in sweatshops and have their unions smashed by Walmart and their homes flooded or turned to dust by climate change. It is the working class that end up wearing poor-quality clothes that easily wear out and are quickly scorned as unfashionable. It's the working classes that are forced by low wages and the homogenisation of high streets into shopping or working at cheap shops like Primark.

It is also the working class that are driven to anxiety and a sense of inadequacy for not being able to keep up with fashion. The feminist academic Sandra Lee Bartky wrote of the double shame borne by impoverished women: the socially created and imposed 'shame of poverty' as well as shame from the inability to keep up with appearance requirements. These are not merely psychological burdens, since the ability to conform to accepted standards of dress and appearance are critical for social mobility.[62]

The ability to buy something should not be confused with freedom.[63] This cheapens freedom by narrowing it to the right to choose between different styles in the shops. Imagining that the right to buy limitless clothes at whatever cost to the planet equals freedom is to lose sight of what freedom actually means. Fast-fashion is not pro-working class; it must be critiqued as a product of corporations' drive for profit, not as the fault of the poor. Arguing that fast-fashion is not the fault of the working class should not be taken for an assurance that life can carry on as normal. If things continue as they are, the working class will just sink together beneath rising sea levels.

To stop environmental devastation, everybody's consumption habits will have to change. The UK has become a society of food banks and homelessness – what clearer evidence could there be that some people, even here, need to consume more? Many others need to consume far less or differently. This is not to be feared. The idea that something will be lost through environmental protection is an inversion of what is real.[64] The term 'inversion of what is real' was coined in response to environmentalists who are ironically concerned more with preserving capitalism than with saving the planet and humanity.[65]

But we must not restrict ourselves to just thinking about consumption. It is counterproductive to create a division between workers' rights and the environment. Too much of the Global North debate has pitted factory workers against saving the planet, with some going so far as to suggest that we just throw millions of Global South livelihoods under the bus. We must find harmony between these two camps; we must accept that capitalism and colonialism – both historic and modern-day – have created a dependency on export-led clothing manufacture across the Global South. This damage must be undone through a just transition that puts people at its heart. For myself and many others, solving overproduction starts with building workers' power in the Global South. Currently there is no democracy in fashion's factories – no choice about what or how much is made, what hours are worked, what chemicals are used, and so on. Take the workforce at the notoriously inhumane cotton-spinning mills of Tamil Nadu, India. Interviews with 725 workers found that, without exception, poverty was the cause of people taking mill jobs. Many had migrated from rural areas where the dry climate had made farming impossible. Some were recruited after a cyclone ruined their crops.[66] Like so many people working on the bottom rung of the fashion industry, they are trapped by the environmental and human catastrophe of overproduction on the one hand and the consequences of climate change on the other.

Imagine a different way – imagine if the entire supply chain was collectively owned. Imagine if a 20-hour work week meant enough resources for a rich and joyful life. Imagine if people had autonomy over the hours they worked, the conditions they worked in, what chemicals touched their skin, what materials were used, what was produced, and where it was sent. The problem of overproduction would not exist. It is no coincidence that for many people it is easier to imagine the end of the world than the end of the fashion industry or of capitalism.[67] Those benefiting from the capitalist system work hard to maintain the idea that capitalism is a natural state of affairs without alternatives. Because an alternative seems unthinkable, capitalism can sometimes seem more real than the planet we live on. Yet maintaining the fashion industry or capitalism is meaningless when compared with maintaining the planet. Only the loss of one would signal the end of humanity. We need to end capitalism; being afraid to say this is to advocate environmental destruction.

'Fashion is inherently colonial, it is the vehicle of capitalism.'[68] This is a quote from Riley Kucheran, an Indigenous scholar and community organiser from Biigtigong Nishnaabeg (Pic River First Nation). I invited him to expand on what he meant by the inherent colonial nature of fashion, and in response he wrote the following passage:

> I'm reminded of 'Amik,' or beaver. In Canada the beaver is a popular cultural icon, but beaver pelts were also a pivotal economic driver during colonization: European luxury fashion markets drove demand for fur production that decimated beaver populations and deprived the Indigenous trappers from sharing in the wealth creation.[69] To Indigenous people, the wealth or 'gifts' that Amik provides extend beyond fashionable attire. Leanne Simpson describes Amik as an Indigenous relative, a life-giving, world-building, engineering marvel that transforms their environment to support intricate webs of relations. Embodied in Amik is cultural knowledge, deep wisdom, ecological science, and powerful lessons about sustainability and living 'in a good way,' but as Simpson points out, Amik's deep wisdom wasn't recognised, Europeans saw Amik as a money-making venture of 'nifty felt hats.' To me the beaver is emblematic of the fashion-colonialism-capitalism intertwinement.[70] I'm cautious not to rely on overly simplistic 'grand narratives,' but from my Indigenous (and trauma-informed) perspective the growth of fashion and the devastating impacts of colonization is all part of the same process.

Much of Kucheran's work involves driving, documenting, and supporting 'Indigenous fashion'. There is an immediate tension between these two words, stemming from the destructive impact of fashion as an industry. As Kucheran writes – 'To me "fashion" recalls and imposes the social processes and structures that deliberately and artificially force change – the "fashion system" that encompasses commodification, mass production, marketing and consumption.' This is in contrast to a localised production system that fundamentally requires 'strong community, and healthy and reciprocal relationships with plant and animal life'.

Indigenous fashion could be explained as a form of sustainable or slow fashion, terms that are now taught and understood as the opposite of fast-fashion. But as Kucheran says, 'Indigenous fashion is even better, there's this spiritual component that makes it far superior to any mainstream consumer fashion'. It is also difficult to define Indigenous fashion with non-Indigenous terminology, nor can there be a single understanding of a concept that encompasses thousands of unique histories and cultures (while this section focuses on Canada, the concept is global). But part of what makes the practice special is that it is the antithesis of the destructive, compulsive, alienated mainstream industry.

'Some of my favourite Indigenous designers classify their work as "art" or "wearable art," but I think that "making" as described by Leanne Simpson is the best alternative to "fashion"',[71] Kucheran writes:

> Indigenous makers embody and interpret ancestral knowledge: the ethical responsibilities, intergenerational relations, and sustainable practices that enabled Indigenous peoples to thrive for millennia. Now some Indigenous designers engage more with industrial production and marketization to stay commercially viable, and their interpretations of ancestral knowledge manifest in diverse ways, but to me, a *truly* Indigenous fashion is grounded in land-based practices. It's smaller, more local, more humble and relational. It's created by communities that embrace Indigenous epistemologies and reject colonialism. This 'resurgent' fashion exists but by its very nature is often unseen by the mainstream industry, and I think for the most part it should stay that way.

Centring Indigenous fashion and making as a vital part of both the history, present, and future of clothing production is a much needed counterbalance to the typically Eurocentric study of fashion,[72] but might it also represent a pathway to dismantling the mainstream fashion system? Indigenous making is inherently political, acting as a challenge not just to the fashion industry but to the structures of capitalist society. At the heart of this question is the fundamental issue of land rights – Indigenous peoples control under 0.02 per cent of land in what is now called Canada.[73] European settlers arrived in the 1600s and by 1670 the Hudson's Bay Company had been established to ship beaver pelts and other goods to Europe – essentially it 'allowed early white settlers to get rich off the vast resources maintained by the Indigenous tribes'.[74] In return for the pelts came industrial goods, guns, and European food, as well as alcohol, smallpox, and measles. The Indigenous population of British Columbia (just one Canadian province) was estimated to exceed 125,000 in the nineteenth century, by 1929 there were just 22,000 Indigenous people left.[75] Corrupt, unfair treaties were signed[76] and the buffalo, an integral part of life, including clothing production, for certain Indigenous tribes in the Canadian interior was all but wiped out. Colonisation was followed by the Indian Act in 1876 which French-Cree-Iroquois journalist Brandi Morin has described as 'a policy that dictates the social, political, economic, spiritual and physical lives of First Nations to this day. It created a reserve system that herded First Nations onto small tracts of land in their traditional territories.'[77]

The Act, which is still in effect today with modifications, also decreed that First Nation children be forced into church-run residential schools to sever them from their Indigenous identity. Children were beaten for speaking their own language as 'the devil's tongue',[78] banned from wearing their own clothes, and forced into 'Western-style suits, and dresses'.[79]

Abuse – physical, sexual, and spiritual – was widespread. To date, the National Centre for Truth and Reconciliation has documented 4,118 children who died at residential schools – a conservative figure based upon detailed analysis of one-fifth of records.[80] The last of these 'schools' closed in 1996.

Today, a report from the Yellowhead Institute states:

Extraction, industrial development, and conservation regimes significantly limit the exercise of inherent Indigenous jurisdiction on their territories. These forms of land use fence off access points to traplines and waterways, impede access to sacred and ceremonial sites, erode sensitive areas, and fragment the land base, prohibiting the establishment of viable and sustainable economies. These are daily, ever-present forms of land alienation that people experience, and they conjoin with all forms of slow violence.[81]

With this as a lived context, of course Indigenous fashion is political. 'We need our land back, we need clean drinking water, we need safety and security, we need our women to stop disappearing', Riley explains. 'That's all required for us to have Indigenous fashion. We need a cohesive community in order to be producing clothing like we used to.'[82] Expanding on this point, he writes of the need for concrete action:

Decolonisation must be expressly tied to the return of stolen land and the restoration of Indigenous sovereignty, but that won't matter if the land and waters are poisoned and unliveable. Indigenous peoples are being increasingly recognised as climate change leaders, so supporting land defenders at pipeline protests, for example, is one way that academics, activists, and concerned citizens could help. It might seem unconnected to fashion, but if you understand Indigenous fashion as relational and deeply connected to Land, you'll see what's at stake.

The study of fashion and the environment can often seem abstract or overly based on science, obscured by statistics and greenwashing, but a roadmap to clothing that does not wreck our planet is fundamentally tied to live political struggles for justice. Kucheran points once again to the findings of the Yellowhead Institute report: 'No notions of "reconciliation" or repair can meaningfully begin until the resounding inequities caused by colonisation are addressed.'[83]

*   *   *

Those wanting the overthrow of capitalism are often accused of being dreamers. Yet there is no greater illusion than that of utopian reformism which believes you can fundamentally change a system without touching its power relations.[84] The scale of change needed to halt our current trajectory towards disaster is not going to be possible under the current system of competition and profit. What we need is a system fundamentally built on respect for the planet and each other, so that the biosphere, including people and animals, turns from a plundered resource into a revered community.

CHAPTER SIX
The Body Politic

Unreachable beauty is a reminder to make an effort.

Karl Lagerfeld

Fashion is an innately visual industry that sells itself as a creator of choice, change, and creativity. Yet it is a world devoid of variety where anyone who does not fit within its slim visual confines is rendered all but invisible. The most indicative instance of this is fashion's approach to the size and shape of women's bodies which this chapter echoes by primarily focusing on women's bodies. I want to be clear that when I use the term 'women' in this chapter and this book, I mean all women including trans women – a transgender woman is a woman and a transgender man is a man. As catwalk imagery has proliferated and the fashion model has become an accepted beauty role model, fashion's influence has spread far beyond just governing what people should wear. The fashion industry has very narrow rules for what it considers 'beautiful'. Carefully policed beauty boundaries traditionally exclude anyone who is not extremely thin, tall, young, non-disabled, cisgender, and white. These confines follow structural modes of oppression which must be proactively addressed and broken down. Freedom of expression for individuals is paramount to a free and equitable society.

Fashion gets in your head. Yet some people baulk at the idea of fashion being able to affect their self-image, seeing it as an insult to their intelligence.[1] Some women experience shame and guilt at not meeting size and beauty standards, then shame and guilt when they try, because they 'should know better'.[2] This cycle of shame and guilt, and not wanting to admit to feeling inadequate, obscures the normalisation of compulsory thinness. To begin to break away from this, we must confront the reality of life under capitalism. It is, therefore, no insult to say that a \$2.5 trillion industry,[3] whose images blanket the planet, has an effect. Nor is it insulting to discuss the over-whelming evidence that fashion has a destructive impact on women employed by the industry as models.

Bodies

The history of human beings is one of body alteration and marking. Bodies have always been used to express the sexual, religious, and cultural practices, and the geography, of specific periods.[4] Yet never have attempts at alteration been so wide-spread nor the 'ideal' so out of reach. The social desirability of an impossible version of beauty serves to torment all those who cannot attain it and as a constant source of pressure for those who supposedly do. This results in normalising body dissatisfaction, which carries serious consequences. Young women do not perform actively at school when they are not feeling confident about their appearance.[5] Around 1.25 million people in the UK have an eating disorder[6] with many more experiencing disordered eating problems.[7] At the same time, obesity – believed to be caused partly by body dissatis-faction and dieting – is rising sharply.

Homogenised beauty is linked to an international rise in body dissatisfaction. In her book *Bodies*, psychologist Susie Orbach outlines how desire for an idealised, slim, Western-ised body has spread with globalisation. Eating disorders followed the introduction of television to Fiji, Chinese women undergo leg-breaking surgery to make them taller, and some of Tehran's 3,000 plastic surgeons carry out five rhinoplas-ties ('nose jobs') a day. Size is intimately linked with race – a Western ideal is promoted at the expense of 'Indigenous bodies'. For Orbach, this is a new frontier of colonialism,[8] with brand iconography replacing religious iconography to determine aesthetic norms.[9]

The Body Politic

Digital Beauty

We live in a world soaked in visuals. People see thousands of images of bodies every week.[10] These images display something unobtainable while simultaneously assuring us of a beauty democracy. Their message is that everyone can and should work towards looking 'great'. Beauty missionaries push the myth that our bodies are in constant need of attention and taming. Life is turned into one long round of 'improvements': plucking, waxing, dyeing, dieting, exfoliating, filing, painting, and squeezing yourself into a particular shape in the vain attempt to resemble an advertisement. The 'advert look' traditionally focuses on two key criteria – thinness and symmetry of features.

The fashion industry collapses the space between aspiration and fantasy.[11] Its rhetoric of 'choice' and 'empowerment', coupled with our ability to consume clothes, means that people are given the impression that they can become what they see. But this beauty democracy does not exist. It is a mirage hiding insurmountable obstacles – obstacles hidden by their very obviousness. Models employed by the fashion industry have a body type shared by just 5 per cent of women in the United States.[12] If you are not born with it then there is nothing that you can do to achieve it. Many women exist without the time or resources to attain a healthy lifestyle, including a nutritious diet, let alone attain a top model lifestyle.[13] One stylist said of models' hair, 'a lot of people don't realise, in editorial, how much is fake'.[14] Plus the images we see in magazines and adverts are not just of augmented supermodels but of digitally enhanced augmented supermodels. One high-profile digital alterations expert described how, for a magazine cover, he altered a woman's feet, knees, and collarbones as well as her temples, the skin around her chin, and a fleshy bump on her

161

forehead.[15] Society's attempt to make reality unpalatable continues with the creation of 'digital supermodels' – women who do not exist but who have been created using computer-generated imagery.

Casting a Glamour

> A lot of magazines that people think are the really cool jobs are the ones that don't pay anything – literally zero. Things can look amazing and you're wearing really fantastic looking clothes but what you're wearing often is more than you'll make in an entire year.
>
> Elliott, Model Alliance

Fashion models appear to hold a deified status as women who have won the 'gene pool lottery'. Modelling is regarded as a glamorous profession but the reality is often anything but. Exploitation and mistreatment abound within this workforce of young women who typically start work before the age of 16[16] and are far from home and traditional support networks. The structure of modelling work and the employment status limbo sets people up for a dangerous imbalance in worker–employer relations. As a result, models are frequently confronted with problems, including wage theft, sexual harassment, unhealthy working conditions, use of child labour with limited rights, and limited recourse for unfair treatment.[17]

Covid-19 hit the modelling industry hard. A survey at the start of the pandemic by the Model Alliance, an organisation established in New York to give models a voice in their work, found one in five respondents did not have enough money to cover their basic needs. More than two-thirds said they were concerned about their ability to pay for housing. Severe hardship was compounded by racial inequality, with a higher proportion of respondents of colour, in particular Black models, having trouble paying for basic needs – both at the time of the survey and after three additional months without income.[18]

Pandemic precarity was compounded by existing exploitation and mistreatment. There is ongoing ambiguity over whether models are direct employees of agencies or 'independent contractors'. One model, Fitz, went on the record to talk about Covid-19:

> We're in an industry that already doesn't have a safety net so I feel double-exposed, almost. I was already having to fight for my own rights and protections ... but I was somehow still getting paid for modelling work, so there was a trade-off. But now that's stripped away ... the industry is non-existent at the moment. There were no policies or regulations in place for us.

The survey found that 55 per cent of respondents were owed money by clients and almost half (49 per cent) were owed money by their agencies. There was also concern about retaliation if models spoke up about dangerous working conditions in the pandemic. Forty-five per cent of respondents said they were extremely or very concerned that they would be proposed for fewer jobs if they refused work or requested extra protections due to the coronavirus. This fear also had a racialised edge to it, with only 22 per cent of Black or African American models reporting that they felt very confident advocating for extra protections compared to 43 per cent of white models.[19]

The Body Beautiful?

What about the impact of the fashion industry on the physicality of fashion models? The debate over the industry's responsibility for eating disorders continues. Anorexia nervosa is a serious psychological illness that can be provoked by a wide range of causes and I would not wish to crudely generalise the disease or those it afflicts. The negative body image that contributes to disordered eating and eating disorders is unlikely to be solved until sexism is expunged and women are no longer taught that their appearance is paramount. There is no doubt, however, that the fashion industry seriously harms its employees by requiring them to conform to a certain aesthetic.

The early 2000s saw a spate of deaths linked to the requirement for extreme thinness. In August 2006, a 22-year-old Uruguayan model, Luisel Ramos, died having just stepped off a catwalk. The cause of death was heart failure caused by anorexia nervosa. Tragedy repeated itself a few months later when Luisel's younger sister, 18-year-old model Eliana, also died from a heart attack caused by malnutrition. A Brazilian model, Ana Carolina Reston, died in hospital also in 2006. Having been told at a casting call that she was 'too fat', the 22-year-old starved herself until, at 5 feet 9 inches tall, she weighed just 6 stone.

What chance did unknown models have when even top fashion models have painful stories about body scrutiny and being told to lose weight? Supermodel Crystal Renn has recalled being told she would make it if she lost 40 per cent of her body weight. She did and as a result battled with anorexia nervosa for years.[20] Another top model, Coco Rocha, was told when she was 15: 'The look this year is anorexic. We don't want you to be anorexic, just look it.'[21]

A Shrinking Industry

The designer Elsa Schiaparelli is credited with first using tall thin models in catwalk shows. Other designers like Charles

Worth and Paul Poiret used a wide range of women as models. A fitter for Cristóbal Balenciaga famously reassured clients that 'Monsieur Balenciaga *likes* a little stomach'. Balenciaga's clothes, created to suit women of many sizes, were often modelled by 'short, stocky' women.[22]

The 1960s saw the introduction of very thin 'waif' models, and during the 1990s the fashion industry was criticised for 'Heroin chic' ('the look of sickness, the look of poverty, and the look of nervous exhaustion')[23] which replaced the more athletic aesthetic of the 1980s. In 1996, Jo Fonseca, director of the Models 1 agency, stated: 'I can think of nothing worse than being fat. The only reason that thin girls look so unusual at the moment is because there are so many fat people.'[24] Then came 'size zero'. In 2013, when I researched my previous book, catwalk models were thinner than ever, with waist measurements comparable to that of a seven year old.[25] 'Size zero' is the US equivalent of a UK size 4. It is as slight as it sounds, particularly in the context of over half of North American women wearing a US size 14 or larger.[26]

It was a highly enforced thinness. Dunja Knezevic, who co-founded the Models Union as part of the British trade union Equity, explains: 'There is such a tiny percentage of girls who are naturally that way and that is mostly because they are young. If you are 20 your hips can't be a certain size when you are six foot tall unless you are starving yourself. Your hips have developed, so it's just impossible.'[27] According to one booker in New York: 'The thin thing now is beyond anything I have ever seen. This is the thinnest time in modelling. It's ridiculous.'[28] Crystal Renn puts it more bluntly: 'Any thinner means dead.'[29]

Models are told to lose weight or get liposuction. The mentality is that you can never be too skinny. I have seen girls come in through agencies who are 15 and haven't developed hips, and they are told 'lose some weight' – just because everybody should lose some weight. It's not even 'eat healthy to be skinny'; it's just 'don't eat'. A lot of agencies recommend living off water. Water, coffee, and cigarettes are a recommended diet still.

Dunja KnezevIC it's just 'starve yourself'.[30]

Why Size Zero?

Women had to die before the dangers of size zero were taken seriously. After Luisel Ramos died, the Madrid and Milan Fashion Weeks banned size zero models and agreed a minimum body mass index (BMI) of 18.[31] Paris and London refused to act. It is hard to convey just how much resistance there was to change. Before she was replaced by Edward Enninful, the *British Vogue* editor, Alexandra Shulman, would tell anyone who would listen just how 'bored' she was of being asked to set a more inclusive beauty standard and how 'nobody wants to see a real person on the cover of Vogue'.[32] She wrote an article in the *Daily Mail* entitled 'Size zero hysteria at London Fashion Week' which dismissed calls for a ban: 'If I started to photograph all our shoots on size 14 women ... would everyone want to look like them? I think not.'[33] This was while studies were showing that restricting photographs of underweight models and prohibiting size zero models was justified as a method of easing pressure on young women[34] – let alone offering some kind of relief to women employed as models.

Much of the industry remained, and indeed remains, vehemently against rights for models – arguing instead for self-regulation to protect fashion as 'art'. As well as starvation, models report being painted with car paint instead of body paint, having their eyes burned with cosmetics, and having their hair fall out after it has been bleached three times on a shoot.[35] These are real people not canvases. This 'art' has consequences. Cries to reject protective regulation exist against a backdrop of some of the most fastidious industry regulations in existence. The Chambre Syndicale de la Haute Couture in Paris, for example, governs haute couture, with legal definitions covering issues such as the number of fittings for each dress and the number of employees a company must have. There is no justification for rejecting health and safety regulations in the fashion industry.

Excuses periodically emerge from within the industry about the 'need' for thinness because it lets clothes hang better and allows buyers to better envisage how clothes will look in the shops. This 'woman as living coat-hanger' argument should not be entertained. Humans model clothes to bring them to life and make them look beautiful; otherwise clothes could just be displayed on rotating racks. What claim can the fashion industry have to creativity if its buyers cannot visualise clothes without extremely thin models or indeed if designers cannot design clothes for a variety of sizes, as Cristóbal Balenciaga did?

Much has been made of models needing to be ultra-thin in order to fit into sample sizes. Some argue that small samples are due to economies of scale since small sizes require less material. But a conglomerate that makes millions in profit can scarcely argue that a few extra inches of cloth will bankrupt them. Sample sizes could be produced in a variety of sizes, something that would reduce pressure on models and benefit the health of society as a whole. Dunja Knezevic describes the refusal of anyone to take responsibility: 'The agencies blame the designers – "How can we stock models who are a size 8 when they only want a size 6?" But the designers say: "They only give us small models".'[36]

A Modern Condition

Such excuses do not justify or explain why young (often poor) people are required to starve themselves to death for the visual entertainment of the rich. So what is really behind size zero?

The economic theories of Karl Marx were his attempt to mirror the relations he observed in the real world.[37] Marx describes the physical condition of the working classes of Victorian Britain – their stunted height, bent backs, gnarled fingers, missing limbs, and deathly pale complexions. This, he said, was the result of labour being external to workers, of their having no choice about what work they do, how it is done, or what is produced. In working, the worker 'does not affirm himself but denies himself, does not feel content but unhappy, does not develop freely his physical and mental energy, but mortifies his body and ruins his mind'.[38] This sheds light on twenty-first-century capitalism's focus on the body and on extreme thinness, because it is startlingly similar to the predicament of the vast majority of women workers in the fashion industry. They have been reduced to 'living appendages of the machine'.[39]

The ultimate poverty or loss of being has been described as being left with nothing to work with except your body, like an animal. This was the original definition of the proletariat.[40] It is the situation for the vast majority of women working as fashion models.

Take Dunja Knezevic's description of modelling: 'You are essentially this object that things are done to. They make you into a product, then they shoot you as this product that they sell.'[41] The way models are treated shows them to be com-modified labour like other workers. The production of fashion is the production of commodities by commodities.[42] These young women are shown no respect.

An agency got a call one afternoon with a request for a model to go and finish off a photo shoot that had started that morning and which was using very strong flashlights. The model sent by the agency ended up having the first layer of her corneas burned off by the flashlights. She was rushed to hospital – the same hospital where the original model from the morning was being treated! They burned the corneas of the model in the morning but didn't change the lights or change anything they were doing – they just called up and got another model

Dunja Knezevic.[43]

Maintaining extreme thinness turns every hour of a woman's day into work. There is no physical or mental rest from dieting. It is an obsession, as this traditional saying describes it: 'A person with bread has many problems, a person without has only one.' For young models, this work is physically and mentally draining.

Models' work is not restricted to catwalk and photo shoots. Behind the scenes, their work is to starve themselves to maintain an illusion that makes money for the fashion and beauty industries. Models are not coughing up soot, but their damaged bodies are a sign of the system at work, a system that has control of them. Strength is replaced by obsessing over extreme thinness. If they are taught that they are weak, women are less likely to fight back against poor treatment.[44] They are also literally less able to fight back against physical attack.[45] Models are also subject to the massive pressure and insecurity of a giant reserve army of labour. If they do not 'measure up', thousands are waiting in the wings to take their job for worse conditions, less money, and less food. This reality is hidden behind statements like this from Linda Evangalista: 'We don't wake up for less than $10,000 a day.'

Enforced thinness – starvation to the point of death – is emblematic of the industry's treatment of people and the planet, of the pressure the industry exerts on all its workers. Making unnaturally obtained or sustained extreme thinness a condition of employment is a reactionary but effective means for the industry to maintain control of employees and to take away people's agency by getting them into a destructive mentality.[46]

Out of the Frying Pan

In *Stitched Up* I wrote: 'As the economy shrinks, corporations may begin to diversify their advertising campaigns in a cynical attempt to attract more customers.'[47] This has happened. Online and high-street brands, particularly those catering to a mass-market audience, have diversified their models and more expensive brands are starting to follow. Jody Furlong, casting director, modelling agent, and founder of The Eye Casting, has worked in the fashion industry for two decades. He describes the ultra-thin white aesthetic as being directly associated not just to a single fashion house but to the brand of fashion itself. This meant there was a reluctance on the part of all fashion companies to diversify because of a mentality that Jody describes as 'fashion models are skinny, therefore we can't have anyone else because it takes us away from fashion'. Then came the rise of, in particular, slash fashion brands who, as Jody says, 'were trying to appeal to ordinary people ... They didn't have to worry about what the fashion press was thinking about them – they were just worried about their consumer. And they know what their consumer looks like and who they're selling to. So, they just went for that.'

Certainly it is refreshing to see models of colour hired, swimwear advertised on a wider variety of bodies, and actual rolls of fat and cellulite – something that was unthinkable for a mainstream brand ten years ago. But what does this really mean? Is this the longed for beauty democracy? Do women finally have attainable beauty ideals? Especially when the latest aesthetic is most associated with the hour-glass curves and hyper-sexualised femininity of the women of the Kardashian family. It is a different look but still one with rigidly patrolled rules regarding acceptable standards for women's bodies.

While Jody describes the aesthetic change as more democratic than the monoculture we faced before, he has no illusions:

> It's gone from one extreme to another. Instead of *this* kind of shape, you now have to have *that* kind of shape. You have to have a certain kind of lips and you have to wear God knows how much make-up just to go to the shops. So, it's out of the frying pan into the fire for women who are looking to aspire to what the world is telling you have to look like.

Diversity is a good business strategy. Research has found that (contrary to what Alexandra Shulman argued) women are more motivated to shop when models in adverts reflect their body size and shape. Purchase intentions are said to rise by up to 300 per cent when models reflect the weight, age, or ethnicity of customers.[48] But as I concluded back in 2014: 'The point of diversity is not to increase profits for corporations.'

In the early twenty-first century, the fashion industry still overwhelmingly equates beauty with thinness and requires models to be thin. The Model Alliance has worked on academic studies on eating disorders among professional models which show that this is far from a historic issue. One such study was published in 2020 after policies in the United States and France had been implemented to try and protect models from pressures to be extremely thin and from sexual harassment. The survey found that a large proportion of respondents reported unhealthy weight control behaviours. These included 54 per cent who reported skipping meals, 39 per cent who used intravenous drips, and 25 per cent who reported self-induced vomiting. The study also documented sexual objectification, with fewer than half of respondents saying they were 'always or sometimes' provided with a private changing area.[49]

More than a Trend

The cult of thinness has spread throughout society beyond just those who have it as a condition of employment. So why do people strive to be thin?

For Susie Orbach, thinness has become fashionable because the West has accumulated vast riches and now has 'some need to exhibit, among this abundance, its opposite: to be free of need, to be highly selective, to be able to control the food that we require, to do away with the materiality of the body'.[50] Orbach argues that if thinness were not in fashion, it would be something else. In the 1950s, companies sold Wate-On and scolded women for being too thin for 'fun'.[51] Today, the fashion industry, along with its 'handmaidens'[52] – the diet, food, and pharmaceutical industries – make billions from body insecurity. Described as 'merchants of body hatred',[53] they 'depend on the breeding of body insecurity [to] create beauty terror in so many people'.[54] Women are too profitable a market to be allowed to relax into their physicality. Instead, they are given an impossible quest for self-perfection which keeps them spending money.

The Lagerfeld quote that opens this chapter reads in full: 'Unreachable beauty is a reminder to make an effort. But if you see something and you can reach what you see, then you do not have to make an effort anymore.'[55] Effort entails buying clothes, accessories, cosmetics, and perfumes. As part of the wider capitalist system, fashion fuels 'consumer demand by creating a craving that can't be satisfied'.[56]

While it might be problematic to argue that there is a natural state of being, women's bodies today are augmented with silicon injections into breasts and buttocks, botox injections, skin bleach, hair dye, enamel teeth, hair extensions, fake nails, vajazzles (crystals applied to the genitals), surgically modified noses and chins, and leg bone grafts. They are also starved. The results are then Photoshopped to within an inch of their life – this is the epitome of the flight from nature.

Alienation leads people to be alienated from the planet, from each other, and from their own bodies, as discussed in Chapter 5. These three things become something to be conquered. Human nature 'splinters'[57] into fractured parts and the body becomes something to be starved and hated, rather than a part of nature, perfect as it is. This conquering of the body comes partly from the way humans are taught to measure themselves by their distance from the rest of the population and 'from nature itself'.[58]

Promoting a fake body ideal is also deeply disempowering. It leaves women feeling so inadequate that they spend large amounts of their time trying to alter their appearance. The promotion of a particular fetishised body shape – in this case airbrushed thinness – forms part of the process of exclusion carried out by the fashion industry. Chapter 7 further explores the idea that the fashion industry defines beauty through a process of exclusion – this time of race – benefiting those that do the excluding and having nothing to do with the actualities of those being excluded.[59]

A particularly pernicious aspect of dieting – of doing it to yourself – has been illuminated by the late Sandra Lee Bartky in *Femininity and Domination*. She outlined the key concept of prisons as being the maintenance of a state of conscious and permanent visibility for all prisoners.[60] Society, she argued, keeps women prisoner by keeping them on display. She describes how women check the mirror half a dozen times a day to see if their make-up has smudged; worry that the wind or rain will ruin their hair; and, being scared of getting fat, monitor what they eat. Women therefore self-enforce their prisoner status: because they know they are being watched, the 'inmates' police themselves.[61]

There has been an important change since *Femininity and Domination* was published in 1990. The rise of the internet means that never before have ordinary people been so on display. If life was a visual prison before the internet, now it is a concentration camp. From sonograms of babies in the womb to photos of funerals, Facebook and Instagram in particular mean that every aspect of our lives is captured and posted online for inspection. Being constantly on display means that 'Facebook facelift' is now a term recognised by the *Cambridge Dictionary*: 'facial cosmetic surgery as a result of vanity brought on by seeing too many photos of oneself on social networking websites'.[62] See also the plastic surgery 'Zoom boom' brought about by people who stared at their on-screen appearance all day during the pandemic.

An illuminating article by the blog *Threadbared* applied academic Rob Nixon's definition of 'slow violence' (violence that occurs gradually and out of sight; an attritional violence that is typically not viewed as violence at all, and which has a delayed effect)[63] to body dysmorphia and eating disorders. For *Threadbared*, adult women tacitly told to strive for a pre-pubertal body is a goal that spawns myriad linked acts of slow violence: low self-esteem, anxiety, depression, and for some drug and alcohol abuse, self-harming, and disordered eating behaviour. In this way, eating disorders can illuminate the society we live in. Rather than being 'a white girl's problem', race and racial violence play a strong role in the development of body dysmorphia.[64] This normalisation of distress adds to women's inequality in society.

Global society is weighed down by war, extreme poverty, financial upheaval, tyranny, imperialism, shrinking resources, nuclear disasters, terrorism, and neoliberalism. If we include the slow violence of climate change – and, I would argue, the alienation of modern life – early twenty-first-century capitalism presents us with perhaps the greatest crisis in human history. It is a time of extremes.

Today's society is also different in that markets have spread to every area of the globe; what is left to conquer is the minutiae of the human body, with product sales dependent on myth and fantasy.[65] Especially in fashion, use-value has been overtaken by the brand fantasies needed for exchange value to work.

Sexual Violence

Models continue to campaign against the sexual abuse that forms an intrinsic part of fashion's workplace culture. There is a long list of industry figures who have engaged in abusive and predatory behaviour. A still longer list includes all those who have enabled abuse by ignoring its existence, covered up for or defended abusers, and dismissed those who spoke out.

The list of abusers includes photographers, model agents, casting directors, brand executives, designers, and industry moguls. It took 17 years of allegations of sexual assault against disgraced photographer Terry Richardson before the most powerful brands in fashion finally stopped hiring him.[66] Many of the women attacked by Harvey Weinstein, before he was jailed for rape, were fashion models. Key to Weinstein's conviction was the brave decision to try and expose his crimes by models such as Ambra Battilana Gutierrez. Paul Marciano was forced to resign as executive chairman of the Guess board over sexual misconduct allegations,[67] while sacked American

175

Apparel founder Dov Charney stands accused of multiple counts of sexual misconduct – though he has never been convicted and denies the accusations.[68] Former Elite model agency boss Gerald Marie is currently under investigation by the French authorities for multiple rape allegations, including from models who were minors at the time. Similarly, in the *New York Times*, 15 current and former male models who worked with Bruce Weber and 13 male assistants and models who have worked with Mario Testino accused the two prominent photographers of sexual exploitation, which they deny. These cases are a sample of the abusive climate fostered by the fashion industry. As supermodel Christy Turlington has stated: 'Harassment and mistreatment have always been widely known and tolerated in the industry. The industry is surrounded by predators.'[69]

The industry has also become notorious for devising fashion shoots that, if conducted outside the industry, would certainly have led to arrests for child pornography. Before regulations were introduced, a particularly disturbing shoot by *Vogue Paris* featured a heavily made-up ten year old in sexually provocative poses. Dunja Knezevic agrees that there is a lot that goes on in the fashion industry that elsewhere would lead to arrests: 'like the sexual harassment, like the child labour ... People don't realise that these girls in the campaigns are 15. The industry just goes "she doesn't look it so who cares if her tits are out."'[70] In a revealing interview, legendary model Kate Moss described how doing provocative shoots as a young girl gave her a nervous breakdown. Of one of her most lauded images, a topless photo shot by Corinne Day, Moss said: 'They were like, "If you don't do it, then we're not going to book you again." So I'd lock myself in the toilet and cry and then come out and do it.'[71]

Industrial struggle is key to empowering models to both speak up and change society. The Model Alliance sets out what it wants to change in its Respect programme: create and implementing a rigorous code of conduct to protect models from sexual harassment and abuse; educate models in their workplace rights and educate stakeholders in their duties; protect the right of models to speak up; end voluntary agreements; and address economic vulnerability to reduce the susceptibility of models to coercion and abuse.[72]

The #MeToo movement has swept the world after originally being founded in 2006 by US activist Tarana Burke to encourage survivors of sexual abuse to speak out. But there is a great deal left to do, not least because sexual violence occurs across fashion supply chains, from catwalks to factories, with women surrounded by a social context which considers them to be inferior, caught at the intersection of gender inequality and inequalities of class, race, ethnicity, age, and migrant status.[73]

Within the modelling industry or factories this is made more difficult because fashion is still dismissed as a 'feminine interest' – devaluing the work of women and lessening the chances of calls for change being taken seriously.[74] Ultimately, social power structures must be smashed to pieces so that men can no longer exploit the power they have over women in workplaces or anywhere else. For now, it remains the case that the fashion industry would not exist without gendered exploitation and sexual violence.

Ableism

Over the years a growing number of stylists, models, and campaigners have persevered with trying to break down the barriers that see people excluded because of made-up fashion rules. (Made up because there is nothing credible or real that says clothes look better on white people or that beauty stops after a certain age or past a certain number on some scales.)

But there is another beauty barrier hidden by its very obviousness – that of ableism.

'In this rigid hierarchy, disabled people often don't get the chance to be valued as stylish and elegant', said Michael Shamash, a former chairperson of the Restricted Growth Association. It is not, he says, a question of increasing profits for corporations: 'There is a moral justification to this. Inclusion is not just about healthcare, housing, transport, education – it is equally about identity and self-worth and how you express it. This that makes access to style so important'.[75]

Model Kelly Knox, who has opened shows at London Fashion Week, says: 'Until I started modelling, I never thought of myself as disabled.' Knox, who was born without her left forearm, adds that 'it's not my impairment that makes me different, but the lack of opportunities given to me because of my arm.'[76] Knox believes that disability is one of the last barriers to break in fashion. 'It is every person's birthright to grow up confidently in their skin with the total freedom to be themselves,' she explains.

These campaigners are carrying a revolutionary message. 'I like the way I look', says Shamash, '[a]nd I like the way I appear, and I am interested in the way I look and appear'. This sentiment is almost unheard of in the fashion industry. It makes for a striking statement, one that is at odds with an industry that could not exist if we all reached this state of self-acceptance.

Steps forward with regards to visual diversity always prompt the question of why it took so long to happen in the first place, and how to prevent it from being a one-off event. Brands and magazines are adept at conducting buzz-generating, box-ticking exercises rather than engaging in real, sustained change.

'They bring you in, and it's like "Diversity Day", and then you go home', model Hari Nef once said. 'Diversity Day is cool – Diversity Day essentially pays my bills. But it's never a blue chip campaign, it's never a contract, or rarely a contract.' Change that makes diversity just a numbers game 'does not lend itself to building a new interface for fashion that is inclusive in a sustainable way', Nef continued. 'It's very difficult to fit yourself into this mould that wasn't built for you – these samples that weren't built for you, these visual contexts that weren't built for you', she adds. 'I think there needs to be a greater awareness invested in who wears the clothes and why they are being included.'[77] Ninety-nine per cent of the population do not fit within fashion's made-up beauty rules – rules that were never supposed to include everybody. In this way, capitalism constantly fills our heads with negative messages: that we're not good enough and must keep trying to measure up by dieting, grooming, and consuming more clothes, shoes, and beauty products.

Fatshionista

'Welcome, fatshionistas! We are a diverse fat-positive, anti-racist, disabled-friendly, trans-inclusive, queer-flavored, non-gender-specific community, open to everyone. Here we will discuss the ins and outs of fat fashions, seriously and stupidly – but above all – standing tall, and with panache.'[78] These were the words of the Fatshionista Live Journal site – an overtly political community which came to define the rise of online fatshion.

I use the term fat because that is what is what bloggers and activists themselves use and because fat is not a bad word.[79] As Dr Charlotte Cooper, author of *Fat Activism: A Radical Social Movement*, has explained: 'Euphemisms and language that attempt to make the concept respectable or medicalized just make everything worse, they enshrine shame, invisibility and powerlessness. How can you have any political thoughts about fat if you can't even say the most basic word? It's really not such a big deal to use this word.'[80]

Sites like Fatshionista provided a platform for people for whom fat stigma directly influences and restricts access to fashion.[81] Kirsty Fife is an archivist, academic, and activist based in Leeds who describes stumbling across Fatshionista and becoming immersed in a radical, free space: 'It was that moment of seeing bodies that were like mine, wearing different things, breaking all the rules, and doing really playful things with clothing – rather than fashion being about "what is it appropriate for me to wear."' Nurtured by the Fatshionista space, Kirsty launched their own blog, *Fatty Unbound*, in 2010: 'I was literally on the dole and bored. I'd grown up in and out of charity shops and at the time there were blogs but I kind of felt like everyone was better off than me. Plus-size clothing was still a wash-out but there were some things emerging if you had enough money.' Their writing, styling, and photography was purposefully from 'the point of being skint', with Kirsty making clothes and buying second-hand bargains.

The blog quickly became popular as part of a soaring movement, calling not just for more clothing options for fat people but for an end to fat oppression across the medical-industrial complex. Fatshion was subversive, powerful, and sticking two fingers up to the establishment but fatshion's growing prominence brought challenges. After a few years, Kirsty found they were being courted by brands and media outlets, with offers of free clothes and invitations to TV shows. 'At the time I was just like "free clothes are great – send them here," but over time it acquired this unexpected sort of ickiness to it', Kirsty says. The pressure grew to maintain 'positive relationships' with brands and to change blog entries if the brands did not like what had been written.

TV shows were a similarly negative experience, with Kirsty pushed to talk about how many calories they ate in a day and what men thought of Kirsty's body. 'It was doubly weird because I'm queer', Kirsty says. 'It was like how I feel about my body needs to be framed for someone else.' Kirsty talked to other bloggers and found they were posting things they no longer believed. The honest, and often scathing, clothing reviews were being replaced by well-paid brand gigs. In 2013, the founder of *Fatshionista*, Amanda Piasecki, told an interviewer: 'My perception of what's happening or what's happened is this deeply queer, alternative type of culture was co-opted by the mainstream ... It's become this exercise in showing how much fat people can be like the mainstream so their worth is questioned less.'[82] Veteran organisers voiced concerns that while it was nice that 'you can just be a fat person who likes pretty clothes', it was dangerous to let the movement stop there.[83]

In Australia, Nathalie Perkins wrote: 'It's foolish to suggest that fat stigma can be solved by the emergence of fatshion bloggers in the mainstream ... Fatshion blogs have largely evolved to be in step with large clothing brands, and I fear that the joining of oppressed and oppressor in brand relationships is not furthering fat activism.' In an extremely insightful passage that can be applied to any subculture movement for change, Perkins continued: 'Is fatshion about fat embodiment or is it about consuming clothes and making up for lost time in a capitalist system that has told us we are unacceptable? If so, is that activism? Who does it leave behind? How can we care for ourselves and other fat people without paying into the system that has fucked us over for so long?'[84]

The question of who was being left behind was one that was increasingly occupying Kirsty's thoughts. They recall a particularly unsettling experience of being invited by *The Times* to be part of a feature on fatshion. A group of fatshion bloggers were assembled and interviewed. Then everyone except Kirsty was invited to a photo shoot. 'They included my words but not my face', Kirsty says:

It was this weird moment of realising that my face didn't fit the mould of what they wanted to present. I think there's a lot of people particularly those who are more likely to be not conventionally attractive – who are queer, who are working class, who are people of colour – a lot of those people were the people that were not moved into these very visible positions.

A cluster of people moved forward, while the rest – including many of those who had laboured to build the movement – got left behind. As another fat activist, Lesley Kinzel, wrote: 'It's easy to cheer for the smashing of beauty standards when most of the people getting credit for doing the smashing are themselves beautiful.'[85]

While there is widespread pleasure that shopping for plus-sized clothing is no longer a desert, becoming a consumer market was never the point of the radical aims of fatshion. Fat positivity has been replaced by 'body positivity', a washed-out version of fat embodiment that is used to 'sell clothing, elevate A-list celebrities, and be a general capitalist tool rather than an anti-establishment movement',[86] and a phrase so overused that it has become meaningless. I agree with Kinzel when she writes that, while it is lovely to tell everyone that all bodies are good bodies no matter what they look like, there has to be an acknowledgement that not all bodies are treated the same by society: body positivity 'places the insecurities of a slender, conventionally attractive young woman in her early 20s on the same level as the psychological gauntlet run by a middle-aged woman wearing a size 28 who dares to go to the beach in a bikini'.[87] Nor is this just about appearance: 'There is a world of difference between worrying about whether your cellulite is showing in a pair of size 6 shorts, and worrying about whether you can physically fit in a seat on an airplane, or whether a hospital will have equipment that can accommodate you during a health scare.'[88]

Fat activism continues, but the fashion scene has largely lost its radical edge. There is, however, still anger and power to be found among those who remained excluded when the lines of acceptability shifted ever-so slightly. Capitalism's new rules of how to look and behave were never intended to accommodate the infinite range of human bodies and experience. Kirsty Fife quit their blog and turned a love of DIY cultural organising into punk bands, making zines, the fat activist movement, and organising plus-sized clothes swaps. 'I still feel clothes are radical', they say. 'For a lot of fat people still at this point in time, clothes form a really important part transforming your feelings about yourself and how you move out into the world.'

'I maintain a lot of faith in clothes swap spaces that are subtly radical', Kirsty continues:

The important thing about clothes swaps is how they centre mutual aid. The ones I run in Leeds have 100 people coming over a day and they all bring from nothing to five bin bags full. And everyone goes away with something and has that experience of an abundance of clothing that is not an experience you have if clothing isn't accessible to you in some way.

The fight against fat oppression continues to be a hard-fought battle against medical, economic, and social discrimination. Dr Charlotte Cooper sums up the importance of fat activism and its place as part of a broad movement towards liberation:

I think of it as a strategy for building really good lives, for making things, connecting with people, developing exciting ideas about what it's like to be human, to be embodied ... It's a method of thinking about politics and power, and for me, though not all fat activists, part of the work of manifesting freedom and peace for all beings.

In the same interview, Dr Cooper states:

Fat queer feminists have been such a powerful force in fat activism because they tend not to value the mainstream. Within this group you are also talking about pioneers of the trans movement, people of the Left, working-class people, people of colour, minority ethnic people, people who are chronically ill or disabled. People who navigate these intersections are often people who will never be let in, so we make our own lives instead. This requires a lot of imagination – it requires politics. It's not something you can buy off a shelf. It is hard fought for and emerges through risk-taking, sharing ideas, believing in the value of your own weird and wild experience.[89]

CHAPTER SEVEN

Is Fashion Racist?

This is not the first time Black people have complained about the fashion industry; this isn't the first revolution. Something's got to give.

Adesuwa Aighewi

Black Lives Matter

Fashion is a highly lucrative business. Because of this, it has historically been guarded as a domain reserved for one demographic: rich, thin, and white. This has resulted in the myth that those outside this demographic do not 'do fashion'. They are relegated to 'the people without history' or, in this case, 'the people without fashion'.[1] This essentially racist premise – that what Paris, Milan, London, and New York produce is fashion and what everyone else produces is just clothing – is the setting for this chapter. It is a premise that allows for white opportunity hoarding; for the dehumanisation, and thus the guiltless exploitation, of the Global South; for the reality that there would be no fashion without racism. The nature of the fashion industry means the entirety of this book should be seen as being about racialised exploitation. This chapter therefore hones in on particular questions of visual representation and the exploitative mining of culture to create trends.

In 2020, challenging racism in fashion gained traction due to the strength of the global Black Lives Matter movement. The police murder of George Floyd in Minneapolis 2020 sent shock waves around the world and led to a racial justice reckoning in multiple areas of society. This meant that a renewed space opened up in the fashion industry, exposing the racist fault lines that make the industry tick. As part of this reckoning, Anna Wintour apologised to her staff: 'I know *Vogue* has not found enough ways to elevate and give space to Black editors, writers, photographers, designers and other creators. We have made mistakes too, publishing images or stories that have been hurtful or intolerant.'[2] She did not, however, resign as editor of US *Vogue* or as Condé Nast's global content advisor.

The strength of the protests also pushed brands to use social media to voice their support, with the now infamous Instagram #BlackoutTuesday seeing brands share black squares and promises to do better. While some welcomed the show of support, others were more circumspect. 'It does come across as disingenuous when a brand says something like "We stand with the Black community." It's like, when have you ever stood with the Black community?' Danielle Prescod, style director for BET.com, told CNN.[3] Supermodel Adesuwa Aighewi echoed this sentiment, saying, 'I don't know if any White person is even able to relate to the emotional turmoil that is being Black and trying to have a business here and trying to survive ... I don't know if there's any sector in fashion where Black people can say we have the same resources, we're equal, we're treated the same.'[4]

Exclusion Zone

In February 1959, photographs of China Machado (born Noelie Dasouza Machado) appeared in *Harper's Bazaar*. It was the first time a model of colour[5] had featured in a fashion magazine, something that Machado's photographer and colleague, Richard Avedon, fought to accomplish. In 2012, China Machado, then aged 82, once again began working as a model. Of her childhood in Shanghai she remarked: 'We [non-whites] had no images. We had nothing that told us we were nice-looking. Nothing. So I didn't think of myself as good-looking at all. It never occurred to me.'[6]

Not until 1966 did *Vogue* magazine put a model of colour on one of its covers. *British Vogue* went first, featuring Donyale Luna. In the photograph Luna's hand covers part of her face –

an attempt, it is thought, to mask her ethnicity. It took another eight years before Beverly Johnson was featured on the front cover of the US edition in 1974. *Vogue Paris* stayed resolutely white until as late as 1988 when Yves Saint Laurent threatened to sever ties with the magazine unless 18-year-old Naomi Campbell was put on its cover.

Decades ticked over but these exclusionary practices continued with all-white catwalks, all-white advertising campaigns, and all-white fashion shoots. New York Fashion Week 2007 was quite literally a whitewash with 101 shows (a third) having no models of colour whatsoever. Even after a public campaign for diversification, New York's 2009 catwalks only allotted 18 per cent of catwalk spots to models of colour. This is even less inclusive than it sounds because repeat appearances from three top models made up half the spots. Out of 35 spots, Calvin Klein used only one model of colour, while Donna Karan selected 3 out of 45.[7]

By industry standards there was only mild segregation in New York. The 2008 Paris Fashion Week, with shows by 40 designers, did not include a single model of colour. Industry insiders talked of endemic racism in Europe: 'In Paris and Milan, if you offer a black girl, they drop the book like it's hot.'[8] Clients were telling casting directors: 'We want a black girl, but don't let her be too black.'[9] While booking agents received casting briefs which said 'no ethnics'.[10] Prada did not have a single Black model on its catwalks between Naomi Campbell in 1997 and Jourdan Dunn in 2008. Amid an accepted level of racism unimaginable in almost any other industry, the July 2008 edition of US *Vogue* led with the story 'Is Fashion Racist?' In September 2013, Naomi Campbell, Iman, and Bethann Hardison wrote an open letter calling on designers to diversify their catwalks: 'No matter the intention, the result is racism. Not accepting another based on the colour of their skin is clearly beyond aesthetic.'[11]

Caricature

When they are offered work, models of colour often face being caricatured. The fashion media routinely casts Black female bodies as illicit, hypersexualised, primitive, or obscene.[12] Commonplace stereotyping of models of colour occurs whenever the industry wants to invoke 'tribal' imagery. Anyone who reads fashion magazines will also be aware of fashion's continuing predilection for portraying women of colour as akin to animals. Jean-Paul Goude's 'Wild Things' shoot for *Harper's Bazaar* in 2009 featured Naomi Campbell running with a cheetah, skipping with monkeys, and riding on an elephant and a crocodile. Other famous examples are Peter Beard's photographs of Iman naked with a cheetah and Maureen Gallagher feeding a giraffe – also while naked.

Fashion shoots also typically utilise everyone from Mongolian herders to Balinese children as mere exotic landscapes. The 'exotic people' are there to provide a contrast to white models and expensive clothes. It is an unoriginal and tedious theme rich with the history of colonialism and exploitation. In August 2008, *Vogue India* ran a 'Slum Dwellers' shoot, juxtaposing impoverished people who survive on $1.25 a day with $100 Fendi baby bibs, $200 Burberry umbrellas, and a $10,000 Hermès bag. Kanika Gahlaut, a journalist at *Mail Today* in India, stated: 'There's nothing "fun or funny" about putting a poor person in a mud hut in clothing designed by Alexander McQueen. There are farmer suicides here for God's sake.' *Vogue* did not list the slumdwellers' names, they are just 'lady' or 'man', unlike the clothes which are fully identified. *Vogue India* retorted: 'Lighten up. Fashion is no longer a rich man's privilege. Anyone can carry it off and make it look beautiful.'[13]

Displacing Whiteness, edited by Ruth Frankenburg, describes how women of colour are fetishised as being 'on a slippery slope from exotic beauty to unfemininity and ugliness'.[14] Because of this, it is also common for models of colour to be chosen for shoots portraying deviance. One magazine editor stated: 'Black girls have a harder-edge kind of look. Like, if I'm shooting something really edgy, I'll use a black girl.'[15] Alek Wek has spoken about how she has been portrayed in the past. She compared a Lavazza campaign where she was pictured as the 'coffee' in a giant cup to previous images of Black people used by the advertising industry: 'There was the big-lipped jungle-dweller on the blackamoor ceramic mugs sold in the forties; the golliwog badges given away with jam; Little Black Sambo, who decorated the walls of an American restaurant chain in the 1960s; and Uncle Ben, whose apparently benign image still sells rice.'[16]

British Vogue

By August 2014, twelve years had passed since an individual Black model had been featured on the cover of *British Vogue*. The previous occasion was Naomi Campbell in August 2002; since then 146 covers had been shot, edited, and distributed. *British Vogue*'s emailed explanation for this editorial policy and specifically why supermodel Jourdan Dunn had not had her own cover (she'd been featured in a group cover six years previously), was: 'Here is a quote from Vogue's Editor, Alexandra Shulman: "We have put Beyonce and Rihanna on the cover of Vogue and at least half our covers do not feature models. We love Jourdan Dunn and she was the cover star of the last *Miss Vogue* which previously had featured Cara Delevingne."'

The online *Vogue* archive showed that since Naomi Campbell, 95 covers had featured models compared to just 58 featuring celebrities, of which Beyonce and Rihanna were just two. In 2014, there had been two celebrity covers and seven

white model covers – two of Cara Delevingne. It is also important to note that *British Vogue* caused hurt and anger among
Black celebrities like Thandiwe Newton who knew they were
also being excluded.[17] Within the fashion industry, landing a
Vogue cover remains an integral part of being booked for the
biggest contracts. It is also a signifier of beauty standards –
and had become resolutely white only. 'There is this fallacy
that "black covers don't sell"', stated Jody Furlong at the time.
'But how do you know? There hasn't been one for twelve
years! You can't say people don't buy it when they're not
given the chance to buy it.'[18] As well as being deeply offensive
to Black women, being used as an excuse for racism is also an
insult to magazine readers. The sidelining of models of colour
reflects the attitudes of those at the top of the fashion industry,
not those of fashion fans.

In February 2015 – 151 covers since Naomi Campbell
– Jourdan Dunn was on the cover of *British Vogue*. There
are roughly 200 pages in that edition; with the exception of
Jourdan Dunn, every other image aside from four adverts
and three small photos are of white people. The long-awaited
profile, written by the then prime minister's sister-in-law and
future editor of a national newspaper, reads: 'Jourdan is not
afraid to give her opinion. On racism in modelling she has the
following outlook: "It's hard being a model regardless, and
then being a black model. I have heard, 'Oh we haven't shown
any black models this season,'" she recalls, delicately chewing
on her chicken wing.'[19]

As I write this, Shulman has not been at *Vogue* for five
years, bowing out with a controversial group photo of her editorial staff – 54 other privileged white people; and a car-crash
interview where she stated: 'I'm against quotas. I feel like my
Vogue had the people in who I wanted it to.'[20] It should come
of little surprise that *Vogue* was in decline – facing a world of
exciting online content and a change in fashion's demographic.

As Estella Tincknell has written, there was an extreme tension between Vogue's culture of privilege and an 'economic imperative to change or perish'. Condé Nast needed to modernise again and needed to work hard 'to reimagine and remediate the intersectional relations of gender, race, and class'.[21]

This job fell to Edward Enninful, who in 2017 made history as the first person of colour to become editor in chief at *British Vogue*. His work, and the work of his new editorial team, has thrilled both buyers of fashion magazines and the accountants at Condé Nast. There is no denying that under Enninful the visual landscape at *British Vogue* has changed. In the October 2021 issue, 42 per cent of all people featured are people of colour (when I wrote *Stitched Up* in 2014, this figure came in at 5 per cent). The cover star is Zendaya, there are two photo shoots featuring fat models, an Icelandic shoot featuring Akon Changkou, Sherry Shi, and Anok Yai, plus profiles of Labour politician Diane Abbott and tennis player Emma Raducanu. It is a far cry from when *Vogue* considered it cutting edge to photograph Theresa May in leather trousers.

While *Vogue* has been carefully repositioned to be more relevant to liberal values, counter-cultures, and youth movements, it is worth remembering the limitations of the fashion press. *British Vogue* remains deeply entrenched in the class system and still goes hand in hand with the financialisation and planned obsolescence that control fashion: £1,500 dresses, £500 hats, and £20,000 watches still rule the pages, along with endorsements for Klarna debt schemes, multinational corporations, and cosmetic surgery.

Intentional?

It would be easy to reduce all fashion race-related stories to the question of whether the wrongdoer is a racist or not. But this approach is generally unhelpful since intention, whether a person intended to offend or not, is only part of the story.[22] It does not matter whether Prada excludes Black models *intentionally*, what matters more is the result. For the majority of people in the fashion industry – and in society as a whole – racism is perpetuated unconsciously and unintentionally, but it is still racism. The notions of racial difference that constitute racism are human creations, not predetermined categories. Because of this they are subject to change.[23] But while race, like sexuality or gender, is a social construct, it still has tangible effects on the world and a very real impact on the lives of individuals.[24]

Racism, in the form of derogatory stereotypes that are constantly rearticulated in culture, supported slavery, lynching, and colonialism. In *A Quiet Revolution*, the Harvard academic Leila Ahmed describes nineteenth-century European ideas about the hierarchy of races and the racial and civilisational superiority of Europeans. This racist narrative aided European colonialism by casting Europeans, not as bloodthirsty, murderous exploiters, but as virtuous men bringing civilisation to backward people.[25] Today, war is still justified by racism. Support for the wars on Iraq and Afghanistan was sought through the idea that the invaders were a civilising force. Women and women's dress have become key issues for neoimperialists trying to justify war. Gayatri Spivak labelled this form of rhetoric: 'white men saving brown women from brown men'.[26] Step one in any war is to dehumanise your opponent so that your actions appear justified. On a local level, negative stereotypes, like those found in the fashion industry, serve to encourage everything from discriminatory police stop-and-searches to subordinate housing, job, and education opportunities.[27]

Frederick Douglass, who escaped from slavery to become a leader of the abolition movement, argued that racism exists to benefit the small minority who are in control of society: 'They divided both to conquer each.' Racism divides people so that they do not unite in action to win higher wages or stage a revolution. By this measure, racism comes from its beneficiaries – those who extract huge profits from a divided and distracted society.

'Ain't I a Beauty Queen?'

There is, however, the question of whether diversifying catwalks and magazines actually ends industry racism or signals integration into an exploitative system. In 1968, there were not one but two important protests at the now infamous Miss America beauty pageant. The first was a feminist protest outside the pageant which rejected the idea of Miss America on the grounds that it was sexist and objectified women. At the same time, in the nearby Ritz Carlton Hotel, the National Association for the Advancement of Colored People held a Miss Black America pageant in protest against Miss America being racially segregated.[28] Segregation was formalised by rule 7 of the Miss America rule book: 'Contestants must be of good health and of the white race.'

Many feminists in 1968 could not understand why the Black community wanted to be integrated into the exploitation of beauty pageants. They did not appreciate the desire to overcome the dominance of Eurocentric beauty that Miss America perpetuated. In *Ain't I a Beauty Queen?* Maxine Leeds Craig explains that being excluded from the dominant beauty ideal does not mean you escape objectification.[29] Instead, you get a double dose of shame – that of being excluded and that of having an 'unacceptable' body.[30] While the protests unfortunately did not unite to find common ground, both carried important messages about discrimination. The first Black contestant was Cheryl Browne in 1970, but there was no Black contest winner until Vanessa Williams in 1983.

Beauty is a site for political resistance, though a problematic one. In *Venus in the Dark*, Janell Hobson questions whether power can ever be achieved from beauty recognition. Do women of colour who have been recognised as 'beautiful' have the power to elevate the status of all women of colour? Are they agents for change or just sex objects?[31] Taking an unequivocal position against the goal of integration, the Black Power activists Stokely Carmichael and Charles Hamilton stated that any Black people 'absorbed into a white mass are of no value to the remaining Black masses. They become meaningless show-pieces for a conscience-soothed white society.'[32]

The token use of models of colour has certainly been used by the fashion industry to excuse racism. *Vogue Italia* has in the past attempted to deflect accusations of racism by producing 'all-black' issues – a tactic that commentators describe as a backward step which reproduces and secures white as 'normal'.[33] The fashion media also wilfully disregards the progress made in combating racism by the rest of society by shooting white models engaging in 'blackfacing', 'redfacing', and 'yellowfacing' (including taping back their eyes). The pathetic excuse is often given that these shoots are 'just art', as if the fashion industry was not merely enacting and compounding age-old patterns of oppression. When the former *Vogue Paris* editor, Carine Roitfeld, was accused of racism for blacking up Lara Stone in 2009, she defended herself by saying: 'I once did an entire issue on a black model.'[34]

Despite the complexities, campaigns for fashion diversity are an important anti-racist struggle. Catwalk shows and magazines define beauty by a process of exclusion. This exclusion extends to questions of size, age, class, disability, and the minutiae of personal appearance, with race as a fundamental category. While the Black Is Beautiful campaigns of the 1960s did not bring change to Black people's economic life, they were a significant cultural victory which ended one form of discrimination.[35]

Behind the Scenes

Across the industry, the visual landscape is slowly changing with a vocal public ready to call out racist practices. Jody Furlong has experienced a dramatic shift in the industry: '100 per cent it is better, I think partly because it couldn't have gotten any worse', he says. But catwalks and magazine covers are just one aspect of the industry – the tip of the iceberg with most of the structure out of sight. From stylists and photographers to make-up artists and hairdressers, designers and CEOs, editors and journalists, the fashion industry has yet to diversify, with the industry suffering from 'white opportunity hoarding'.[36] Student selection committees at art schools have also been found rejecting Black applicants for citing hip hop as an influence while waving through white students who they acknowledge are less talented.[37]

Jody lists the problems with systemic racism that still dictate many of the rules of society: 'It's things in the structure of society that make it more difficult for some people to succeed than others, and you can't even notice it as coming from a racist place it's just because it's the norm, whether it's lack of opportunity, lack of education, lack of money, lack of entry point into these kind of workplaces, all different things, lack of confidence.' He continues: 'A lot of those things are tied up as well, class and race are inextricably combined. There's no point just employing lots of Black people who went to Oxford and came from Marlborough ... it's a class issue as well as a race issue.' This is particularly pertinent regarding the expectation that young people will complete unpaid or poverty waged fashion internships and entry-level jobs in expensive cities like New York or London.[38]

Photographer Campbell Addy has also talked about the need to diversify staffing at traditional media brands: 'The foundations hold up the structure. If you want change in a genuine manner, you've got to change the foundations ... I want the industry to come 360 degrees. Not just what we see, but the people creating the content.'[39] It is also vital that representation extends beyond catwalks, because as Aurora James, founder and designer of Brother Vellies, has said: 'When you have just Black models or Black musicians as the only Black women in your sphere, it's really objectifying. It doesn't really allow us a space to be intellectuals or businesspeople.'[40]

Take, for example, the fact that LVMH had never named a Black woman to the top creative post of any of its brands until 2019, when it hired Rihanna to start Fenty, her own luxury apparel line, a project that closed down in 2021.[41] In September 2020, Stella Jean, a Haitian Italian designer and the only Black person ever appointed to Italy's influential Fashion Council, announced a boycott of Milan Fashion Week as a protest over racism: 'As the first and only Black designer in the history of the Fashion Council, it is my responsibility to explain to those who haven't noticed the extreme marginalization in which my minority lives', she told the press, saying she could no longer remain silent in the face of a rise in Italian fashion houses producing racist products.[42]

Ultimately, leadership representation alone will not change the structural inequality and racism that hold up the fashion industry. Diversifying boardrooms will not bring better working conditions for garment workers or bring equal rights to such an undemocratic industry. It is one thing to see more diverse magazine covers but quite another to achieve the emancipation of workers across the Global South. This kind of change would need an intersectional feminist and anti-capitalist approach, whereby power is not just the preserve of a small elite of people but is democratised right down to the grassroots. Only by challenging the system itself could you start to see the fashion industry (in a very altered state) being serious about anti-racism, workers' rights, and environmental justice.

Inspiration or Appropriation?

While the people of the world may be rejected by the fashion industry, their cultures are commodified and vociferously consumed.[43] In 2012, Urban Outfitters produced a 'Navajo' range of clothes and accessories. The range had no links to Navajo designers or artisans, the items merely displayed a faux tribal print. The marketing of inauthentic products using Native American tribal names is outlawed under the Indian Arts and Crafts Act. Amid popular protest, the Navajo Nation served Urban Outfitters with a cease and desist letter, highlighting their particular objection to the 'Navajo Hip Flask' and the 'Navajo Hipster Panty', which contravened their spiritual beliefs about modesty and the reservation-wide ban on the consumption of alcohol. Refusing to apologise, Urban Outfitters were sued by the Navajo Nation.

Urban Outfitters argued that 'Navajo' was a generic term for a style or design and so they had a right to use it. The corporation went as far as to argue that the tribe's federal trademark registration of the word 'Navajo' should be cancelled. In 2016 the two sides reached an agreement, in which Urban Outfitters acknowledged the validity of the trademark. The two parties also entered into a supply and licensing agreement for a collaboration on a line of jewellery.[44] The fashion industry is notorious for profiting from the co-option and reproduction of cultural dress from across the globe. Fashion has rightly been compared to Godzilla for devouring everything in its path.[45]

Fighting the Misuse of Cultural Possessions

There is a growing movement of Indigenous communities around the world taking legal action to try and prevent the theft of their intellectual property. One group that continues to campaign for legal rights is the Women's Association for the Development of Sacatepéquez (AFEDES), a Mayan women-led organisation that fights for Indigenous rights and the autonomy of Indigenous women in Guatemala. For centuries, Mayan artisans have woven intricate, brightly coloured designs which contain history, stories, spiritual beliefs, and the value systems of a vibrant living culture. These designs, many of them sacred, were being ripped off, commodified, and sold by both national and international fashion brands as well as the Guatemalan government. 'When the state wants to promote tourism, they use the Indigenous. They use the photos of the women with güipiles – the traditional blouse of the Indigenous women', explained Angelina Aspuac, an organiser from AFEDES. But in reality, she said, the state was benefiting from the weavers' work while discriminating against Mayans.[46]

'The phrase "dispossession of identity" encapsulates what all Indigenous people of Guatemala are suffering from', Mayan weaver Petzey Quiejú told *Truthout*. 'Fifty years ago, the majority of families made their own clothing, which was based in their relations with the cosmos; the weavings were not decorations, but rather something that had symbolic meaning that was connected with the life and nature that surrounded them. But then came the [capitalist] system.'[47] Resisting cultural annihilation was part of a long history of Mayans resisting invasion, imperialism, and genocide. In 2016, AFEDES took their case to Guatemala's Supreme Court and demanded a legal framework to protect their ancestral heritage from companies who had no respect for the origins of the designs they were stealing.

Indigenous Designs Are Not in the 'Free Bin'
Beyond Buckskin

In 2015, London-based brand Kokon To Zai (KTZ) produced a striking black-and-white men's jumper. But when catwalk photos of the jumper appeared, they horrified a family in Nunavut in what is now called Northern Canada. The jumper was instantly recognisable as having been copied from a sacred design on a caribou parka created by an Inuit shaman named Ava in the early 1920s. 'This is a stolen piece', Salome Awa, Ava's great granddaughter, told CBC Radio. 'These are sacred images that they are using', she said. 'They are breaking the Inuit sacred laws of duplicating someone else's shaman clothing ... and for profit of all things.' It was not the first time KTZ had been criticised for copying Indigenous designs. On this occasion the brand apologised and withdrew the jumper. 'They didn't even mention an apology to my great-grandfather', Salome Awa said. 'They didn't mention his name ... and they didn't even offer any monetary gains to our family ... In terms of, "We are so sorry that we're going to give the money back that we've stolen from you," is not there.'[48]

If we lived in an equitable global society, the respectful intermingling of cultures could be taken as a sign of progress, of an inspiring, globalised world in which different cultures are celebrated.[49] Artists, after all, do not live in isolation and it is impossible not to be influenced by our multi-layered world of international foods, music, clothes, religions, ideas, and art. Yet in the current world, this approach cannot be applied to brands as it ignores the historical and political context of the spread of culture. While the mutual fusing of cultures can, in part, be celebrated as exchange, for the most part it is the outcome of domination.[50] The cultures of the world have not spread and merged through an organic process of cross-cultural harmony; instead, colonialism and neocolonialism have resulted in the supplanting and harnessing of those cultures they have encountered.[51] Vast profits from fake cultural products rarely translate to jobs or benefits for Indigenous communities whose artists are left struggling to make a living from authentic products.[52] Dior once provided a disturbing example of this with its 'Fertility Goddess' shoe from Galliano's 'tribal chic' collection. The heel of the strappy shoe was a miniature replica of an African fertility goddess statue. Each step caused the wearer to tread on the goddess, replicating the colonial relationship between Europe and Africa.

The use of Native American designs by giant multinational corporations reflects this deeply unequal relationship whose history is one of subjugation and terror. They represent the theft of cultural identity and lost homelands.[53] In imitation goods, history and meaning are lost: 'Native American people are reduced to one dimensional outdated stereotypes, or worse, as an extinct exotic race that once roamed the land, but who no longer live and breathe and resist today.'[54] This inequality dictates who is allowed to do the appropriating. The sociologist Erving Goffman noted that '[i]mmigrants can impersonate Native Americans in dress and in patterns of decorum but it is still a doubtful matter to Americanise one's name or one's nose'.[55]

Cultural appropriation remains a sensitive issue. Many consumers remain resistant to the idea that their $5 feathered earrings are an offensive by-product of oppression and colonialism. Métis writer Chelsea Vowel explains the need for sensitivity by asking: 'What does the Victoria Cross, the Order of Canada, a framed Bachelor's degree, the Giller Prize, and an eagle feather all have in common?' The answer is that each is a visual recognition of a certain kind of achievement that is imbued with important symbolism. Each of these symbols has rules governing its use and imitation will cause offence.[56] Picture, if you will, the effect on a decorated war veteran of seeing fake Victoria Cross earrings being worn to a rave and then tossed in a bin, then add to this scenario that the vision triggers reminders of centuries of dispossession, dehumanisation, and genocide by a colonial regime.[57]

Fashion's penchant for imitating culture reinforces the idea that cultural dress is fabulous and exotic when worn by some but backward when worn by minorities.[58] Chanel can show a *faux* Indian 'Paris–Bombay' collection at Paris's Grand Palais, Hermès can sell saris costing from $1,800 to $100,000, but the same styles when sold or worn by Indians are considered 'backward'. Similarly, a white US citizen, for example, can wear fashions from the subcontinent of India without taking any of the 'heat' of oppression that goes with these clothes when worn by Indians in the United States.[59]

Calling for cultural traditions to be afforded respect does not mean that people should dress only according to their national identity and eschew all contact with other cultures. As Chelsea Vowel says: 'It's OK to love our stuff.'[60] Elsewhere, Riley Kucheran has advised people of the responsibility of wearing the occasional handcrafted Indigenous piece:

> If you purchased a beautiful beaded necklace from the Santa Fe Indian market, it becomes your responsibility to be proud of that and to share that. When someone says, *Oh my god, that necklace is so stunning.* You can say *It's this artist, they're from this nation, it's from this family.* Then, you can actually take on that role of educating others.[61]

While the fashion industry needs to diversify to afford Indigenous artists the same opportunities as corporations to determine what their culture looks like and how it is represented in the global fashion arena, this is not a problem-free journey.[62] As Riley Kucheran points out, ending cultural appropriation, racism, and inequality does not just mean inviting artists, designers, students, and practitioners into a fashion system that is a 'structurally colonialist, capitalist, and white-supremacist institution'.[63] 'The danger', he writes, 'is that domestication turns an overtly political movement into a "culturalist project of representation."'[64] Instead, the power structures that cultural appropriation mirrors must be overturned in a process that ends the racism that appropriation stems from and the imperialism that it reflects. As such, Kucheran offers strong words of caution to Indigenous fashion designers and those engaging with Indigenous fashion for the first time:

> There's an Indigenous fashion 'movement' right now that is hurtling itself towards new heights of visibility, but this is cause for concern. Indigenous fashion challenges stereotypes and can make political statements, but every engagement between Indigenous designers and the fashion industry thus far has ended in disappointment. Inclusion or an invitation to the table (however fashionable) can detract from the movement's broader goals. Representation and 'visual sovereignty'[65] has its risks, and equating cultural identity with consumption is rarely a good idea. Instead, a resurgent Indigenous fashion that is highly political, which protects ancestral knowledge while carefully navigating any 'strategic concessions' it makes with capitalism when refusal is not an option, is the 'critical' Indigenous fashion I propose we pursue.[66]

Shifting Power

For decades, Europe's and the United States' control of fashion went all but unchallenged. Partly this was because fashion hubs tend to be located in powerful centres of industrial capital. The industry needs cities full of skilled workers, customers with plenty of money for shopping, and media industries for promotional purposes. Fashion houses need the political and economic clout of a powerful country that can negotiate advantageous terms for its products and establish cultural hegemony for its ideas. As an industrial fashion centre, Paris benefited from industrialists, financiers, and the historical encouragement of the French government, which passed laws to prevent copyright infringement. Likewise, Italian industrialists worked closely with their government after the Second World War to create an export-led fashion industry that could rejuvenate the economy.[67]

By seeing the fashion industry as a source of power for multinational corporations and states, we see why its racial identity is so closely guarded. Fashion in France directly generates €35 billion in sales each year and employs 150,000 people. France is the world leader in perfumes, cosmetics, *haute couture*, and *haute joaillerie* (exclusive jewellery);[68] it does not want to share this clout. Becoming inclusive would mean losing the power to exclude. Edward Said wrote in *Culture and Imperialism*: 'The power to narrate, or block other narratives from forming and emerging, is very important to culture and imperialism.'[69] Blocking narratives in fashion is characterised by the simultaneous commodification of culture and the rejection or racist portrayal of people.

As the centre of economic power shifts and giant fashion corporations are no longer just American or European, the question the established industry will ask itself is how to expand its market while keeping the club doors closed. With the rise of China as an economic superpower, the fashion industry has tried to appeal to China as a market by recruiting more Chinese models and producing collections so targeted they were problematic. Susanna Lau described the look as sometimes replicating 'those weird connotations that traditional Asian dress signifies in Western cultures (docility, demureness, opium-den slutiness, etc.)'.[70]

The designer Robert Wun told *Vogue*: 'One of the biggest problems with anti-Asian racism is the normalization of it – when it's categorized as a joke or a punchline – or when it's compared to racism experienced by other communities and then played down like it's insignificant.' The coronavirus pandemic saw a rise in anti-Asian hate crime, spurred on by figures like Donald Trump who used the phrase 'Chinese virus' to refer to Covid-19. In March 2021, eight people, including six Asian women, were shot dead at three spas in Atlanta, Georgia. With the fashion industry rightly under fire for tolerating and propagating racism, industry figures shared their experiences of anti-Asian racism and called for change across society. 'Stop ignoring our existence until it is convenient for you: We are more than a box on your politically correct checklist,' stated model Fernanda Ly. 'It is a prevalent thought that Asia and Asians are to be taken advantage of – for example, through cheap labour or monetary gain by the selling of luxury goods. Please understand that we, too, are human beings with a very rich history – we are not lower class citizens whose existence is only for your benefit.'[71]

'Anti-Semitic, Homophobic, and Ridiculously Snobbish'

In February 2011, John Galliano was arrested following complaints that he had hurled racist and anti-Semitic abuse in a Paris café. The incident had been filmed and the video went viral. As more reports of racist outbursts surfaced and Natalie Portman, Hollywood star and face of Miss Dior perfume, publicly severed ties with Galliano, he was sacked by both Dior and his namesake label. He was subsequently found guilty of anti-Semitism by a French court. Avoiding jail, he was fined a mere €6,000.

Galliano's role as chief designer at Dior renewed speculation over the behaviour of Christian Dior himself during the Nazi occupation of Paris. Having spent much of the war employed by the couture house of Lucien Lelong, Dior's clients were the wives of Nazi officers and French collaborators.[72]

While she despised Dior's New Look, Coco Chanel also became deeply embedded with the Nazis in Paris. She is described as 'a wretched human being. Anti-Semitic, homo-phobic, social climbing, opportunistic, ridiculously snobbish, and [she] actively collaborated with the Germans during the Nazi occupation of Paris'.[73] Closing down her fashion house, Chanel spent the occupation of France in the Paris Ritz with Hans Gunther von Dincklage, a spy sent to Paris as part of an advance party preparing for the Nazi invasion. Chanel used laws banning Jewish people from owning businesses to try to rob her partners, the Wertheimers, of the perfume business they had co-founded. Chanel moved in the highest Nazi circles in Paris and even played a part in the failed 'Operation Modelhut' plot, which involved her being an intermediary to Winston Churchill.

Disgraced and arrested in post-war France, Chanel was inexplicably released. Fearing attacks and being forcibly shaved as a *collaboratrice horizontale*, she fled to Switzerland with von Dincklage and lived there in exile for 15 years. Her comeback in the 1950s was coolly received in France. Only the American market saved her from disappearing into obscurity.

Despite this history, Chanel is usually portrayed as a woman who struggled through hardship to liberate women from restrictive clothing and create the 'little black dress'. The film biopic of Chanel starring Audrey Tautou crudely ended before the Second World War. At the time, Tautou was the face of Chanel and the film was effectively an hour-and-a-half-long advertisement for the brand, which had an estimated net worth of $18.5 billion in 2013.[74]

Louis Vuitton is another fashion house that aligned itself closely with the Nazi occupiers in Paris. Under the stewardship of Gaston Vuitton, grandson of the founder Louis Vuitton, the company benefited from a close relationship with the occupying forces. The company went so far as to produce busts of the Vichy regime leader Philippe Pétain in their factory. Gaston's son, Henry Vuitton, was commemorated for his services to Nazi Germany. This history was purposefully suppressed until being exposed in Stephanie Bonvicini's book, *Louis Vuitton: A French Saga*. The book was met by silence from the French press – for LVMH (owners of Louis Vuitton) are among France's biggest advertisers. A spokesperson for LVMH denied being involved in the lack of coverage of the book: 'We haven't put any pressure on anyone. If the journalists want to censor themselves, then that suits us fine.'[75]

The German designer Hugo Boss owned a small textile company in Metzingen, Germany. One of his early contracts was to manufacture brown shirts for the emerging Nazi Party. By 1938, the firm had become a key supplier of Nazi uniforms, including for the army, the Hitler Youth, and the paramilitary SS. As the war progressed, Hugo Boss's factories were staffed by forced labourers from France and Poland, most of whom were women.

These details came to light in 2011 with the publication of the economic historian Roman Koester's *Hugo Boss 1924–1945*. The book was commissioned by the Hugo Boss corporation but Koester denies that this influenced his findings. More than just a business relationship, Hugo Boss was ideologically aligned with the Nazis, having joined the party as early as 1931. He was prosecuted and fined for his involvement after the war.

The Spanish designer Cristóbal Balenciaga designed numerous dresses for Carmen Polo, wife of the fascist dictator General Franco. Fleeing the Spanish Civil War in 1937, Balenciaga moved to Paris, where he also became a designer for the Nazi elite, though he did turn down the opportunity, when asked by Hitler, to help make Berlin a centre for couture. Having closed his fashion house in 1968, Balenciaga came out of retirement in 1972 for just one commission: a wedding dress for General Franco's granddaughter, María del Carmen Martínez-Bordiú.[76]

Should artists be judged by their political beliefs? If so, should we judge their art by the same standards? While disappointing, it should come as no surprise that so many lauded designers collaborated with fascist dictatorships. The Russian revolutionary leader Leon Trotsky described artists as living 'in a bourgeois milieu, breathing the air of bourgeois salons, they receive and are receiving hypodermic inspirations from their class'.[77] Many top designers would have been sympathetic to Nazism because it was what surrounded them. By 1939, fascist and authoritarian ideology had become the dominant force of the political right across Europe.[78]

Bourgeois business interests would have also been paramount for these designers: if it is your job to create anything from yachts to furniture to fashion for the very rich, then you are destined to bow to their wants and opinions. In this way, life determines consciousness.[79] It is of course these same fashion houses that continue to clothe dictators today.

Yet making dictators look powerful, and siding with a reactionary authority, involves a criminal loss of principle. Nor is it automatic. Dior's sister Catherine became a noted member of the French Resistance and Elsa Schiaparelli repeatedly turned down invitations to work with Benito Mussolini's fascists in Italy. Who knows how many other creative minds were lost through resisting fascism. So if we reject people's opinions, should we reject their art?

Sometimes an artist's political sympathies are expressed in the content of their work. Dior's collusion with the Nazis is arguably echoed in his designs. The Nazis believed women should look virtuous and feminine, and restrict themselves to *Kinder, Küche, Kirche* (children, kitchen, church). It was an ideal that Paris fashion houses catered for during the occupation. Dior's restrictive, hyper-feminine form was arguably 'more than merely reactionary, nostalgic and backward looking; it became the persistence in the late 1940s of the romantic styles that had flowered under Nazism'.[80] Portraying this Nazi ideal of womanhood also intersected with the aims of Dior's capitalist cotton-baron backer.

When art and such politics merge, we must reject the art. Beauty should not take precedence over political meaning, as Elizabeth Wilson explains in *Adorned in Dreams*. It would be wrong to view patterns made by people being blown up by shells as 'beautiful' as the Futurists did; or to view Leni Riefenstahl's film of Hitler's Nuremberg Rally simply as a great work of light and shade. To do so would be to ignore the meaning of events and allow the pursuit of style to justify cruelty and death.[81]

Yet someone like the resolutely anti-Semitic Coco Chanel could produce an aesthetic that challenged sexist assumptions about women. Sometimes abhorrent people produce art worthy of consideration. This is not to say that wearing Chanel is a progressive act. Chanel products are stamped with the name Chanel and her symbol of linked 'C's. Ironically, people wear them as symbols of liberty and élan as well as luxury and expense. But Chanel was anything but a symbol of freedom: she was a homophobic, anti-Semitic bully who sought to crush liberty. When asked if he thought Coco Chanel was a feminist Lagerfeld replied that she 'was never ugly enough for that'.[82]

It is also possible to argue that Chanel's far-right ideology is reflected in her designs. Bearing in mind what we know about her beliefs, her clothes – with their minimalism and austere uniform aesthetics – start to look different. They seem less progressive and more like an expression of the idea that a particular type of white European minimalism is superior to cultures that use colour, pattern, flamboyance, volume, and the shape of the human body in modes of dress. There is an 'othering' and an exclusion that runs throughout Chanel's work.

Another idea that is useful here is from Lola Olufemi, who writes that, '[w]hile it is possible to have a positive experience of art produced by an individual who has perpetrated harm, perhaps it is more important to realise that art alone cannot repair harm. If we want art that reflects the true complexity of our lives and the true range of human emotion, then we must eradicate the harmful conditions in which we live.'[83] This idea that art alone cannot erase harm prompts the question of why we could ever believe that a documented history of active Nazism can be erased by clothing designs. Do we sell our freedom so cheap that we consider its price to be padded handbags?

To edit out the industry's role in bolstering such regimes is a betrayal of those that suffered at the hands of fascists. Edward Said wrote that we are better off exploring history rather than repressing or denying it.[84] Accepting that the fashion industry has a racist past and continues to perpetuate racism today is a step towards preventing a racist future. This involves recognising the realities of the fashion industry – that it is premised on the ability to exclude groups and individuals. This exclusion benefits those that do the excluding and has nothing to do with the actualities of the excluded.[85] Ending racism in fashion cannot be achieved in isolation. It requires ending racism in society. This requires a systemic change to remove a tiny minority's ability to exclude everyone else; it requires an end to the system that needs racism: capitalism.

CHAPTER EIGHT

Resisting Fashion

The charge sheet against the fashion industry reads as follows: fashion reinforces racism, sexism, gender stereotypes, class, and unequal power relations. Fashion seriously exploits its impoverished workers and stifles social progress and freedom of association, while fostering gender-based violence and authoritarianism. Fashion also exploits its customers, pushes the values of wealth and greed, and promotes body insecurity and dissatisfaction. Fashion is a monopolised industry with large corporations controlling both the luxury and mass market. Corporations control the factories and the shops, the fashion magazines and the cotton fields. Fashion's endless quest for profit means scant regard is ever shown for people, animals, or the environment. Fashion is destroying the planet. In an industry that sells itself as a promoter of individuality, the reality is one of conformity with billions of pieces of trend-based clothing churned out each year and sent to identikit stores from Birmingham to Bangkok, with magazines, websites, and social media on different continents promoting the same styles.

And yet fashion is for many people an immense source of joy and a means for creative expression. These final three chapters examine attempts to change the fashion system – resisting, reforming, revolutionising – so we can keep the good and exorcise the grim.

Protest Fashion

The ideas of the ruling class are in every epoch the ruling ideas, i.e. the class which is the ruling material force of society, is at the same time its ruling intellectual force. The class which has the means of material production at its disposal, has control at the same time over the means of mental production.

Karl Marx[1]

Fashion is ideology. What we have seen in Chapters 6 and 7 – that 'thin is beautiful' or 'Black models are not aspirational' – are examples of ideology pushed by the industry. These ideas necessarily benefit the status quo; as Marx said, ideology is power turned into ideas. These ideological ideas reinforce class relations and allow the ruling class to establish, sustain, and reproduce positions of power.[2]

Because of this, fashion is used to define people's roles, status, and gender. One demand of the Peasants' Revolt in Germany in the sixteenth century was the right to wear red because under sumptuary laws certain colours and materials were illegal for all but the nobility.[3] Today, the pricing of brands enacts the same class hierarchy. If you are rich you can dress in Dior, Prada, and Lanvin; if you are poor your options for shop-bought clothes are roughly Primark, Tesco, and Boohoo. This makes fashion a signifier of difference that lets class appear legitimate – with the upper classes frantically trying to naturalise their higher status through clothing.[4]

But as well as being a means of expressing power, clothing is also a time-honoured site of protest against ideology and unfair material conditions. As I write, Afghan women are posting photos of themselves in beautiful, traditional Afghan dress using #DoNotTouchMyClothes and #AfghanistanCulture in protest at the Taliban. And in a much publicised move, Congresswoman Alexandria Ocasio-Cortez wore a white dress emblazoned with the red slogan 'Tax the Rich' to the Met Gala. For hundreds of years people in politically organised groups have adopted modes of dress to convey a singular non-verbal message. Sometimes this non-verbal message accompanies extremely verbal and active forms of protest, sometimes rebellion through clothing is all people can get away with – and even this act carries the threat of imprisonment, violence, and death.

Protest fashion remains a staple in the toolbox of the oppressed – it is resistance enacted by women, LGBTQ+ groups, Indigenous groups, marginalised groups, and working-class movements around the globe. It continues to enrage those in positions of authority – legislation recently passed by China to quell protests in Hong Kong went as far as to ban imports of the black clothing favoured by protesters.

Protest fashion, which I am defining as clothes deliberately made or chosen for a protest, is radical because it is part of challenging not just the dominant ideology of the fashion industry but also capitalism itself. To be clear, I am talking here about progressive protest, not the styles or ideologies invoked by the right or far right. Protest fashion disobeys the fashion industry – people wear what they actually want to wear rather than what the industry says is appropriate or on trend. Take, for example, the clothing worn at Pride Parades or at Black Trans Lives Matter protests – a space opens up that is incalculably more free and fantastic than anything in the industry's narrow confines. Second, in the same way that a protest reworks reality and power – roads are closed, uncontrollable crowds are in charge – protest fashion also creates an alternative reality, if only for a few hours. Capitalism states that fashion is about making money for corporations, maintaining the status quo, maintaining demand and the economy through endless shopping, feeling insecure, and keeping our creativity within certain narrow confines – protest is the opposite of this.

Rebel with a Cause

Another part of protest fashion are the people who use dramatic, norm-defying dress on a *daily basis* to reject ruling-class beauty ideals and the naked emperor's demand for silent social obedience. Punk, for example, with its confrontational assault on the aesthetic values of the dominant classes, is arguably ideologically opposed to capitalism itself.[5]

Straight away there is the question of whether dressing differently is just an expression of personal style rather than a significant attempt to change society. Certainly, there is no single reason why people use their clothes for rebellion.[6] Some people dress differently merely to shock and gain attention, some do it to lampoon something in society they detest, some are relieving boredom, and sometimes fashion is alienation masquerading as individuality.[7] A jaded photographer summed up the Harajuku scene in Tokyo: 'The rest of their lives are going to be crap, so they might as well enjoy themselves while they can.'[8] Others avoid fashion as 'conservative sceptics'; they are opposed to the latest bizarre trend the industry is attempting to foist on them rather than against fashion per se.[9] But there are people for whom style is protest, a way of making a deliberate political point.

Whatever the reason, challenging ruling-class ideology is a dangerous path to take. To prevent disobedience, society metes out punishments to those who disobey fashion etiquette. Dress can influence the ability to gain employment, rent a flat, avoid assault or arrest, be found 'not guilty', get a visa, appear in the media, win elections, get on planes, make friends, or marry the person you love.

Is It Really Resistance?

Despite these risks, and the role of fashion in enforcing ideology in society, does dressing differently really count as rebellion against the fashion system? After all, donning, for example, the anarchist uniform of vegan trainers and all-black clothes is hardly guerrilla warfare. What would a serious challenge to society's material relations look like? When trying to bring about change, does it matter how we dress? Is how we dress really anything more than an individual act? Does it count as resistance?

In his autobiography, Malcolm X rejects attempts to use style to defy the system despite having been a rebellious 'zoot-suiter' in his youth. The 'zoot suit riots' took place primarily in Los Angeles in the early 1940s. White servicemen and the authorities clashed with disaffected Latino and Black youth who wore the zoot suit to reject a society that rejected them. Zoot suits were flashy. With long jackets and wide legs, they used far more material than was considered patriotic while rationing was in place. Zoot suit 'girl gangs', like the Slick Chicks and Black Widows, wore feminised versions of the zoot suit.[10]

For Malcolm X (later influenced by the conservative mindset of the Nation of Islam), dressing outlandishly became a distraction from 'real' resistance. Today, some argue that fashion acts as a pressure valve, enabling disgruntled elements in society to let off steam that would otherwise build up.[11] There is no reason, however, why dressing differently should necessarily be a substitute for politics or engagement with serious issues.

The correct way to define resistance is widely debated in James C. Scott's *Weapons of the Weak*. Conventional political wisdom states that 'real' resistance needs to be 'a) organised, systematic and cooperative; b) principled or selfless; c) have revolutionary consequences; and/or d) embody ideas or intentions that negate the basis of discrimination itself'. Dressing as a Goth is arguably none of these things, even if done en masse. It could be dismissed as token, incidental, and not aiming to change the structures of society because it is 'a) unorganised, unsystematic and individual; b) opportunistic and self-indulgent; c) has no revolutionary consequences; and/or d) implies in its intention/meaning an accommodation with the system of domination'.[12]

Scott makes the compelling argument that it was scattered and isolated (though numerous) desertions from the Tsarist army in 1917 that made the Russian Revolution possible.[13] According to Scott, while acts are rare and isolated, they are of little consequence, but when a consistent pattern appears it is resistance.[14] He argues that to dismiss individual acts of resistance is fundamentally to misconstrue daily life for those living under oppression, because most people are simply trying to survive day by day.

A similar argument has been made with regard to rebellious dressing by African American women in the 1960s. The popularity of the Afro hairstyle grew in support of the political prisoner Angela Davis. As Davis herself states, this led to the largely forgotten arrest and harassment of hundreds of Black women who were persecuted as Davis lookalikes.[15] While for some, clothes, accessories, and hairstyles might be their only means of political engagement, what links desertions from the Tsarist army with Afro hairstyles is the fact that there were significant movements behind them both. In Russia there was a large Bolshevik-led revolutionary movement agitating wholeheartedly for dissent, and in the United States there was a growing Black Power movement.

While the punks of 1970s Britain endured a certain level of oppression, there are far more extreme examples of people using clothing to resist. Under the system of slavery in Jamaica, plantation owners instigated practices designed to strip enslaved people of 'their pride, their dignity and, most of all, their African identity'.[16] Steeve O. Buckridge describes in *The Language of Dress* how enslaved people were given clothes made of osnaburg linen, a uniform meant to humiliate and rob them of their cultural dress practices. Yet these fabrics were fashioned and accessorised to reflect African modes and aesthetics. This was one way for people to prevent cultural alienation and hence psychic annihilation. Clothes became the means to rebel, signifying absolute resistance to the theft of self-definition, history, and culture.[17]

There is a long, powerful history of marginalised people, especially women, using dress to resist oppression, particularly while under colonial rule. Yoruba women resisted the British occupation of Nigeria by wearing only their traditional clothes and speaking to the authorities only in Yoruba – their medium for expressing far-reaching dissent.[18] For women in Palestine during the First Intifada, Palestinian flags and colours were banned in public, so women made 'Intifada Dresses' embroidered with doves, rifles, and political party symbols, worn to signify resistance to the Israeli occupation.[19]

A more recent example concerns the transformation of oppressive objects into a symbol of resistance. Abigail Echo-Hawk is a Pawnee artist and chief research officer at the Seattle Indian Health Board. In March 2020, the board urgently requested PPE and Covid-testing kits from local and federal partners. What arrived instead was a box of body bags. 'It was almost the perfect metaphor for what the federal government has been doing to us for centuries', Echo-Hawk told CBC Radio. 'Giving us the things to bury our people in and not giving us the resources so our people can live.' As a population, Native Americans were hard hit by Covid-19, with one study finding double the infection rates and two and a half times the death rates of white people.[20]

Feeling horror, but not surprise, at being sent body bags, Echo-Hawk spent months transforming them into a traditional ribbon dress as a symbol of the 'hope, resiliency, strength and absolute resistance and fierceness of Indigenous survivors'. Echo-Hawk placed red handprints on the dress to represent Missing and Murdered Indigenous Women and Girls, and added jagged 'autopsy' stitching. She glued on mirrors to reflect the scale of the injustice back to the government. On Woodlands fabric, Echo-Hawk wrote her personal mantra: 'I am the tangible manifestation of my ancestors' resiliency.' 'So much has been taken from us for the last 500 years', Echo-Hawk said. 'We are fighting for every piece of it back, and we are restitching that in bold, brilliant, beautiful colours of ribbon dresses and ribbon skirts and regalia, and words and poetry and art.' Ribbon dresses also formed an important part of the protests against the Dakota Access Pipeline at the Standing Rock Sioux Tribal Reservation.[21]

Alongside the ideas of refusal and reversal examined below is the idea of resurgence – 'a set of decolonising theories that comes from the latest generations of Indigenous academics' with the aim of dismantling and rebuilding systems. Primarily through the work of Riley Kucheran, this book has intermittently explored the process of an Indigenous fashion resurgence, which aims to challenge and take apart the mainstream fashion industry. But as resurgence challenges, it is still restricted by colonial and capitalist systems of oppression.[22] Dress *can* be an act of resistance and a powerful force in resistance movements, particularly among women and non-binary people. It has the power to be bold, embodied, and defiant. Its significance regarding changing the structures of society, however, depends on whether there is a movement behind it. In this way, fashion and clothing are a form of simmering dissent rather than a decisive and final revolutionary act.[23]

Refusal and Reversal

In *Fashion as Communication*, Malcolm Bernard identifies 'refusal' and 'reversal' as two key forms of resistance in dress: refusal being the attempt to separate yourself from offensive power structures, and reversal being the attempt to reverse the power and privilege around which the power structures revolve.[24]

Punk

In Britain, punk was most prominent in the late 1970s and early 1980s, decades when disaffected working-class youth faced rising unemployment and limited opportunities. A severe form of refusal, punk was an anti-authority reaction to a system that left many people disenfranchised: 'Beneath the clownish make-up there lurked the unaccepted and disfigured face of capitalism.'[25]

The Women's Liberation Movement

The radical women of the Women's Liberation Movement refused the outlandish make-up of the 1980s and the decade's high heels, tight clothes, and short skirts as sexualised and repressive.[26] Intertwined with LGBTQ+ movements, a 'Women's Libber' was stereotypically portrayed in a boiler suit and Doc Martens, with a make-up free face and cropped hair. The movement resented society's fixation with youth, beauty, thinness, and a narrow sense of the erotic. They believed that women had been indoctrinated into spending far too much time on their appearance, and that clothing designated for women actually (not just symbolically) subjugated them.[27] Fictitious bra-burning stories gained notoriety because they fitted so well with the tabloid belief that feminists wanted to destroy anything they felt oppressed them.

The hijab

Hijab fashion is widespread and diverse; there are literally hundreds of ways to wear the headscarf. After the 2001 bombings of the World Trade Center and the start of the so-called War on Terror, the wearing of the *hijab*, *niqab*, and *burqa* suddenly emerged as a matter of state for Western nations. Anti-feminist, pro-war hawks in both the United States and the United Kingdom repeatedly used Muslim women to justify imperial war and domination. This was the same hypocritical tactic used by the colonialist Lord Cromer in Egypt in the late 1800s.[28]

Historically, when faced with such a climate, movements like Black Is Beautiful have reacted to painful prejudice by proudly reasserting their scorned identity.[29] This is what happened with the *hijab*. Faced with attack and a polarising society, many women chose to take up the *hijab* as 'an affirmation of identity and community, of pride in heritage, of rejection or resistance to, or even protest against, mainstream society'.[30] Further polarisation is taking place in Europe, with bans on religious clothing in multiple countries. A ban on face coverings in France, which was upheld by the European Court of Human Rights, led to fines for nearly 600 Muslim women in fewer than three years and France's 2004 law banning the wearing of headscarves in schools stopped some Muslim girls from finishing their education.[31] French philosopher Alain Badiou described the ban as a capitalist law that removed a woman's right to undress only when she wants to.[32]

Attacks on Muslim women's dress have been part of an imperialist agenda seeking support for war. If Muslim societies can be framed as needing to catch up with 'civilised' societies, then war looks justified as a liberating force. Certainly, there is a feeling among many Muslim women that they are exhausted by the debate over their dress and that they want to be judged by what's in their head not what's on their head.

* * *

Refusal styles encounter one insurmountable problem – there is no escape from planet fashion. You can refuse to participate in the system, but unless you overthrow it, it will still be there when you open your eyes. Regardless of how you dress, you are still living in a capitalist system. Even the most covered-up woman will still encounter thousands of fashion messages telling her she is too fat, too dark, or too ugly. Committing to wearing a boiler suit for the rest of your life does nothing to help the oppressed women in China who made that boiler suit. Home-made or second-hand clothes are still produced using materials made under capitalism. It is impossible to refuse to participate.

Reversal

Reversal is an act of resistance that attempts to reverse positions of power and privilege. It has most frequently been used as a tactic by women or women's advocacy groups in an attempt to change the position of women in society, particularly with regard to the right to wear controversial, bifurcated articles of clothing – in other words, trousers.

Trouser-wearing women

It is important to note that while trousers for women were controversial in Europe and the United States in the nineteenth century, they were worn by women in many other parts of the world. Albanian Muslim women wore trousers in the nineteenth century as did Mughal Indian women in the early seventeenth century and Mongolian, Inuit, and Japanese women throughout the ages.[33] Debates about trousers for women often ignore these cultures as people without fashion.

The dress reformers of nineteenth-century North America chose fashion as their site to challenge long-standing beliefs about women. In *Pantaloons and Power*, Gayle Fischer describes how reformers wanted to show that rather than just being a covering for the body, clothing was a powerful cultural symbol, emblematic of women's place in society.[34] Fashion consisted of debilitating corsets, layers of petticoats, and floor-length dresses that restricted movement. Dress reformers advocated knee-length dresses worn over pantaloons. Amelia Bloomer, after whom the bloomer outfit is named, wrote: 'The costume of women should conduce at once to her health, comfort, and usefulness.'[35] Personal adornment, she said, was of secondary importance.

As a campaign, dress reform emphasised individual change rather than changing state or national laws; having failed to gain momentum, it fizzled out by 1879.[36] Over the next century, trousers for women slowly gained acceptance in Europe. During the two world wars, women agricultural and munitions workers wore trousers to work. In the 1920s, leisurewear became more daring, and cycling and swimming became acceptable for women. Hollywood stars like Marlene Dietrich and Katharine Hepburn eroticised and glamorised trousers for women. In 1964, André Courrèges showed trouser-suits for his Spring collection. By the late 1960s, jeans had become widespread for women.

Trousers threaten conservative elements because they represent male power, independence, ease of movement, physical work, and sexual independence – the alarming spectacle of both promiscuity and non-participation. In December 2019, the Sudanese government repealed a controversial Public Order Law which gave police the power to arrest or flog women wearing trousers. Ten years earlier, in 2009, Sudanese journalist Lubna Ahmed al-Hussein was put on trial for wearing trousers – an act that at the time was considered indecent under Sudan's strict morality laws and carried a possible punishment of imprisonment and 40 lashes. Far from being an isolated case, in 2008 alone 43,000 women were arrested in Khartoum state for clothing offences, with the chief of police unable to say how many of these women were flogged.

Rather than use the immunity granted to her by her job as a UN worker, Hussein resigned from her post and insisted on a public trial to which she wore the trousers that had resulted in her arrest. The court found Hussein guilty and, while sparing her the lash, fined her the equivalent of $200. 'Islam does not say whether a woman can wear trousers or not', stated Lubna Ahmed al-Hussein at the time. 'The clothes I was wearing when the police caught me – I pray to my God in them. Let them show me what the Qur'an or Prophet Muhammad said on that issue. There is nothing.'[37]

I Want to Create My Own Vision

Florent Bidois is a fashion artist originally from Brittany but now settled in London. 'Fashion is important', he says. 'In this patriarchal society being LGBTQ doesn't fit the norm, so you obviously get into things that are going to help you know yourself better and embrace your quirks. Fashion is a definite tool to set yourself apart but also to recognise each other. It's like a sixth sense.' His fashion artistry is an endless source of visionary joy. A glimpse of a world without enforced conformity. 'My intention', he says, 'is to create beauty. It is very personal but as a creative, I want to create my own vision of what I think is beautiful and I use myself and my body as a canvas.' Part of this work is a refusal to 'forbid' himself from wearing something he considers beautiful. 'I am a cis-gender gay man but I do want to wear heels, I do want to wear make-up, I do want to wear dresses sometimes and this is not for me to shock anyone – I might shock by default without realising, or even with realising, but this is not my intention.' He continues:

I don't mean to disrupt anything – I just do not want to forbid anything to myself. I can't say this enough, this is very personal, I'm not trying to be anything other than myself. All these elements – the makeup, the hats, the heels, the dresses – it's just for me to feel good, to feel fabulous. What comes out of my mouth – whether I'm dressed up or down remains the same, I do not become another person. It emphasises my confidence, it enhances my looks and assurance but I'm not a different person.

We live in a society based upon a gender binary which says that boys do a certain set of activities and wear a certain set of clothes, while girls do a separate set of activities and wear a different set of clothes. Among the gatekeepers of this made-up set of rules is the fashion industry with its rigid adherence to 'menswear' and 'women's wear' – follow the stairs down to menswear in the basement, watch the women's wear collection on the catwalk. Since *Stitched Up* was published, the concept of gender-fluid clothing (while not new) has blossomed. Some companies insist on trying to make 'gender fluid' mean shapeless beige items, but outside of the mainstream, gender-fluid fashion is capturing the hearts of more and more people. The reality is that gender-fluid fashion can and should be absolutely any item of clothing when worn by anybody. As one commentator has said: 'The notion that clothing as an expression of our personality belongs to one gender or another is the social construct that needs disassembling.'[38]

We are not yet at the stage where people's gender identity has been delinked from what they choose (or have) to wear – whether that is dresses and heels or suits and brogues. People still draw a direct line between how an individual dresses and assumptions about gender. In reality, there is of course no need to dress a certain way to be gender non-conforming or any other part of the myriad human experiences that make up the LGBTQ+ spectrum. One day it will not be considered shocking for Billy Porter to wear an iconic Christian Siriano tuxedo gown on the red carpet, for Lena Waithe to wear a rainbow cape or a 'Black Drag Queens Invented Camp' suit to the Met Gala, or for Kurt Cobain, Pharrell Williams, or Harry Styles to wear a dress on the cover of a magazine. More importantly, acceptance and adoration will also be automatic across the board: 'Make no mistake: trans femmes of colour started this and continue to face the backlash from it. Our aesthetics make it to the mainstream, but not our bodies. We are still dismissed as "too much" and "too queer" because we aren't palatable enough to whiteness and heteronormativity,' gender non-conforming writer and performer Alok V. Menon wrote recently. 'I hope that people will remember that what is manifest in a magazine does not necessarily materialize on a moving train: when it's you against transphobia with no one to defend you.'[39]

Clothing reversal does not automatically challenge the underlying structures of society. It is not enough to reverse roles and clothing in order to challenge the underlying structure that has created such inequality. We need a world where challenging gender stereotypes does not turn into chauvinism or internalised sexism – 'attacking femaleness, deriding "girly stuff" and rolling your eyes at "women's issues"'[40] – and where gender neutral or gender fluid does not mean any singular appearance or mode of dress. We also need a world where people do not feel the need to wear earphones on the tube as armour against taunts and unkind comments, where no one is afraid for their physical safety as they walk home – or when they get home – and where any form of violence directed against the LGBTQ+ community has ended utterly and finally. With 2020 being the worst year on record for transphobic killings in the USA since this data started being recorded, fighting for this world will never stop being vital.

The Anti-Capitalist Book of Fashion is not a fashion advice book, but I couldn't help but ask Florent Bidois what he would say to someone who wanted to explore expressing the link between clothing and identity. 'I have a very simple piece of advice that I've followed myself, and that is to start small', he said.

> Believe it or not, but my foray into colour was with socks, it was such a big thing for me to wear colourful socks. I had always worn black socks all my life and then I just thought okay I need to make a change. I felt I was doing something crazy but I wanted colour. So start small – an accessory, a little bit of make-up, and then you will notice that you want more. I know it will happen because it does – you start feeling comfortable with one thing, two things, three things.

Shock Value

Punk is on the catwalks, Che Guevara T-shirts are everywhere, the Palestinian *keffiyeh* has become 'as ubiquitous as leopard print',[41] and 'Liberty' is a shop not a slogan. Nothing is sacred; everything is up for replication – a precedent set in the 1800s when African headwraps styled by enslaved women in Jamaica were copied by rich white women as an 'island fashion'.[42]

There is an almost numbing inevitability to co-option. Punk, while a genuine movement, was nonetheless propelled by shrewd entrepreneurs who were key to both defining and marketing the punk look.[43] Vivienne Westwood and Malcolm McLaren (manager of the Sex Pistols) ran the Kings Road shop SEX which stocked punk and S&M-style clothing. While they did not invent punk, much of their work captured and commodified the movement. Punk's strategy of refusal was no defence against appropriation, and in the end punk was both a product and a victim of capitalism. After a few explosive years it was incorporated into the mass market.[44]

Yet its political roots mean there are examples of punk surviving among disaffected youth. In Myanmar there is an underground punk scene which does everything from feeding the homeless to taking part in anti-coup protests against the Generals. And of course there is the Russian punk scene, made famous by persecuted punk band Pussy Riot. For many, punk is not a trend or a game.

The incorporation of the Women's Lib aesthetic was more subtle but no less real. Malcolm Bernard notes that the 'make-up-free' look is big business, with 'how to get the natural look' articles clogging magazines – with at least eight cosmetic products needed to get a 'natural' face. The custom of going bra-less, and as a result having visible nipples, which started as a protest against patriarchy and female-specific clothing, has also become highly eroticised.[45]

Before the aesthetic and political values of punk and women's liberation were appropriated, society used them to push the politics of both movements to the fringes of society. This is yet another risk faced by any group refusing fashion – they can become isolated[46] as society dictates: *They look mad, so they must be mad – just ignore them.*

The co-option of a style partly depends on the proximity of a subculture to the fashion industry. New York's gay scene and the city's Black and Latino communities have a close sociological proximity to the New York fashion industry, and have a greater influence on fashion than, say, the farmers of Utah, who are sociologically separated from the fashion industry.[47]

This demonstrates the dialectical relationship of fashion and resistance fashion: they are interdependent and need each other to evolve. Resistance fashion must necessarily acknowledge and oppose mainstream fashion.[48] The wearing of Yoruba clothing by Nigerian women was empowering *because* they were casting aside the dress of the British authorities which they had been told was the 'civilised' way to dress. Mainstream fashion, on the other hand, gains enormous financial benefit from the constant flow of rebel fashions that emerge.

Keffiyeh or Topshop tea towel?

Fashion has been called 'capitalism's favourite child'.[49] It has the ability to take even the most controversial fashion and make millions from it. The *keffiyeh* is a symbol of Palestinian resistance against Israel, its black-and-white chequered pattern historically seen in newsreels of Yasser Arafat, Leila Khaled, and Palestinian resistance fighters. With the Second Intifada and Israel's barbaric Operation Cast Lead in the winter of 2008–9, support for the Palestinians grew, and in Europe – and London in particular – *keffiyehs* became fashionable as a symbol of pro-Palestinian and anti-imperialist sentiment. Fast-forward a few months and the *keffiyeh* had transitioned into a 'multi-ethnic desert scarf' available in every shop and stall on the high street, in a wide range of colours. Balenciaga sold *keffiyehs* for $2,000 each.

Fearing it would lose its political meaning, tracks by pro-Palestinian rapper Lowkey were littered with references like 'I rock a keffiyeh not a Topshop tea towel'. While sections of the pro-Israeli lobby hoped the mass manufacture of 'desert scarves' would take the sting out of the *keffiyeh*, this did not happen. No lasting damage was done to the pro-Palestinian movement by its popularisation. Demonstrations and campaigns continued regardless. Throughout the 'trend' it was easy to tell a *keffiyeh* from a Topshop tea towel and conversations about Palestine were sparked across the globe.

Brands that brought out imitation scarves certainly benefited, while these companies could not neutralise the politics behind the print, they used the trend to make money. Companies took the ideas of rebellion and freedom associated with the *keffiyeh* and transferred it wholesale into their brand.

229

The Palestinian cause is, however, big and potent enough to weather a storm-in-a-teacup like the 'desert scarf'. Palestine is recognised for Palestine, not for a fashion trend.

Co-option

There are smaller movements that have not been as lucky. In 1980s New York there was an underground network of young, gay, primarily Black men who danced and posed dressed as glamorous cultural icons – an impressionistic dance style that became known as 'Voguing'. One academic described the young men as being deeply oppressed as outsiders – racially, sexually, and because they were effeminate and poor. The Vogue Movement both parodied and affirmed the dream of being on the front cover of a magazine.[50] The co-option by Madonna and Warner Brothers that took place with the song 'Vogue' is common knowledge, unlike the backstory of the oppression of the Vogue Movement. While some argued that Madonna gave the movement a voice, the fact that the original message was 'lost in a sea of hand gestures' implies that what took place was little more than the exploitation of an oppressed minority.[51]

The sad truth is that resistance styles never really threaten the fashion industry. The industry is highly adept at not just absorbing shocks and controversy but of benefiting from them. This is also what happens when resistance takes place outside the fashion industry. While punk is confrontational statement dressing, anti-consumerist grunge was, and is, small wardrobes of mostly thrift store finds that are beautiful or scruffy or both. Nirvana's Kurt Cobain was famous for wearing the same items – band T-shirts, cardigans, plaid shirts, and the occasional dress – over and over again and for customising clothes himself.

Despite the political, anti-consumerist origins of grunge, the fashion industry swiftly set to work. Several designers co-opted it. Marc Jacobs was fired from Perry Ellis for a collection so controversial (and inauthentic) it was never produced. Grunge was not a popular style for the fashion elite. Journalist Suzy Menkes led the opposition by handing out 'Grunge Is Ghastly' badges – an ironic use of the badge which is a staple of the grunge look.

Thus, even the ultimate not-making-a-statement fashion can become a fashion statement. One commentator noted the 'painful irony in social rebels having to view the signs of their rebellion sported in exquisite materials by those they thought they were rebelling against'.[52] When Jacobs sent part of his grunge collection to Kurt Cobain and Courtney Love they promptly burned it. The dialectical relationship between the fashion industry and resistance fashion means that resistance is simply absorbed, repackaged, and sold back to us.

Resisting fashion

The reproduction of subversive styles should not be mistaken for democracy. First, the ability of multinational corporations to reproduce items like the *keffiyeh* and retain all the profits is far from democratic. There is no social equality in this system and no means for people to exercise control over the corporations they buy from (the idea of shopping and 'dollar votes' as democracy is discussed in Chapter 9). This approach also confuses democracy with the so-called free market.[53] What does it matter if you can buy a 'Feminist' slogan T-shirt if it was made in a sweatshop and the underlying problems that mean women need to smash the patriarchy go untouched?

Second, we are far from the tolerant utopia imagined by some postmodernists. Authorities react to baggy jeans by expelling children from schools and preventing people from boarding planes. Denim Day is still held every year in April to mark the day the Italian Supreme Court overturned a rape conviction because the judges decided that a young woman's jeans were so tight she must have helped her rapist remove them which implied consent. Similarly, women are being blamed for being raped if they wear mini-skirts, or sacked, excluded from school, and attacked for wearing the *hijab*. Transphobia remains rife in society. A true aesthetic democracy will only be possible once full democracy has been attained, when neither the ownership of beauty nor society's means of production are in the hands of the few, and when racism, sexism, and class are no more.

The movements showcased in this chapter have been resisting more than just fashion, but they have used clothes to make their point. At the start of this chapter, I mentioned the creation of alternative realities by both protest and protest fashion. These two things collided on International Women's Day 2020 when Women's Strike shut down Oxford Street with a giant free clothes swap. Thousands of people marched through central London before blockading Oxford Street – tarpaulins were laid out and covered with clothes which anyone was free to take. This was in direct opposition to the corporations that line Oxford Street, with shoppers encouraged to abandon the shops and join the protest and free shop instead.[54] For a few hours protest clothing was used to challenge not just fashion but the capitalist system that underpins it.

Resistance both challenges and fuels fashion. Dress is most useful as a tool to keep resistance alive, to maintain cultural identity in the face of oppression, and to inspire people towards a new dawn. As with African enslaved people in Jamaica, rebellious cultural practices have been described by the feminist academic bell hooks as nourishing the capacity to resist.[55] Imagining and enacting what dress can look like in a society without stereotypes and oppressive restrictions causes the imagination to soar. The role of art in prompting imagination is essential, since without the ability to imagine new worlds, we have little hope of building one. To quote something I read by the writer Jessie Lynn McMains, 'maybe art won't save the world, but it makes the world worth saving'.[56] Encouraging freedom of expression for individuals can also lead people to see that fashion and beauty ideals are just ideologies put in place to benefit the ruling class. This is part of bringing capitalism into focus rather than it being too close to the lens to be objectified. Once capitalism is visible, it can be challenged. So what would happen if the often disparate nature of protest fashion was replaced by a movement with a more organised purpose that united people around key aims? This is the subject of Chapter 9, which examines movements that aim to act collectively in their fashion choices.

CHAPTER NINE
Reforming Fashion

Reforming Fashion

Join us in rejecting the ti(red) notion that shopping is a reasonable response to human suffering.

Buylesscrap.com

Of all the tragic and disturbing issues discussed in this book, it is the subject matter in this chapter that often proves the most provocative. To reform capitalism or to overthrow it, that is the question. These positions are sometimes incorrectly paraphrased: stick plasters over gaping wounds and try to save a few souls while millions are condemned to barbarism, or wait hopelessly for an almighty change that may never come.

The setting for this chapter is not a factory in China or a mall in New York but a family kitchen in the north of England. On the table was a brochure for an Indian clothing co-operative, and I (unhelpfully) offered to tell my stressed-out, overworked acquaintance everything that was wrong with both the company and the premise of 'ethical fashion'. Since she had ordered clothes for her children from the catalogue, it is unsurprising that a heated argument ensued. She yelled that waiting for a revolution before doing anything was immoral and I yelled back that trying to reform capitalism was a naïve and damaging distraction from reality.

Eventually, we agreed that we had the same outcome in mind but were suggesting different means of getting there. Arguments about the politics of clothing, like arguments about the politics of food, become heated very quickly because they feel so personal. Clothing is presented to us as a question of individual choice. On the surface the choice seems simple: 'good clothes' or 'evil clothes'. If you choose the 'good' clothing you are virtuous; if you pick the 'evil' clothing you are wicked. While it makes sense to buy the least harmful option when purchasing any product, what about the myriad factors that determine 'choice'? Class is the primary factor. You buy what you can afford. If you cannot afford £30 for a pair of knickers, then it does not matter that they are handcrafted in Britain from organic cotton; you will have to buy five pairs for £5 from Primark – and will probably feel guilty and ashamed for doing so.

It is no coincidence that we have been steered into the dead end of viewing only clothing as an individual issue. This goes right to the very heart of neoliberalism – a system that teaches us that empowerment comes from acting individually (not collectively), that freedom means variety in what we consume, and that we should trust in the system and shop (not fight) our way to a new world. What you do as an individual does count and choosing to tread as lightly as possible upon the earth is essential, but it is not enough to take us off the dreadful trajectory that we are on.

There is no way out of sweatshop labour or environmental devastation via an individual route. You cannot shop workers in China to freedom. You cannot shop the Aral Sea back to life. The neoliberal mindset that permeates the fashion industry must be shaken off because it is dangerous nonsense. Rather, we must confront the issues in this book critically and with a collectivist anti-capitalist attitude. We do have agency on an individual level and high individual carbon footprints must be brought down, but we must confront the challenges ahead collectively and with a realistic assessment of the barriers that people face. Marx defined this contradiction: 'Men and women make their own history, but they do not make it as they please; they do not make it under self-selected circumstances, but under circumstances existing already, given and transmitted from the past.'[1]

That is why constructive argument over the issues contained in this chapter is important. We must recognise who the real enemies are, and all those wanting change must learn to work together on their common ground. The differences in opinion between people wanting change are tiny when compared to the gulf between us and that of, say, Kansas oil barons like the Koch brothers. Angela Davis quoted a Betsy Rose song on this point: 'We may have come here on different ships, but we're in the same boat now.'[2]

Contention arises in the last three chapters of this book because they represent the starting point for action. Once you decide you want to change the world, you then have to decide how to go about it, and there will naturally be differences in opinion. Realistic assessment and debate over what works and what does not is the only way forward. In this chapter, I look at several methods for organised reform of the fashion industry: people organising collectively as consumers, shopping differently to change the world; government-led reform; the 'language not action reform' of multinational corporations; and finally the international labour movement.[3]

An Early Challenge

The fashion industry has long caused revulsion. In 1889, horror at the sweatshops of newly industrialised North America prompted the social reformers Jane Addams and Ellen Starr to found Hull House in Chicago, a community of reformers who worked on education and healthcare projects. One Hull House resident was Florence Kelley, a social reformer and friend of Engels.[4] Kelley conducted fieldwork in the square mile surrounding Hull House and found children as young as three working in tenement sweatshops.[5] She later attained the unprecedented position of the state's first factory inspector. Her research led to the state of Illinois prohibiting the employment of children under the age of 14 and limiting women and children to a maximum eight-hour day. In 1895, however, the Illinois Association of Manufacturers had the law declared unconstitutional.

Alice Woodbridge, another campaigner and secretary of the Working Women's Society, carried out detailed research into the working conditions of women in the New York retail sector. Her reports prompted the social reformer Josephine Shaw Lowell to found the New York Consumers' League in 1890. The League researched and publicised the plight of exploited women and children and sought to protect consumers from overpricing and poor-quality goods. One of the first investigations carried out by the League was into working conditions for those making cotton underwear.[6] The League emphasised the ability of consumers to bring about change by buying only from companies who treated their workers with respect.[7] It published a 'White List' advising shoppers which companies paid fair wages and had reasonable hours and sanitary conditions. As other cities established consumers' leagues, in 1899 Josephine Shaw Lowell and Jane Addams chartered the National Consumers' League and invited Florence Kelley to New York to become its general secretary.

Kelley's pioneering programmes included the issuing of a 'White Label' that could be used by certified companies to prove that their products had been made under fair working conditions and without child labour. She organised consumers to boycott sweatshop-produced clothing, stating: 'To live means to buy, to buy means to have power, to have power means to have responsibility.'[8] As a committed socialist, she taught that real change would not come until the roots of social ills were addressed rather than just its symptoms.

Ethical Calculus

Our wardrobes are today the meeting point for two premises – that the fashion industry is responsible for widespread devastation and misery and that it is our behaviour as consumers that is to blame. When I first wrote *Stitched Up*, 'ethical fashion' held an exceptionally low market share at just over 1 per cent of the overall apparel market.[9] Today it is no longer just small businesses that offer 'ethical fashion' as a solution. Practically every brand on the planet, including Boohoo, has a 'sustainability' section – prompting the question that if a corporation can make one line of shoes or jeans in a more responsible manner, why make the rest in the usual ultra-destructive way? Data from 2020 analysed by the Business Research Company states that the global ethical fashion market reached a value of approximately \$6.3 billion in 2019. The research states that this market is expected to grow to \$9.8 billion in 2025 and to \$15.1 billion in 2030.[10] If we take \$2.5 trillion as the value of the fashion industry this still leaves 'ethical fashion' with a current market share of 0.25 per cent, meaning solutions that rely on encouraging more shopping in this area ignore what is happening with 99.75 per cent of fashion production.

But a major question remains: What the hell even is ethical fashion? The fashion industry is a deregulated, subcontracted system where brands are free to make up their own rules and words and then print them on labels: *eco, eco-innovative recycled, upcycled, vegan, conscious, fair wage, fair trade, locally made, carbon neutral, organic, made with renewable energy, made with love, circular, biodegradable, zero waste* – it is little wonder that even Stella McCartney now says, 'I barely even know what the word sustainable means any more.' These random label words should be viewed as feeding a dynamic where instead of helping people question what they are purchasing, the intention to purchase is just reinforced. As one commentator stated: 'It's a bunch of coded language so that we think, yeah I'm comfortable with that, I can buy that.'[11]

Kate Harper, a fashion researcher in Norfolk, says a conceptual impurity regarding the word 'sustainable' is rendering the concept almost completely meaningless, with brands using it however they please. 'It's almost like a grammar issue, or a misunderstanding of how to use the word', she says. For something to be sustainable, it has to be able to be done forever. Sustainability is a process, it is not a fixed moment and definitely not an individual object. 'You can't have a sustainable pair of jeans because "to jeans" is not a thing that you do, it's not a verb, you can't "jeans".' Instead of applying the verb 'sustainable' to an inert object, Kate explains that it is the hundreds of processes which brought a pair of jeans into existence which must be judged as sustainable or not.

'It's changing the way people think about sustainable behaviour, by reducing it down to *I'll buy this thing and not that thing*', Kate says. Attaching the word 'sustainable' to the properties of a garment is not just a linguistic issue, rather it protects big business from scrutiny regarding their manufacturing processes and governance. 'Encouraging people to think about something as having innate positive qualities or innate negative qualities is really misleading and unhelpful', Harper continues. 'It's not about the qualities of the thing, it's about how this thing came about and what's going to happen to it.' No matter, then, if an item is made from recycled polyester or organic cotton when millions of them are being churned out, flown round the world, then dumped in landfill. Further food for thought comes from a point highlighted by Riley Kucheran (see Chapter 5): 'Several sustainability debates have asked: *what exactly are we trying to sustain?*' A question that reminds us that truly sustainable fashion is not about preserving the fashion system.[12]

To go with all the labels, an abundance of books advise on ethical fashion. Many share recurring themes which limit their ability to provide a satisfactory solution to fashion's problems. A central dilemma for ethical fashion is how to prioritise all the issues thrown up by the industry. One book explains that there is no 'simple list of moral ticks and crosses' with which to decide which is most important.[13] Is it better to buy a dress sewn in a co-op in India which uses thousands of freight miles or a locally manufactured dress from a company that uses fur trim? Is it better to buy organic cotton jeans from a retailer who shuns workplace safety regulations or conventional pesticide-ridden jeans from a regulated retailer? How about a recycled polyester fleece which sheds synthetic lint fibres and contaminates oceans, beaches, and marine life?[14] Is it better to buy vegetarian shoes made in a Chinese sweatshop or leather from a designer who says fat people are ugly?

The unhelpful solution proffered by ethical fashion books is for consumers to try an 'ethical calculus' to figure out which issues matter most.[15] This inability to provide a decent answer stems from not wanting to name capitalism as the cause of the problem. This leaves consumers with what one ethical fashion guide called 'the knotty question of which ethical standards matter the most'.[16] By not recognising the capitalist system as being responsible for the ills of the industry, these books seek other sources of blame, like consumer apathy, human greed, or cod psychology.

Because they do not name capitalism, ethical fashion books are forced to look to unlikely sources for salvation. As well as urging people to buy less, most ethical fashion books often read like a shopping list, with brands and products advertised on every page, including big businesses listed as 'high-street heroes'. Predicting that these lists might appear contradictory, *Green Is the New Black* states: 'If you have a problem with big corporations, remember that they are the ones with power, and if they change, it creates big waves that really make a difference. Even if it is all a big PR promotion, what does it matter?'[17]

It matters both because this is a neoliberal mindset and because PR promotions obscure the reality of corporate practices. Brands state the most outrageous things: 'By using our unique size and scale, we are empowering women around the world' (Walmart); 'We are committed to doing our part in keeping the world a healthy and safe place worth living in' (Hanes); 'We're working to change things, for everyone' (Primark); 'We are dedicated to supporting the communities where we operate' (GAP). As Naomi Klein explains, 'every company with a powerful brand is attempting to develop a relationship with consumers that resonates so completely with their sense of self'.[18] When the language, images, emblems, and rhetoric of each of these brand campaigns comes across as empathetic and convincing it is because they are lifted directly from social movements. Time after time, ad campaigns from GAP, Levi's, and so on sell us back our ideas devoid of original meaning and used as a screen for human rights and environmental abuses. The language has changed, the practices have not – in fact, they have gotten worse. Research from the Global Fashion Agenda in Copenhagen found that progress on everything from carbon reduction to living wages was 30 per cent slower in 2019 than the year before. Then there is the rocketing volume – with apparel and footwear forecast to increase by 81 per cent to 102 million tonnes by 2030, according to the same report.[19] Corporate 'causumerism' (promoting the idea of shopping for a better world) is, therefore, a direct opponent of progressive social movements.

The embracing of ethical language by multinational corporations comes from the upsurge in public interest in ethical consumption.[20] As we saw in Chapter 2, for the first time we are seeing a global movement against corporate climate arsonists like the fossil fuel industry, the agricultural industry, and the fashion industry. This leaves brands falling over themselves to appear part of the solution and not the problem. It is important here to remember that fashion brands are not people; they don't have personalities or hopes or dreams. They are corporate entities with one goal: to make more money than their competitors. If they perform a hollow imitation of sounding progressive it is because they are responding to swells in public opinion which they are no longer able to ignore. We have seen this with feminism, with climate change, and with Black Lives Matter. But these moves have nothing behind them other than the drive to co-opt dynamic social electricity, make people believe that they see a reflection of themselves in a brand, and above all to pretend that they are part of the solution rather than being the problem. Social change will never come from fashion corporations and it is wrong to believe that it ever could. Marx noted in the rules of the First International that 'the emancipation of the working classes must be conquered by the working classes themselves'.[21] Corporations do not intend to free us, nor are they able to. Freedom can only come from within.

Change the World Not Just Your Wardrobe

There are more general problems with the idea of causumerism. Purchase or dollar votes are cast in direct accordance to how many dollars you have.[22] How can you influence the labour practices in Kering's vast supply chains if you cannot afford a £100 bottle of perfume let alone a £2,500 handbag? Dollar votes entrench the position that to have power in society you must have money. I experienced a bizarre example of this way of thinking when I witnessed a panellist at a university event tell an audience of students that a good protest would be to stop buying diamond jewellery – if they didn't like the mining practices of companies like De Beers, they should boycott them! Trust me when I say that we can do better than this.

Causumerism shifts all the blame for the world's ills from capitalism onto individuals. As discussed, products are considered 'ethical' are often the most expensive on the market, so ethical consumption is unfortunately deeply class-based. It is wrong to blame those with the least individual power in society for the destruction of the planet or the existence of sweatshops while ignoring the huge carbon footprints of wealthy shoppers. Particularly as we enter yet another economic crisis it is vital to remember that we will not change fashion in a vacuum but must aim for an overhaul of society that redistributes wealth equally. It is vital to attack the systems that oppress people and not to attack the oppressed. There are multiple stages before an item gets to the point of consumption, including design, material selection, manufacture, and transport. By placing responsibility only onto consumers, we render these myriad decisions and the profit motives behind them invisible. Above all, ethical consumerism can cement people's identities as passive consumers rather than as active citizens. If you are aware enough to be reading a book about capitalism then you must not limit yourself to individual action but must act collectively and politically and bring others with you. Life is about more than just retail, and we must not allow all major functions of society to be subordinated to the task of shopping, lest we waste away our lives and power.[23]

Sit Back and Wait?

People who argue against reform only are often accused of being unwilling to act in the here and now, but this is a misrepresentation of their political stance. Why would those who most want change be content to sit back and wait for it? 'They cannot and dare not wait, in a fatalist fashion, with folded arms for the advent of the "revolutionary situation"',[24] declared the revolutionary Rosa Luxemburg. It is not a simple choice between reform and revolution; rather, they condition and complement each other.[25]

There is a long, radical history of people gaining rights for themselves and for others by acting as political consumers. The Russian Revolution began with women's protests over bread prices. The Montgomery Bus Boycott of the American Civil Rights struggle – 'Walk in dignity not ride in humiliation' – was so widespread that it ended racial segregation on buses after 13 months. The Harlem Housewives' League carried out a 'Don't buy where you can't work' campaign to force shops to hire Black employees. There have been rent strikes, Gandhi's boycott of imported Lancashire cotton, and the global consumer boycott of South African goods.

What links these campaigns is that consumerism was a means to an end, not an end in itself. The Russian Revolution began with women's protests over bread prices, but the end was not cheap bread. Political consumerism, as opposed to causumerism, works with the knowledge that capitalism cannot be reformed. It uses consumption to bring about a specific change, it does not make a different type of consumption the end game.

The following questions distinguish causumer campaigns from political consumption campaigns: Is the campaign being organised by a corporation? Is a corporation making money from the campaign? Does the campaign see itself as an end in itself or does it challenge political power and capitalism? Does the campaign empower people to do more than just shop? Who or what does the campaign blame for exploitation? I do not take the view that people should never engage in consumer campaigns. Indeed, it makes sense to buy the least harmful products possible, and many consumer campaigns have been successful in raising awareness about issues like climate change and sweatshops. What I am saying is that action must not stop at the checkout.

For my second book, *Foot Work*, I developed a concept I call the Triangle of Change. This came about at a Clean Clothes

Campaign Faircademy in Germany after I observed a discussion among activists which repeated the same arguments about shopping differently. On one side was the idea that shopping is the most important thing people can do to change the fashion industry so campaigns should focus on education and encouraging people to shop ethically, swap clothes, make clothes, and buy second hand. On the other side was the argument that this is too passive, too individualised, and too class-exclusive. These arguments were presented as a continuum – with the two sides posed as polar opposites. The Triangle of Change changes that by bringing together Individual Change, Political Change, and System Change, and helping us move forward to remake the world.

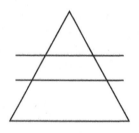

At the top of the triangle is Individual Change because this is generally where people start thinking about how to change the world. Because items like clothes and shoes are so personal, it is natural that people start here, with their own wardrobe. Individual Change is valid, but as you see it is only the tip of the problem. The danger therefore is staying at this level and thinking that aligning your personal life with your convictions will fix everything. The next step is to move down to the second part of the triangle: Political Change. This level is the start of actively connecting with groups of people and the powerful systemic elements that block change. Here we confront free trade agreements, the lack of legislation, corporate law, wage laws, land rights, fights for trade union freedom, questions of taxation, and transparency, and we work in solidarity with workers, environmentalists, and human rights defenders across the globe. We work to force governments and brands to change their behaviour and regulate the worst ills of capitalism. It is here that we work intersectionally and in complete connectivity and alignment with the people most affected by the fashion industry – workers' groups in the Global South.

The third level is quite literally the foundation of the problem and it is what this book is about – confronting capitalism and creating System Change. This is where we confront the fact that the fashion industry would not exist without the systemic exploitation of women, the exploitation of the Global South, colonialism, the creation and maintenance of racism, widespread environmental destruction, and the imposition of class and poverty.[26] This form of activism, one that aims to replace capitalism with a new, equitable way of living, is vital because we must not neglect to see clearly where power lies. It is where we leave aside the idea that capitalism can be reformed for the better. This stage involves much of the same work as political change but with the addition of understanding capitalism by reading, learning from, and sharing intersectional revolutionary ideas as a tool for social change. It involves building and participating in revolutionary groups that are working to build movements (base-building) and rebuilding working-class institutions like unions, tenant groups, anti-racist campaigns, mutual aid groups, and environmental protection groups to name a few.[27] Ultimately, this involves organising progressive social forces into an international power bloc that can challenge the injustice of capitalism.

Regulation?

What we have seen over the past few decades is a huge expansion in corporate power which has not been matched by accountability mechanisms like laws and regulations. One worthwhile aim of some campaigns is to get governments to legislate in favour of better labour practices or environmental protection. But governments are unwilling to legislate to control corporations because, as Rosa Luxemburg wrote a hundred years ago, '[s]tate control is penetrated with the exclusive interests of the ruling class'.[28]

Under current international law, states get to pick and choose which agreements they sign up to and which they reject. The approach of the British government with regard to protecting garment workers and the environment is to trust in voluntary corporate social responsibility (CSR) schemes. Happily for corporations this is precisely the approach they favour, as it means they can avoid legal regulations. One case close to home that illustrates this is Leicester in the English Midlands. Leicester's motto as a proud textile hub used to be 'Leicester Clothes the World'. Today its giant red brick spinning mills might have fallen silent, but they have been replaced by thousands of sewing machines whirring across a network that criss-crosses the city. These newly formed small factories – some no more than lean-to sheds – employ approximately 11,000 people on wages as little as £3.50 per hour. Leicestershire garment workers are typically women from either South Asian or eastern European backgrounds who have extremely limited employment alternatives. In these 'dark factories' that churn out £6 dresses, there are often no contracts, no sick-pay, and no health and safety measures.

These factories hit the headlines once again in the summer of 2020 when it was revealed by Labour Behind the Label that conditions in Leicester's factories, primarily producing for Boohoo, were putting workers at risk of Covid-19 infections and fatalities.[29] Leicester is an interesting case because it is the story of British brands manufacturing in Britain under British law and employing British people. It shows the culture of corporate impunity, the failure of regulations to protect people, and the total lack of supply chain liability in the fashion industry. Another income stream flowing into Leicester's industry also comes from the state in the form of benefits as corporate subsidies. The minimum wage for over-25s is £8.72. It is possible to pay people £3.50 an hour because such wages are topped up by housing and unemployment benefits. Protecting workers against exploitation right here in Britain requires the state to act – to create binding supply chain laws, to not cut down the factory inspectorate, to close tax loopholes, and to end the risk that workers who report abuses will face harassment from the immigration authorities. Instead of the threat of deportation which empowers employers, workers should be offered at least a three year leave-to-remain guarantee in exchange for reporting illegal working practices, as has been implemented in Argentina. Workers who are victims of corporate abuse should also have access to legal aid and services to reclaim wages and compensation.

There are often calls for greater transparency in the fashion industry. As a starting point, it should be made compulsory for companies to publicly disclose an annual, searchable, full list of supplier facilities which states the names of authorised supplier facilities at all levels (including homeworkers), site addresses, parent companies, types of product made, number of workers, and wage levels. Added to this should be the demand that products sold within the UK are labelled to include a database-linked product code which provides information about production facilities and a verifiable record of the raw materials used throughout the production process. A standardised, fully public shipping database at an EU level which stores records for all exports and imports of cargo entering European ports would also be a step forward. While this information would be useful, transparency must not start to function as a regulatory mechanism in the place of laws. As has taken place in other industries, like chemical and food, there is the danger that '[a]greeing that people had a right to know, politicians could argue for warning labels and more data while avoiding hard or unpopular decisions. Corporations could comply – and find ways to use their reports to improve their market position.'[30]

The (RED) Manifesto

The Davos Summit of 2006 saw the launch of the (RED) brand by U2 frontman Bono. Its premise seems simple: buy specially branded (RED) products from brands like Giorgio Armani, Gap, Converse, and American Express and an undisclosed portion of the cost will be donated to the Global Fund which provides HIV/AIDS medicine in Africa. The (RED) website asks: 'Has there ever been a better reason to shop?'[31] A critical appraisal of (RED) can be found in Lisa Ann Richey and Stefano Ponte's *Brand Aid: Shopping Well to Save the World*. (RED) has been charged with allowing corporations to raise their CSR profile without having to make any progressive changes to their business model. (RED) focuses solely on the symptoms of disease and poverty rather than their causes.

(RED) even has its own 'manifesto', but there is nothing in it about the social conditions that underpin poverty, inequality, and disease. There is no mention of the exploited workers who make (RED) products. Nor is there any mention of the environmental impact of the products. Instead, HIV/AIDS is presented as an emergency that justifies ignoring race, gender, and global inequalities.[32] When pressed about this, Bono did his own 'ethical calculus' and responded: 'Labour issues are very, very serious, but six and a half thousand Africans dying is more serious.'[33] Far from asking people to consume less or to consume differently, (RED) advises: 'You can look chic enough in Armani, hip enough in Converse, pay for your goods with American Express, and feel good about yourself ethically.' The 'conscious consumer' is replaced with the unthinking 'compassionate consumer'[34] who trusts multinationals to do good and find a cure for AIDS. This is a deliberate attempt to undercut gains made by ethical consumerism campaigns and social movements which have encouraged people to become conscious and critical. It is the deflection of attention away from the causes of crises like the AIDS epidemic.[35]

For a campaign designed to alleviate the HIV/AIDS pandemic in Africa, critics swiftly pointed out that there was no African agency in the campaign. The special (RED) edition of *The Independent* disgracefully featured Kate Moss blacked up on its cover. Many (RED) products are not even available in Africa.[36] Instead, the suffering of people across Africa is used to market designer products.[37] *Brand Aid* recounts the story of the talk-show host Oprah Winfrey wearing a GAP inspi(RED) T-shirt on her show ('the most important T-shirt I've ever worn in my life'). Oprah gave each audience member a T-shirt, explaining that half the profits from the audience's T-shirts would provide medicine for 14,000 pregnant women. At face value this is compelling, but what Oprah did not explain is that buying a GAP T-shirt provides just two weeks' worth of medicine. It would take 27 T-shirts to care for one person for a year and countless numbers for a lifetime of medication.[38]

AIDS medicine should be globally provided to everyone who needs it as a matter of course rather than being a sideline for multinational corporations. Health care should not rely on the free market. The economic crisis and the resulting downturn in consumer spending make the vulnerability of these campaigns particularly pertinent. What happens when HIV/AIDS medication no longer generates profits for multinational corporations? It is not enough to give the poor medicine; we must ask why they do not have it in the first place.

The amount (RED) donated in its first five years was tiny: 1 per cent of the Global Fund's donations.[39] (RED)'s primary

251

aim, however, is the rehabilitation of global commerce as a force for good. Multinational fashion corporations are more scrutinised than ever. Campaigns like (RED) provide a safe way for them to repair their image and move from talk of sweatshops to talk of curing HIV/AIDS in Africa. Sweatshops, environmental devastation, and the increasing concentration of wealth and power in the hands of the rich are all hidden behind a veneer of beneficent, life-giving corporations. Giorgio Armani stated of his participation in (RED): 'Commerce will no longer have a negative connotation.'[40]

(RED) still exists in 2021; its website says its corporate 'cavalry' is 'proudly fighting the urgent threat of COVID'. I asked Professor Richey if she was surprised to see (RED) move into 'fighting' Covid as well as HIV/AIDS? She said she was not surprised in the least:

> Given that all sorts of corporations were unable to resist 'Covid branding' and (RED) already had a clear infrastructure in place to successfully promote their Brand Aid collaborations. Also AIDS is moving out of the humanitarian communications radar as Covid became 'the' global virus of concern, it was certainly beneficial for (RED) to also claim that space.

(RED)'s Twitter account is currently selling precision cookers – 'Every purchase helps fight global health emergencies like AIDS and COVID' – and trucks which 'help fund life-saving programs'. There are also suggestions for 'Last-Minute Halloween Costumes that Save Lives' consisting of (RED) items you might already have bought.

Sweatshop Warriors

As we have seen in the preceding chapters, the international labour movement remains the most dynamic and effective part of fashion's movement for change. This is in no way an exhaustive list, but it is here that we find trade unions like the Free Trade Zones and General Services Employees' Union, which represents thousands of garment workers in Sri Lanka, or the TTCU in India. It includes grassroots workers' rights organisations like the Bangladesh Centre for Worker Solidarity, or the Association Glasen Tekstilec (Loud Textile Workers) in Macedonia, and large transnational unions and organisations like UniGlobal and IndustriALL. It encompasses migrant worker 'guerrilla groups', workers' rights organisations like the Asia Floor Wage Alliance, the Garment Worker Center in Los Angeles, the Solidarity Centre, and the Workers' Rights Consortium, and campaign groups like the Clean Clothes Campaign, Labour Behind the Label, United Students Against Sweatshops, War on Want, and many others. It also includes anti-corporate campaigns and political movements fighting back against evils like war and climate change. This sector constantly brings new opportunities for building cross-class, cross-sector, multiracial fronts involving the radical labour movements, youth, intellectuals, and professionals.[41]

Miriam Ching Yoon Louie's anthology *Sweatshop Warriors* is, among other things, an effective anthology of garment workers' struggles against neoliberal policies in the United States. One case study details the Asian Immigrant Women's Advocates' early watershed struggle to expose the inequalities of the fashion industry and make manufacturers take responsibility for their subcontractors. The campaign was initiated to try to get back-pay for twelve Chinese workers after one manufacturer, Jessica McClintock, pulled a contract and their sweatshop closed. Jessica McClintock denied any responsibility for the Chinese workers, but after a campaign of consumer boycotts, pickets, media exposure, and political pressure the company was forced to negotiate.

In 1996, after a four-year struggle, the immigrant women workers won an undisclosed cash settlement, an education fund for garment workers to learn about their rights, a scholarship fund for workers and their children, a bilingual hotline for workers to report any violations of their rights in shops contracted with McClintock, and an agreement from both sides to work to improve conditions within the industry.[42] The case discredited the idea that manufacturers were not responsible for the abuse suffered by workers in sweatshops.

A key element in this movement is solidarity. Big gains were made, for example, when Honduran trade unionists worked with United Students Against Sweatshops to implement the biggest ever collegiate boycott of a single company. Fruit of the Loom is the largest private employer in Honduras, and over 100 universities cut ties with the company until it was forced to enter into an agreement with the union. Recognising that sweatshop workers are not mere victims led United Students Against Sweatshops to adopt a quote from an Australian Aboriginal activist as its motto: 'If you have come to help me, you are wasting your time. But if you've come because your liberation is bound up with mine, then let us work together.'[43]

In March 2015, a group of people including Kalpona Akter, executive director of the Bangladesh Center for Worker Solidarity, and Mahinur Begum, an 18-year-old survivor of the Rana Plaza collapse, visited the New Jersey headquarters of The Children's Place. They had come to ask the brand's CEO to increase compensation to victims of Rana Plaza. But when they went into the offices the police were called and the activists, including Akter and Begum, were handcuffed and charged with trespassing. News of this injustice spread like wildfire through networks – activists launched 'OrphansPlace.com' and planned to picket Children's Place stores across the USA.

Faced with a PR nightmare, the company paid more than $2 million into the compensation fund.[44]

While sections of the international labour movement are anti-capitalist in one form or another, I have placed it in the reform chapter because, as we have seen with the Covid-19 pandemic, under capitalism all the gains won by labour can be rolled back. There is no labour rights change – increase in minimum wage, trade union agreement, factory safety regulations, etc. – that is set in stone under capitalism. History is not a linear march towards progress; rather, it is a struggle between two sides – the working class and the ruling class. Gains for one represent losses for the other; the myth of Sisyphus was an apt analogy for Rosa Luxemburg to make about the struggle for reform. Trade union work becomes increasingly difficult during periods of economic crisis when shrinking numbers of jobs and falling rates of pay sometimes divide workers and lower their confidence. When this is the case, trade union work can be reduced, at best, to trying to defend the few rights that you still have.[45] But this critical work must continue. It is out of this movement that the real gains for garment workers have been made. What this movement demonstrates is that the way we change the world is as people, as citizens, as workers. This is the power we have over governments and companies. They need us more than we need them.

Is a Just Capitalism Possible?

Arguments in favour of reform often (accidentally or not) turn into pro-capitalist arguments. The economic crisis of 2008 made the idea of an unstable 'casino capitalism' widely accepted; Covid-19 also made it easy to see the structural flaws in this system. And yet there remains the myth of a 'just capitalism'.[46] This implies that capitalism can be fair. It recommends trusting in the neoliberal values of the free market.

The idea of 'just capitalism' is an illusion that promises fundamental change without the need to alter the balance of power.[47] Even worse, it proffers the same economic system that has wreaked such havoc as the solution to the problems it has generated.[48]

In a system racked with exploitation and environmental destruction, surface modifications are not enough. 'The quixotic quest to construct a capitalism that might be ethical and just will have to be abandoned', wrote David Harvey. 'At the end of the day it matters not one whit whether we are well intentioned and ethically inclined or self-indulgently greedy and competitively destructive. The logic of endless capitalist accumulation and of endless growth is always with us.'[49] The problem, therefore, is not that I do not believe in a 'just capitalism'; the problem is that it does not exist.

Some of the methods for organised reform discussed in this chapter are fragments of a blueprint for an ideal society. The international labour movement and solidarity campaigns have vital parts to play in changing the world and fashioning a new one. Organised campaigns can unite, engage, educate, and inspire people. What they cannot do is produce clothes that are free of exploitation or environmental degradation. This is impossible under capitalism. As disappointing as it may be to hear this, there are no ethical clothes for sale. Temporary disappointment is, however, a small price to pay for taking part in the biggest challenge ever faced by humanity – the overthrow of capitalism.

CHAPTER TEN

Revolutionising Fashion

257

Dress suitably in short skirts and strong boots, leave your jewels in the bank, and buy a revolver.

> Fashion advice from the Irish revolutionary
> Countess Constance Markievicz

Why is it that, when it comes to our economic system, we have so readily swallowed the line that capitalism is the only possible option and we shouldn't even think about creating something better? Why are we so wedded to the dusty dogmas of this old sixteenth-century model, to the point of dragging it doggedly into a future for which it is manifestly unfit?

> Jason Hickle[1]

Revolution

The word revolution signifies two things. First, it captures the scale of the problems facing humanity today, problems that only revolution can answer. Second, it represents the spirit of people fighting injustice in pursuit of a better world.[2] This chapter imagines a post-capitalist society where capitalism has been overthrown and the world is in a state of permanent revolution. While this might seem a distant possibility, it is important that this chapter be set in a revolutionary future because the problem with raising only partial demands is that partial demands face a pre-established framework and the limitations set by capitalism.[3] To reach revolution and create a new world requires the liberation of the imagination and hope. This is in contrast to an overall social climate that promotes disillusionment and despair.[4] That is why this chapter has permission to envision and dream.

Marxism is not a blueprint for a future society, nor is it a set of rules or a creed by which to live. Rather, it is a demand for recognition that a new form of society *can* exist. How can we imagine an epoch that we have not experienced? Trotsky noted that what this society will look like is unwritten because 'the development of art is the highest test of the vitality and significance of each epoch'.[5] In one sense, how things will look is immaterial because what happens under freedom is less important than reaching it.

While the main task is to achieve freedom rather than worry about what happens next, I want to use this chapter to showcase some of the countless ideas for the creation of a fair society, to show that we have a world brimming over with ideas for attaining justice and equality. I have also sought to answer some of the questions about revolutionising fashion that repeatedly arise. There is nothing inevitable about progress and nothing in this chapter is 'destined' to come true. What I discuss in this chapter are possibilities. Whether they become realities depends entirely on what we do.

The invitation of this book has been to envisage a new society – one based on equality, freedom, and joy – and then to think hard about *what fashion is for* in that society. At the moment the purpose of the fashion industry is to make billions for the already stinking rich and to maintain a system of subjugation for the rest of us and the Global South in particular; to tear up the land, poison the water, exploit animals, and enslave human labour. I promise you once again that we can do better than this. I also hope that by now you have your own long checklist of things you want to change and can envisage a fashion industry that is vastly smaller and slower, localised and environmentally aligned. This does not sound too extreme, except when you consider what it would take to create this future for the entire industry, not just 2 per cent of it. Then it becomes not about creating perfect capsule wardrobes but the overthrow of a catastrophic economic system.

The Vast Storehouse of Potential:
Let's Democratise Design

> However sugarcoated and ambiguous, every form of authoritarianism must start with a belief in some group's greater right to power.
>
> Gloria Steinem

Art plays a hugely important role in society. It has the power to make life beautiful, to make us dream, to challenge us, and to lift our gaze above the horizon to picture a better future. This includes clothing. Yet art and fashion are tangled in a web of commerce, competition, and exclusivity. Once, while admiring the Central St Martin's graduate collections, a friend quipped: 'Don't worry, this time next year they'll all be broke and unemployed so you can buy up their collections for peanuts.' She spoke from bitter experience.

Even designers graduating at the top of their class face the prospect of unpaid internships, unemployment, or 'succumbing' to employment with a brand they neither like nor respect. A designer's fate, like that of our common cultural heritage, is determined by a relatively small number of private financial and industrial institutions which are completely unaccountable to the public. These corporations, now including social media companies, hold the power to block and control which narratives will emerge in society.[6]

Corporate power is ideologically bolstered by the Romantic idea that the famous fashion designer is a God-like figure capable of summoning their ideas out of thin air.[7] This idea of art was critiqued by Bertolt Brecht and Walter Benjamin as an individualistic and mystified concept which omits the artist as a worker rooted in a particular history with specific materials at their disposal. Fashion designers do not make the materials with which they work. The constant recycling or reinvention of ideas in the industry shows that just as car assembly plant workers use already processed materials to make cars, so too do fashion's forms, myths, symbols, and ideologies come already worked on.[8] One curator described how 'the core function of most creative people in an information glutted age is not innovation but rearrangement'.[9]

Artistic work should not be oversimplified. Clothing design is a skilled art form which differs from machine work.[10] Yet the idea of the designer as a 'rearranger' is an antidote to the elitism and deification that is rife in the fashion industry, showing instead that all the materials and skills that produce great works are socially produced. Just as even the greatest pianist needs a socially produced piano to perform on,[11] the most lauded designer needs socially produced pencils and paper, materials, a set of skills learned from teachers, and a history both to follow and to rebel against – not to mention huge assistance in the form of design teams, administrators, financiers, and domestic staff. Yet with power so concentrated in the industry, people sycophantically flock around key figures in the hope of gaining their share.

Nor is design a level playing field where talent automatically wins over hardship. Fashion can appear to be an egalitarian industry with a significant number of women, working-class, and LGBTQ+ designers. Yet it is still the case that class limitations combine with race and gender barriers to exclude many people from creative work. Student selection processes at art colleges have been found to be openly racist, replicating the inequalities found in wider society.[12] The economics of aesthetic production (buying materials and having spare time) also limit opportunities.[13] The risk involved in becoming an impoverished creative producer is far less for those who know, for example, that they will inherit a house from their parents.[14] This is replicated to a greater extent on a worldwide scale:

261

how many Schiaparellis or Balenciagas have lived and died in cotton fields and sweatshops?

Why should it be like this? There is nothing to say this is the correct way of living, so what if we democratised design? Hierarchy sharply and criminally limits human potential. There exists at present a gross underuse of talent. This probably means that the cure for cancer is trapped in the cortex of someone working as a waste-picker in India. It undoubtedly also has a profound impact on our creative and fashion worlds. The public is 'barred' from participating in the process of artistic fashion creation. We are allowed to make purchases and to style ourselves, but that is it. People create marvellous beauty with their limited purchases, often in dire circumstances. Does this offer a glimpse of what might be possible in terms of design creation? The Marxist professor Bertell Ollman asks that we imagine a society where everyone is free to be creative, when for each person 'the vast storehouse of their potentialities is at last emptied'.[15] What, then, might we see in terms of clothing design?

Currently, the confines of the market means that creativity comes second to what can be sold to produce maximum profit – with artists bogged down in mediocre bourgeois taste.[16] A designer's work is not art for art's sake but art for profit's sake – an alienated means to an end that hampers creativity and potential. We must sever the link between design and money, to reach the point where art and design are not stepping stones in a career but have been set free. We must reject entirely the notion that ultimate creativity exists in a small cabal of white Europeans.

But what, some might ask, if there was suddenly an excess of designs, an outpouring of creativity and ideas? How would we decide which was the best? An excess of art is surely the point. In an ideal society the floodgates will open and everyone will be unrestricted. After the Russian Revolution, art led a feverish existence.[17] It would be the same in the world that this chapter envisages: a tidal wave of new influences and inspiration – 'above the ridge new peaks will rise'.[18]

Attempting to restrict or contain art is capitalism's habit whereby art is a commodity rather than a social good. The Parisian couturiers fought tooth and nail to keep fashion for the rich. If this elitism ended, an excess of designs would not matter. We might at last see the freedom of choice that capitalism pretends to give us. Competition and elitism are concerns only under capitalism, as John Berger notes: 'The arranging of artists into a hierarchy of merit is an idle and essentially dilettante process. What matters are the needs which art answers.'[19] Young designers graduate to discover that their peers are now competing for the same few jobs. What if, instead of promoting individualised entrepreneurship and competitive achievement, society valued collaboration, mutual recognition, solidarity, and compassion?[20] In today's industry, a few individuals decide who works in fashion; in an ideal society there would be unlimited creative space.

Revolutionary Fashion

For a few years before and after the Russian Revolution of 1917, art in Russia experienced a movement that remains unique in the history of modern art in terms of its creativity and powerful, relevant engagement with everyday life. In *Art and Revolution*, Berger describes how this process evolved. The liberation of the serfs in 1861 allowed for the development of capitalism and a small urban proletariat which swiftly became the most militant and revolutionary in Europe and directly opposed to absolutist and undemocratic Tsarist rule.

Russia's avant-garde artists, as part of the intelligentsia, were deeply concerned with the political and spiritual future of their country. The cultural backwardness of Russia and the

263

absence of bourgeois patrons left them somewhat out on a limb: 'Instead of a present they had a past and a future. Instead of compromises they had extremes. Instead of limited possibilities they had open prophecies.'[21] Russia's avant-garde saw themselves as representing a liberated future. It was an art scene where women were considered equal to men,[22] and there was a common belief in art having a social role that was affirmative rather than critical.[23] Thus, after the revolution there were several years during which artists freely chose to serve their state and the revolution.[24]

Until Liubov Popova and Varvara Stepanova were invited to work as designers at the First Moscow Textile Printing Factory in 1923, all designs there had been Western imports. The two women worked at the factory for a year, producing 150 textile designs, of which about two dozen were put into mass production.[25] They were artists designing for mass factory production and their work was celebrated as the first implementation of the slogan 'art into production'.[26] While only a small proportion of their designs were mass-produced, they were hugely influential. They made prints achieve the level of 'real art' and were described by art critics as having 'brought the rich colours and intense ornament of contemporary art to the cities'.[27]

Originally from a wealthy background, Popova, who died prematurely in 1924, regarded her artistic work as a duty and a social obligation.[28] Yet her art is not dogmatic. Instead it is full of 'vital creativity itself', having embodied the spirit of creative progress, renewal, and inquiry.[29] Displaying an attitude unimaginable in her European contemporaries, Popova once said: 'No single artistic success gave me such profound satisfaction as the sight of a peasant woman buying a piece of my fabric for a dress.'[30]

The designs of these two women are rich, graphic, complex, colourful, and well ahead of their time, certainly in terms of fashion design. But in a sense, like many Russian artists, Popova and Stepanova were too dynamic for the social and economic realities of the period[31] and their designs were often seen as too 'fashion forward'. 'There is always the danger that the relative freedom of art can render it meaningless', argues Berger. 'Yet it is this same freedom which allows art, and art alone, to express and preserve the profoundest expectations of a period'[32] – comments highly applicable to Popova and Stepanova.

Simply placing fashion designs by Popova and Stepanova alongside designs by their European contemporaries speaks volumes. Their prints encapsulate the hope, audacity, and dreams of the Russian Revolution. Across the rest of the world, fashion was the plaything of the rich. This was a time when working people were supposed to be no more than drab factory and cannon fodder, yet Popova and Stepanova saw them clothed in light and colour. Their designs speak of a new world, bright, beautiful, and defiantly shining forth the phrase the Russian working class was throwing at its adversary: 'I am nothing and I should be everything.'[33]

Linking Design with Production

Being an environmentalist does not mean aiming for a society of scarcity. Humans differ from animals in that we free ourselves from need through production. It is important for culture that we are not in a position of scarcity because, as Trotsky explained: 'Culture feeds on the sap of economics, and a material surplus is necessary, so that culture may grow. Art needs comfort, even abundance.'[34] While it is essential to free ourselves from scarcity through production, there is no reason for life to be segmented and compartmentalised.[35] Sweatshops and compartmentalised Taylorist methods of production compound alienation. They turn highly skilled, autonomous artisans like the silk-weavers of Lyon into workers on assembly lines passing objects or parts of objects in front of them during twelve-hour shifts.[36] More recently, Indian spinning mill workers described life enthralled to machines: 'Most of my life I am spending with the machines. There is absolutely no contact with the outside world', said one worker. Another worker explained that because the machines run constantly they cannot stop working: 'The machines are on 24 hours per day. I get no proper sleep. They are continuously asking us to work both the day and night shift.' The machines have a dual repressive role, with women reporting that the noise of the machines is used as a cover by male supervisors to make sexualised and abusive comments against them.[37] Ending this gendered, racialised exploitation is key to the emancipation of the global working class. The rush that keeps machines running 24 hours a day is not our rush, it is the greedy rush of the drive for profit. If we take profit out of the equation we can slow down to the pace of real need, not corporate greed.

Stepanova was against an artificial divide between clothing designers and producers. A textile designer, she believed, should discover what happened to fabric once it left the factory gates.[38] With the Design Council reporting that 80 per cent of a product's environmental impact is decided at the design stage,[39] and the charity WRAP (the Waste and Resources Action Programme) reporting that 300,000 tonnes of clothing ended up in household residual waste in 2016,[40] this approach is more important than ever. The question of waste reduction must be paramount in design and specialist knowledge must not be separated from decision making. Designers should participate fully in society's production decisions rather than being passive.[41]

Another false divide that should be scrapped is that of consumers and producers. Passive consumption means people are presented with ready-made products they have had no hand in creating,[42] resulting in the alienated mystification of clothing and a visual world we did not make for ourselves.[43] Roland Barthes wrote that capitalism needs consumers who do not calculate the real cost of their purchases: 'If clothing producers and consumers had the same consciousness, clothing would be bought (and produced) only at the very slow rate of its dilapidation.'[44] If people helped to make their clothes they would undoubtedly consume less, respect more, and lose the alienated need for so many possessions. In *Foot Work*, I wrote about the concept of 'prosumers', where people transform from 'consumers' into 'prosumers' by working 20 hours a week then using another 20 hours a week to repair, produce, and share goods completely independent of industrialised production systems.[45]

Before fashion was mass-produced, clothes were often home-sewn. Some argue that making your own clothes is a more sustainable method of production, with efforts like Fibreshed going one step further to push regional land-based textile and dye production.[46] Alexandra Kollontai wrote in *Communism and the Family* that the danger of seeing households as units of production is that the burden falls on 'the active fingers of the wife'.[47] On top of work and domestic duties she must now make clothes. Women have fought to free themselves from the domestic yoke; an ideal society would not send them back to it.

There already exist positive moves to localise collective production. As we have seen in the creation of Indigenous clothing, 'makers typically draw on certain universal Indigenous cultural values like respect and responsibility' while nurturing a sustainable relationship to land. Riley Kucheran writes that:

Indigenous modes of making are also inherently communal because the process involves reciprocity and requires par-

267

ticipation of many different kinds of knowledge holders. The 'supply chain' of Indigenous fashion consists of Elders who share stories that provide direction to hunters, hide tanners, plant dye and medicine cultivators, weavers, sewers and the designers who coordinate the process. This means that more of the community participates and shares in an economy that regenerates culture. I see this in growing Indigenous collectives and entrepreneurs who are investing in their communities, like Bethany Yellowtail of the B. Yellowtail Collective and Tania Larsson.[48]

Degrow and Democratise

The global corporate economy based on the idea of limitless growth has become a permanent war economy against the planet and people.

Verdanda Shiva[49]

We are dangling on the edge of an environmental precipice, but the good news is there is no mystery to be solved; we already know what has to be done to avert climate breakdown. The answer is: 'We need to actively scale down fossil fuels and mobilise a rapid rollout of renewable energy ... to cut world emissions in half within a decade and get to zero by 2050.'[50] This is the biggest fight we face – a battle for the only known life in the universe.

In his book *Less Is More*, Jason Hickle talked about 'growthism' as a structural imperative, a hegemonic ideology that no one stops to question.[51] Growthism is the idea that all sectors of the economy must mindlessly grow all the time, no matter the consequences. Degrowth, on the other hand, is a planned reduction of excess energy and resource use. Some sectors of the economy could be selected to grow – healthcare, clean energy production, regenerative agriculture. But other sectors could be selected for degrowth (or demolition). In this list would be the arms industry, SUVs, and fashion. We must absolutely shrink fashion production and consumption. But we must also centre garment workers in the Global South. It is true that, as Hickle writes, '[g]lobal ecological break-down is being driven almost entirely by excess accumulation among the very rich while the consequences hurt the [Global South], and the poor, disproportionately'.[52] We cannot allow for 'solutions' that compound this inequality and punish the Global South all over again.

This is why, along with degrowth must come democracy. There is no democracy in the fashion industry. It is currently a corporate dictatorship. The workers of Rana Plaza in Bangladesh died because they had no control whatsoever over the factory they worked in. They were coerced into entering a building they knew was unsafe due to fear of violence and destitution. This was possible because the factory, and thus the lives of the workers, were controlled by a rich businessman who was in thrall to the needs of multinationals.

But what if the means of production were collectively owned? What if the dictator was overthrown? What if every clothing factory, cotton field, technology developer, and the Chambre Syndicale de la Haute Couture in Paris were under collective ownership? What if, instead of operating to produce profits for the few, they were run for the benefit of humanity and the planet?

Social production organised by workers would end unsafe working practices because no one is going to vote to work in a death trap. With equality of power, there would be no more Rana Plazas. The building owners would be working in the factory like everyone else and so it would also be their life at risk from criminal practices. This levelling of society would end other dangerous and polluting practices like sanding jeans, the dust from which causes silicosis, and there would be no hazardous generators as solar-powered electricity production would be under collective control and we would stop making fabrics from fossil fuels. If everyone took turns working in factories, no one would sanction such deadly and unnecessary practices. As discussed in Chapter 5, socially organised production would end overproduction because no one not reliant on wages is going to vote to work 15-hour days, seven days a week, on an assembly line that produces 20 billion pieces of clothing. The only people that need such vast quantities of clothing are the people that sell them at a profit; under collective ownership their role would have ceased. The end of the drive to make a profit would bring about a return of use-value over exchange value because people would make things to use them (and enjoy them) rather than to sell them. What was produced could be the best, most durable clothing we can make – all from renewable and recyclable fabric. Happily, socially organised production would also result in far more leisure time.

During the transition, we could implement a 'public job guarantee'[53] so that anyone who wants to can get a job doing socially useful work. Typically this is described as things like care work or renewable energy work, but in the fashion industry there is so much to do – upgrading or demolishing buildings, electrical and fire safety implementation, sorting and recycling vast quantities of waste from material and thread scraps to buttons, devising ways to safely dispose of chemicals like glues, dyes, and tannery chemicals, water cleaning and river, sea, and lake rejuvenation, land and ecosystem regeneration, and vast animal rehabilitation as billions of animals are released from the conveyor belt of slaughter. The people who currently work in the factories would be in charge of transforming and creating a new industry. There is more than enough work to be done, we just have to share it out equally and make sure everyone is cared for.

There is also the possibility that some people will want to shut down factories and return to work on the land. Many countries in the Global South were pushed into creating export-oriented economies. Sri Lanka's ruling class embraced the idea of building hundreds of garment factories across the country and herding workers into them. War, poverty, and mechanised industry further undermined people's ability to survive by farming small plots. But research has found that women who are already leaving Sri Lanka's free trade zones to return to small-scale garden farms say it is already a better life option than factory work because they have much healthier food, spend far more time with their families, and are independent.[54]

Going forward, job diversification – everyone taking turns at certain forms of labour – could mean that everyone played a part in clothing production, which would end the separation of consciousness between consumers and producers and prevent any one person or group becoming stuck in one job.[55] Robots and automation would certainly be part of changing industry, doing many of the most dangerous tasks, though they remain unable to cope with the floppy fabric needed to make clothes (for more on this see *Foot Work*). Under capitalism, people choose, or are assigned, a certain trade and more or less stick to it to avoid starvation, whereas in an ideal society people would be able to spend some of their time designing or making clothes without being pigeonholed as a designer or factory worker. Currently, reserving art and design for the few is inseparable from its suppression in the masses.[56] Most importantly perhaps, common ownership would end the present scenario where people do a full day of back-breaking labour yet still go hungry:

What he produces for himself is not the silk that he weaves, not the gold that he draws up the mining shaft, not the palace that he builds. What he produces for himself is wages; and the silk, the gold, and the palace are resolved for him into a certain quantity of necessaries of life, perhaps into a cotton jacket, into copper coins, and into a basement dwelling.[57]

In a post-capitalist society, the 'fashion industry' would be shrunk to the point that it was unrecognisable. Tens of billions of bits of clothing would simply never be made. Production would be much slower and more localised. In Marge Piercy's speculative fiction book *Woman on the Edge of Time*, utopian clothes are made from algae by machines that disgorge them like paper towels. In this world, there remains the question of how to keep eight billion people clothed and shod. It is useful here to think about *associate producer communities* – a concept based on István Mészáros' work in *Beyond Capital*, which was used by the administration of Venezuelan President Hugo Chávez to develop the concept of an 'elementary triangle of socialism', to which the environmentalist John Bellamy Foster added an ecological element. The three concepts, which must be accorded equal weight, are: (1) social ownership of the means of production and social use, not ownership, of nature; (2) social production organised by workers and the regulation by communities of the relationship between humanity and nature; and (3) the satisfaction of the communal needs of present and future generations and of life itself.

In a post-capitalist society, associate producer communities are small, localised production hubs; they are similar to but not the same as present-day cooperatives as they are based on genuine collective ownership of all the world's resources. Unfortunately, under capitalism, workers in cooperatives have to become the capitalist entrepreneur. They have to discipline themselves, cut their own wages, and potentially fire each other.[58] Collective production is by far the most efficient form of production, and clothes are likely, for the most part, to be made in small factories collectively owned by communities of associated producers.[59] Maybe you are reading this as a maker and you love spending time stitching clothes together; this is wonderful and I salute you, but it is not for everyone, plus there is still the question of where individual makers get the textiles, threads, wools, beads, etc. that they use. Some collectively organised production will be necessary, but it will not be outsourced sweatshop production.

I think it is likely that we will entirely pause mass clothing production for years in order to allow the land to regenerate, to perform a clean-up of the industry, and to sort, categorise, mend, upcycle, and redistribute what clothing we already have. Many of these resources will go into vast clothing libraries for communal ownership, leading to greater access to clothing but smaller personal wardrobes. Mending and tool workshops would spring up for repairs and skills sharing, along with communal laundries.

When some production is needed, how would these producer communities decide what to make? The communities of associated producers (the parts) would function democratically as part of society (the whole). Currently, fashion operates in a top-down structure whereby there is a perverse centrality which destroys any chance of collectivity. Think, for example, of companies like LVMH or Inditex which undemocratically determine production. Post-capitalism, the whole and its parts would work together in a non-adversarial manner. Substantive democratic decision making would occur within the parts. At the same time, conscious planning and coordination of the parts by the whole – for example, ensuring that all society's clothing needs are being met – would ensure the parts functioned democratically as part of the whole.[60] There is a need to satisfy communal requirements on a global scale. Satisfying these needs means that an abundance of food, housing, sanitation, clean air, water, health care, education, and socially owned transport takes precedence over clothing production.[61] Because we live on an 'island planet',[62] the idea of communal needs must work on a global scale until economic inequality becomes a historical memory. These communal needs include the planet itself. First and foremost would be clothing production that has no lasting adverse consequences for biodiversity or the planet.

Can we really do this? We can because worker control produces the possibility for far more variety and innovation than under capitalism.[63] In 1976, an innovative scheme called the Lucas Aerospace Plan asked workers at an armaments factory what they would rather make. The result was 150 worker-devised schemes for socially useful goods that could have been made instead of military hardware, including wheelchairs, artificial kidneys, and solar heating kits. Hope thrives on reason and experience, and we have all the skills we need to refashion society, a truth kept secret by the present system.

Decolonise

I am often asked if I *really* believe the fashion industry can be changed. It is a question that snaps my mind to a single place – the Matuail rubbish dump on the outskirts of Dhaka. The truckloads of rubbish that arrive are municipal, domestic, and commercial. Much of the commercial waste is direct from Dhaka's endless web of garment factories – textiles, chemicals cans, buttons, old thread spools. Matuail is the hidden side effect of an outsourced industry and '[a]n enactment', as Dr Max Liboiron's seminal book *Pollution Is Colonialism* states, 'of ongoing colonial relations to Land'.[64] This vast landscape is home to a community of waste pickers (a term first adopted at the First World Conference of Waste Pickers in 2008 as a non-derogatory term that recognises people's contribution to public health and environmental sustainability),[65] who sort through the dump for bones, glass, metal, and garment factory remnants. It is highly dangerous, dirty work done wearing sandals.

In a podcast discussion with Dr Liboiron, Professor Michelle Murphy, from the Environmental Data Justice Lab, has talked about how any 'being or land that's already been harmed' then gets stigmatised, rendered disposable, or considered cheap and up for further injury: 'If this land has garbage on it, let's put more, let's concentrate the garbage there. We live in a world where certain people are rendered disposable and they have the burden of intensive violence coming at them from many angles, with the world hostile to their existence.'[66] Matuail exists now as the current home and livelihood for hundreds of people who live and work in a community formed around dignified labour. Many of the people I met there were climate refugees – driven from their ancestral farmland by rising seas and melting snowcaps. Already, in a country viciously marked by colonialism, their farms were seen as inconsequential by the world, and the land covered by the rubbish dump was deemed disposable by corporations outsourcing production to Bangladesh. In such a place the super-yachts of the owners of these corporations seem even more obscene and it is even more apparent that the colonial pathways of extraction were never erased.[67]

The climate crisis means the fashion industry will change – either it will evolve to small, holistic, zero-carbon production centres as part of a green future, or it will drag us over the cliff to a climate apocalypse in which the survivors search for scraps in rubbish dumps. Either way, what is happening now has no long-term future. We live in a time where our actions determine which of these futures will come true.

Calls to 'decolonise fashion' spring from a desire to critically revaluate the industry and its practices. While decolonial approaches mean different things in different regions and contexts (as Max Liboiron has written, 'different colonialisms will have different decolonialisms and anticolonialisms'[68]), the word 'decolonise' must not be watered down to mean just reading books, having discussions, or putting new managerial systems in place. Themrise Khan, a researcher based in Pakistan, has called 'decolonisation' a 'loanword' since it does not exist in multiple languages from Urdu to Arabic to Spanish. Instead it is a Eurocentric word, first used by British colonial administrators and politicians as they watched their empire crumble. Khan writes that 'for them, decolonisation was the disappointment of the imperial illusion of permanence – the end of empire'. In reality, decolonisation was not a beneficent political change or a subtle rebalancing of power; it was a violent and bloody struggle. Anyone who has lived through decolonisation (or even watched *Battle for Algiers* or studied the Vietnam War) will understand that these struggles were, as Khan writes, 'a violent end to a violent occupation, which had to be fought for with equal violence by the occupied *against* the occupier. If left to the colonisers, they would have never acquiesced.' To decolonise is not just to hand the reigns of power over to more localised masters; it is not to 'soften power imbalances'[69] but to engage in the wholesale transfer of power from one social class to another.

Because of this, it has rightly been pointed out that to *actually decolonise* global institutions like the World Bank or the international aid sector would be to render them non-existent. The same goes for the fashion industry – to actually decolonise the industry, in a successful struggle to end exploitation and colonial practices and complete a transfer of power, land, and material resources from rich to poor and from Global North corporations to Global South workers, farmers, and Indigenous communities would be to end the industry. As we have seen, the fashion industry cannot exist without the exploitation of women, of people of colour, of the Global South, and of the planet. End this exploitation – the real aim of decolonisation – and you end the industry.

Writing from his territory on the shores of Gchi-gamig (Lake Superior), Riley Kucheran has his own misgivings about the concept of 'decolonising fashion'. He writes that: 'I fear that a new "decolonising fashion" is itself recolonising.' He rightly states that the current fashion industry and its accompanying academic sector is not up to the task of decolonising itself because it is a 'structurally colonialist, capitalist, and white-supremacist institution' – neither a safe place for Indigenous students or practitioners nor a healthy place for anyone to exist. It is crucial that, as Kucheran writes, the political project of decolonisation does not to turn into a 'culturalist project of representation'.[70] He writes:

> It becomes essential that any decolonizing discourse does not act as another 'settler move to innocence' by focusing solely on 'decolonizing the mind' without explicit material consequences like repatriation of stolen Indigenous land and reinstatement of Indigenous sovereignty,[71] decolonised fashion is therefore a lofty goal: arguably incommensurable and absolutely something to not take lightly.[72]

For Kucheran, decolonisation is a dual process: 'a simultaneous dismantling of colonial systems and a rebuilding of Indigenous worlds'. But we must be clear that true decolonisation has earth-shaking and reworking consequences: 'decolonisation must be recognised and understood as an expressly material process: it must involve financial reparations and the return of stolen and occupied Indigenous land – at a minimum'.[73]

'I think the pandemic has demonstrated how fragile global supply chains are', Kucheran continues:

I'm beginning to see Climate Change as an opportunity to end the fashion industry: we're going to be forced to stop purchasing cheap disposable clothing, we're going to be forced to mend clothing. I often think, after the storm, are we going to be able to feed ourselves? Clothe ourselves? Indigenous peoples are preparing for the worst future climate scenarios with resurgence of ancestral ways of being and making.

We will not get to this future point without ensuring we have an intersectional present. This means explicitly ensuring that fashion's movement for change is not itself acting in a colonial fashion. Consider this quote given to me anonymously by someone in the Global South who felt unable to speak freely in case of angry repercussions: 'Global North organisations feel they are the ones doing all the thinking, that they are the ones with the ideas and they know how to solve our problems – this is really problematic.' They went on to describe a movement culture that lacks dialogue and discussion, where workers' groups in the Global South are excluded from decision making and there is an assumption that one size fits all because all garment-producing countries have the same history and political system: 'Take a step back and listen to the Global South and its voices rather than telling them all the time what to do and what you need', the anonymous source said. 'Otherwise it's a coloniser perspective. I see it a lot in the movement right now. I think we need to decolonise the language and the way we think and act.'

Many well-meaning Global North groups still approach fashion activism from a charity perspective instead of that of solidarity and building workers' power. This is a movement that must be led by workers on the front line of the garment industry, as the source explains: 'Worker leaders need to believe they are the ones who actually know what is best for us. They don't have that if they feel they need to go to Global North organisations for ideas, and if Global North organisations think "we know we know what is best for you".'

I urge you to bear in mind the slogan held by HomeNet International which was once relayed to me by Janhavi Dave: 'Nothing for us, without us. Don't offer or plan anything without our participation or voice.' Being involved in fashion's movement for change means listening to those on the front line of exploitation at all times.

Again, this paragraph from Riley Kucheran about Indigenous communities is applicable and useful for the wider movement:

> It's key to understand that decolonisation is already happening on the ground, in communities, generated from the everyday practices of Indigenous individuals and collectives that are actively building decolonised futures. It is largely up to fashion studies to get out of the way, to listen to and support Indigenous fashion resurgence, to create and hold space for Indigenous leadership without co-opting and commodifying Indigeneity.[74]

Human history is full of shameful atrocities, many of which are still in motion. But as a human collective, we have never faced a crisis like climate change. It is an existential crisis not for the fashion industry but for humanity. In the face of this threat, remember that capitalism's speciality is making us feel powerless and making us feel divided. Our task is to focus on our commonality – no matter our differences in regions, races, genders, and so on. This commonality exists in our need for this planet and in the fact that as a global working class we do not need capitalism.

Anti-capitalism, but Make It Fashion

We're in a crisis, but do not get depressed – we have so much to gain from the fight for a better world. Fashion is often a horrible thing to write about, but one of the joyful elements is wondering what post-capital fashion might look like. In some ways it is easier to imagine the impact of these post-capitalist changes on a worldwide scale than to envisage their impact at street level. How would these changes affect the visual world that we each inhabit? Would daily life change? And what would people look like? Again, it is important to reiterate that we cannot know how people would dress in a post-capitalist world. There is no one answer to this question. Art, and fashion, resonate with people because they mirror and represent the world they are living in.[75] Fashion thus changes over time because it arises in different social environments. A post-revolutionary society would have unimaginable consequences for clothing.

We can, however, try to imagine whether 'fashion' would still exist. Fashion has been defined in this book as *changing styles of dress and appearance adopted by groups of people*, a definition that aims to keep fashion in the material not the ethereal world. Fashion has the ability to sum up an epoch, to evoke the spirit of the times, which is why Varvara Stepanova wrote: 'It would be a mistake to think that fashion can be abolished, or that it is haphazard or unnecessary. Fashion gives us the lines and shapes to suit a particular time.'[76]

Art is not static any more than life is static, and it would be odd to argue that there is an ultimate way of dressing (or doing anything) that should remain unchanged for all of time. But while fashion as a concept of change may exist after the revolution, fashion as an industry would be unrecognisably different. Clothing is consolidated into fashion via a series of social constructs.[77] Like a solid gold picture frame, it is everything that goes *round* clothes that makes them fashion – the catwalks, the media prestige and hype, the elaborate shops, and ideology all combine to produce a false religiosity.[78] This false religiosity both celebrates wealth and ownership and cements it. As Kanye West once said: 'They made us hate ourself and love their wealth.'[79]

False religiosity exists to help the fashion system produce maximum profits for corporations. Commodities like bags and shoes are placed on pedestals for worship. Worship is the flipside of the industry. Fashion is needed to produce money for corporations, but it is certainly *wanted* by its consumers. On closer inspection the pleasure that fashion brings to people (myself included) does not actually afford an escape from the very things that make us seek pleasure in the first place.[80] Fashion is worshipped because life is alienated and mundane for most people: 'The more monotonous the present, the more the imagination must seize upon the future',[81] Berger argued. Fashion's startling ability to make people believe in 'the heady possibility of making a new start'[82] keeps people coming back for more. It is wanted because it is linked to the ability to get a job, a partner, or greater social standing.

What if life was on the whole joyful and stimulating? What if you were assured of prosperity and a meaningful existence? What if private property and competition were not enshrined? What if work, love, and standing in the community were not based on appearance? This would result in people not being compelled to worship at the altar of fashion, praying for success. Some people might still want to partake in studied dress but gone would be the barbarity of fashion and cosmetics that stems from their obligatory nature.[83] We might reach a situation where the only chastisement given to a woman who does not paint her face is that given to someone who decides not to paint a watercolour – none.[84] A society without capitalism would necessarily be a society without the fashion industry as we know it.

Mao Suits?

The Cultural Revolution, which took place between 1966 and 1976, aimed to rid China of 'old' thinking and culture. For the authorities, this new society had no middle ground – everything and everyone was either revolutionary or reactionary.[85] To be labelled reactionary had dire consequences, fear of which led people to speak, act, and dress as inconspicuously as possible. As a result, the *zhongshan zhuang* ('Mao suit') became the prevailing fashion of the time.

Interestingly, as Juan Juan Wu outlines in *Chinese Fashion: From Mao to Now*, there was no government decree *ordering* people to wear the *zhongshan zhuang*; rather, its prevalence was the result of an atmosphere of conformity, fear, and revolutionary fervour.[86] Given, however, the banning of items like Western suits and the threat of death for being reactionary, the government's role in this style should not be underestimated. The ubiquitous drab blue or grey Mao suits could also be taken as a sign of the government's professed allegiance to working people and the need to clothe nearly a billion people at a time of great scarcity.

What the Mao suit was *not* was the end of fashion. Quite the contrary, in fact, due to a perverse twist of fate that saw people become 'aware of dress and appearance to an unprecedented degree', for during the Cultural Revolution a fashion faux pas could mean death. This meant that people studied 'prevailing fashions down to the minutest detail with a singular intensity'. Juan Juan Wu explains that rather than exterminate fashion, the Cultural Revolution produced one of the most fashion-conscious (to the point of paranoia) nations in history. One simply couldn't *not* care about fashion.[87]

In the same vein, strict uniforms are adopted by certain political groupings who purport not to care about fashion, for example Europe's anarchists. Among such groups the parameters of the accepted uniform are strictly policed so everyone wears the same thing. This indifference to fashion is so studied, and such care is taken not to step outside the lines, that the obsessional and self-policing nature of fashion becomes clear.

The fashion academic Ulrich Lehmann has rightly argued that uniforms are not always a joyless way to dress; he points to the joy people get from wearing identical football shirts.[88] Yet, just as we are not aiming for a society of economic scarcity, nor are we aiming for one of cultural uniformity brought about through repression. A fully post-capitalist society which was democratically structured through associated communities of producers rather than ruled in a top-down manner would not need, want, or be able to repress people in this manner. Instead it would enshrine democracy and freedom of expression for individuals.

Gender, Race, and Class

That it is 'ideological' is an accusation commonly thrown at the art of those on the Left, as if the work of Johannes Vermeer, Paul Gauguin, or Christian Dior was not ideological and as if free marketeers were somehow neutral. As bell hooks explains, there is no art that is politically neutral.[89] This includes fashion. The way people dress today is defined by prevailing ideologies. So what might the impact on fashion be in a post-capitalist society where ideological constructs like gender, race, and class have been renounced?

The likelihood is that some obvious gender fashion rules will be cast aside as relics of an old oppressive order: pink for girls, blue for boys, trousers for men, dresses for women. But what of items such as high heels and corsets? Heels have long been rejected as the antithesis of the ideals of feminism.[90] So would they be banned post-revolution? The same question can be asked about items like the *hijab*, which sections of the French feminist Left campaigned to have outlawed. The short answer is no, items would not be banned. It was a huge mistake to ban the *hijab* in France just as outlawing high heels or mini-skirts would be a mistake. Liberation is not, as some French feminists mistakenly believe, about the substitution of rules for more rules. You do not seek to free women from what you consider to be a cage by placing them in a bigger cage. Self-emancipation is the only route to freedom. Anti-*hijab* legislation covering schools or workplaces risks what one cultural commentator described as 'creating a geography where Muslim women's bodies are not welcome in certain places, and policing where they can and cannot venture'.[91] The key with clothing for women is choice. It will be fine to wear heels but also to not wear them – ever.

A single vision of anything is not freedom of choice. The fashion industry's loss of power would also mean an end to the exclusion of bodies that do not 'measure up'. Body insecurity would be replaced by the loving acceptance and celebration of all kinds of beauty. Women must have the freedom to be whatever they want and not be subject to negative or critical messages if they decide not to give two hoots about their appearance. The struggle for emancipation is 'nourished by the image of enslaved ancestors rather than that of liberated grandchildren', argued Walter Benjamin.[92] Certainly, this is how I feel about women's clothing, it is the spectre of past restrictions on life-roles and dress, encapsulated by 1950s dress, that make me work for such change.

Under capitalism, racism in the fashion industry manifests itself in the exclusion of models of colour and by the exclusion

284

and appropriation of culture. If those powerful elements in society who depend on excluding people to secure their own power were removed then there would be no need to exclude people. The ending of race as a means of exclusion would end for good the idea of beauty having one colour. It would also end shame and oppression in dress, allowing people to wear their own cultural dress without becoming targets for abuse.[93] Commodification and cultural co-option occur because art is viewed as something to be bought or sold rather than celebrated. What is needed are ways to fulfil our humanity that go beyond possession.[94] This would end cultural appropriation as a means to fill up the monotonous nature of modern life with escapist fantasy.[95] Rather than alienation, a post-capitalist society would be one of fulfilment and creativity.

Under capitalism, the definitive factor in fashion is class, with people branded by their net worth. Ancient Egyptians had different-coloured robes for different ranks. Thousands of years later, Britain had cloth caps, bowler hats, or top hats – 'the higher the crown, the higher the social ranking'.[96] The same divisions are replicated in dress for leisure time. If you want to display your wealth, simply attach expensive objects to your body. An end to a hierarchical society would mean an end to people fighting to keep their place at the top of society. Currently, fashion underpins the power of a particular social class.[97] If there was no class, there would be no fashion as we know it because there would be no need to signify wealth through clothing, to own commodities in order to prove your difference from those who cannot afford what you have, and to express class power through clothing. Instead, there would be freedom of expression for individuals and an equality that would not separate the makers from the wearers of beautiful clothes.

Myriad of Possibilities

Capitalism should be regarded as a failed system.[98] It cannot provide the people of this world with adequate food, shelter, clothing, health care, or education. Its impact on the planet is devastating and may well lead to planetary catastrophe unless we act. Its impact on people is to cripple them physically, mentally, spiritually, and artistically. Riven with contradictions, capitalism will only ever bring crisis, war, and devastation. For every advance made there are a thousand more locked away in denied potential.

The production of fashion exemplifies this state of affairs by devastating the planet, maiming its workers, and rigidly implementing the idea that there is only one way to look and to live. Fashion will never be free without an end to capitalism. And yet fashion can contribute to the remaking of the world. It has the ability to replace the old with the new, to make us hope and dream. That is why, for every division in clothing that must be torn down, there is a myriad of possibilities that could spring up. This will be the adventure experienced by the new society. The poet Alexander Blok described the task ahead: 'To redo everything. To arrange things so that everything becomes new; so that the false, the dirty, dull ugly life which is ours becomes just life, pure, gay, beautiful.'[99]

About the Illustrator

Jade Pilgrom is a freelance illustrator currently working from Orlando, Florida. She received a BFA in Illustration in 2011 and specialises in editorial work. She has been featured in Hallmark, *Huffington Post*, Etsy, Paramount Pictures, Apartment Therapy, and the long-running *POETRY* magazine.

For feedback or work inquiries, please contact her at:
jadepilgrom.com
jadepilgrom@gmail.com

Notes

Foreword

1. Leon Trotsky, *Literature and Revolution*, edited by William Keach, translated by Rose Strunsky Lorwin, Haymarket Books, 2005, p.189, 207.

Introduction

1. https://cleanclothes.org/news/2013/10/23/resolveuid/1339b9f126e74206b7e9aeb75f262fee.
2. Ingrid Loscheck, *When Clothes become Fashion: Design and Innovation Systems*. Berg, 2009, p. 135.
3. Colin Gale and Jasbin Kaur, *Fashion and Textiles*. Berg, 2004, p. 20.
4. Dana Thomas, *Deluxe*. Penguin, 2007.
5. István Mészáros, *Marx's Theory of Alienation*. Merlin, 2006, p. 175. Virtuoso piano players need socially produced pianos.
6. Kaisik Wong's work, copied by Nicolas Ghesquière for Balenciaga: www.businessoffashion.com/2013/03/op-ed-who-watches-the-watchmen.html?utm_source=Subscribers&utm_campaign=5d6286da05-&utm_medium=email. Dior, Prada, and Celine were caught copying historic designs: www.fashionista.com/2013/04/raf-simons-miuccia-prada-called-out-for-copying-historic-designs.
7. I agree with the approach taken in Linda Welters and Abby Lillethun (eds), *The Fashion Reader*. Bloomsbury, 2007, pp. xxv–xxix. See Sandra Niessen and Jennifer Craik's chapters for more on this argument.
8. Radu Stern, *Against Fashion: Clothing as Art 1850–1930*. MIT Press, 2004, p. 2.
9. Valerie Steele, *Paris Fashion*. Berg, 1988, p. 18.

Notes

10. Jean Allman (ed.), *Fashioning Africa: Power and the Politics of Dress*. Indiana University Press, 2004, p. 2. 'The people without history' is a quote from Eric Wolf which was adapted by Allman to 'The people without fashion'.

11. John Berger, *Art and Revolution*. Writers & Readers, 1969, p. 157.

12. www.hyllanderiksen.net/blog/2018/12/13/whats-wrong-with-the-global-north-and-the-global-south.

13. www.forbes.com/sites/pamdanziger/2020/11/22/china-is-headed-to-be-the-worlds-largest-luxury-market-by-2025-but-american-brands-may-miss-out/.

14. Thanks to the Society for the Promotion of Area Resource Centers, an Indian NGO partnered with the National Slum Dwellers' Federation.

15. Terry Eagleton, *Marxism and Literary Criticism*. Methuen, 1985, p. 59. Eagleton makes this point about writers, books, and publishing houses.

16. Giannino Malossi (ed.), *The Style Engine*. Monacelli Press, 1998, p. 30.

17. Jean Rostard, quoted in Rachel Carson, *Silent Spring*. Houghton Mifflin, 1987, p. 13.

18. www.businessoffashion.com/2012/10/springsummer-2013-the-season-that-was.html#more-37507.

19. Jeanette A. Jarrow and Beatrice Judelle (eds), *Inside the Fashion Business*. John Wiley & Sons, 1966, p. vii.

20. https://allpoetry.com/A-Worker-Reads-History.

21. R. T. Naylor, *Crass Struggle*. McGill-Queen's University Press, 2011, p. 26.

22. Speech by Audre Lorde, 'Learning from the 60s', 1982, www.blackpast.org/african-american-history/1982-audre-lorde-learning-60s/.

23. Manfred B. Steger and Ravi K. Roy, *Neoliberalism: A Very Short Introduction*. Oxford University Press, 2010, p. 53.

24. www.unicefusa.org/press/releases/unicef-too-many-children-dying-malnutrition/8259 and www.bain.com/about/media-center/press-releases/2019/fall-luxury-report/.

25. Phrase typically attributed to Werner Sombart (1902) or Elizabeth Wilson (1985).

26. CEO Johann Rupert, www.businessinsider.com/how-the-10-biggest-luxury-brands-came-to-dominate-the-world-2012–6?op=1#ixzz2M6Y16Yhk.

27. www.bain.com/about/media-center/press-releases/2020/covid_19_crisis_pushes_luxury_to_sharpest_fall_ever_but_catalyses_industrys_ability_to_transform/.

28. Terry Eagleton lecture, Counterfire Conference, London, 5 November 2011.

29. James C. Scott, *Weapons of the Weak: Everyday Forms of Peasant Resistance*. Yale University Press, 1985, p. 301.

30. Eagleton, *Marxism and Literary Criticism*, p. viii.

31. Neil Faulkner, *A Marxist History of the World: From Neanderthals to Neoliberals*. Pluto Press, 2013, p. 152.

32. Ibid., p. ix.

33. Eagleton, *Marxism and Literary Criticism*, p. 5.

34. John Berger, *Ways of Seeing*, documentary, part 1.

35. Eagleton, *Marxism and Literary Criticism*, p. 5.

36. Malcolm Barnard, *Fashion as Communication*. Routledge, 1996, p. 145 and chapter 1.

37. Neil Faulkner, interview, 26 February 2013.

38. Terry Eagleton, *After Theory*. Allen Lane/Penguin, 2003, p. 100.

39. Louis Althusser, quoted in Eagleton, *Marxism and Literary Criticism*, p. 18. Hélène Rytmann was an important Jewish sociologist and an active member of the French Resistance during the Second World War. She was murdered by Althusser in 1980. They were married but he did not stand trial as he was declared unfit. After learning of this I have deleted his name from the text of *The Anti-Capitalist Book of Fashion* as I do not want promote him despite his work on social class. I am leaving this footnote as I do not think enough people know about the life of Hélène Rytmann or of Althusser's crime.

40. Bertolt Brecht, quoted in Ibid., p. 49.

41. Ibid., p. viii.

42. I am grateful here to points made by Clive Lewis MP during his speech at the March 2021 Media Reform Coalition event: The Solution or the Problem? What Should We Do with Our Public Service Media?

43. South End Press (ed.), *Talking about a Revolution*. South End Press, 1998, p. 7.

44. Terry Eagleton lecture.

45. www.ursulakleguin.com/nbf-medal.

Chapter 1

1. www.theguardian.com/global-development/2021/mar/09/female-workers-at-hm-supplier-in-india-allege-widespread-sexual-violence.

2. Friedrich Engels, *The Condition of the Working Class in England 1844*, 'The Great Towns'.

3. Eric M. Sigsworth, *Montague Burton: The Tailor of Taste*. Manchester University Press, 1990, p. vii.

4. Ibid., p. 28.

5. Diana de Marly, *Working Dress*. Holmes & Meier, 1986.

6. Ibid., p. 145.

7. Sigsworth, *Montague Burton*, p. 42.

8. *Wadsworth Review of Economic Studies*, quoted in Christopher Sladen, *The Conscription of Fashion*. Scholar Press, 1995, p. 11.

9. Ibid., p. 18.

10. Ibid., p. 23.

11. Ibid., p. 37.

12. Ibid., p. 39.

13. Alison Settle, *English Fashion*. Collins, 1959, p. 47.

14. J. Anderson Black and Madge Garland, *A History of Fashion*. McDonald (Black Cat imprint), 1990, p. 245.

15. Valerie Steele, *Paris Fashion*. Berg, 1988, p. 263.

16. Ibid., p. 269.

17. www.designmuseum.org/design/christian-dior.

18. Steele, *Paris Fashion*, p. 270.

19. *Harper's Bazaar*, February 2012.

20. Lindsey German, *Sex Class and Socialism*. Bookmarks, 1998, p. 105.

21. Steele, *Paris Fashion*, p. 274.

22. www.designmuseum.org/design/christian-dior.

23. Sladen, *The Conscription of Fashion*, p. 76.

24. Ibid., p. 76.
25. Kurt Lang and Gladys Engel Lang, 'The Power of Fashion', in Linda Welters and Abby Lillethun (eds), *The Fashion Reader*. Bloomsbury, 2007, p. 84.
26. Sladen, *The Conscription of Fashion*, p. 54.
27. George Orwell, *The Road to Wigan Pier*. Victor Gollancz, 1937, chapter 8.
28. Sladen, *The Conscription of Fashion*, p. 104.
29. Faulkner, *A Marxist History of the World*, p. 255.
30. Ibid., p. 253.
31. German, *Sex Class and Socialism*, p. 106.
32. Steele, *Paris Fashion*, p. 279.
33. Colin McDowell, *The Designer Scam*. Hutchinson and Random House, 1994, p. 20.
34. Tobé Coller Davis, 25th Annual Boston Conference on Distribution, 1953. Quoted in Jarrow and Judelle, *Inside the Fashion Business*, p. 246.
35. Jarrow and Judelle, *Inside the Fashion Business*, pp. 158, 160.
36. Ibid., p. 246.
37. Steele, *Paris Fashion*, p. 282.
38. www.mckinsey.com/business-functions/sustainability/our-insights/style-thats-sustainable-a-new-fast-fashion-formula.
39. www.vice.com/en/article/n7j43m/boohoocom-uploads-every-day-fast-fashion.
40. www.bbc.co.uk/news/world-55793575.
41. www.nytimes3xbfgragh.onion/2021/03/30/technology/amazon-market-size.html.
42. www.theguardian.com/fashion/2020/dec/03/christopher-wylie-amazon-is-one-of-the-biggest-threats-to-the-fashion-industry.
43. www.forbes.com/sites/pamdanziger/2020/01/28/amazon-is-readying-major-disruption-for-the-fashion-industry/.
44. www.retailgazette.co.uk/blog/2021/04/asos-profits-skyrocket-253-in-first-half-as-sales-almost-hit-2bn/.
45. www.thetimes.co.uk/article/mahmud-kamani-net-worth-sunday-times-rich-list-97r67xcp8#.

46. www.forbes.com/sites/markfaithfull/2021/02/10/shein-is-chinas-mysterious-15-billion-fast-fashion-retailer-ready-for-stores/.

47. www.publiceye.ch/en/media-corner/press-releases/detail/75-hour-weeks-for-shein-public-eye-looks-behind-the-chinese-online-fashion-giants-glitzy-front.

48. www.nytimes3xbfgragh.onion/2021/03/30/technology/amazon-market-size.html.

49. https://stories.publiceye.ch/respect-by-zara/.

50. www.forbes.com/billionaires/#page:1_sort:0_direction:asc_search:_filter:All%20industries_filter:All%20countries_filter:All%20states.

51. Lucy Siegle, *To Die for: Is Fast Fashion Wearing out the World?* Fourth Estate, 2011, p. 15.

52. www.thetimes.co.uk/article/weston-family-net-worth-sunday-times-rich-list-8ln5orjp6.

53. www.selfridges.com/GB/en/features/info/our-heritage/.

54. www.retailgazette.co.uk/blog/2021/10/selfridges-owners-in-talks-with-qatar-about-potential-4bn-sale/.

55. Sigsworth. *Montague Burton*, p. 98.

56. Naylor, *Crass Struggle*, p. 12.

57. www.bbc.co.uk/news/uk-58804504.

58. www.bbc.co.uk/news/business-39118566.

59. www.bbc.co.uk/news/business-54831374.

60. www.thetimes.co.uk/article/pandora-papers-lady-green-spent-millions-on-london-properties-as-bhs-collapsed-b9x9prvtf.

61. www.bbc.co.uk/news/uk-45987084.

62. www.telegraph.co.uk/news/2019/02/08/sir-philip-green-claims-revealed/.

63. www.bloomberg.com/news/articles/2014-02-26/ortega-s-zara-fashions-tax-avoidance-by-shifting-profits-to-alps.

64. https://wwd.com/business-news/financial/fashion-world-figures-panama-papers-10407011/.

65. www.forbes.com/profile/bernard-arnault.

66. Bernard Arnault, quoted in LVMH Net Boosted by Louis Vuitton, WWD Issue, 13 September 2003.

67. Thomas, *Deluxe*, p. 18.

68. *Libération*. www.wwd.com/business-news/business-features/newsmaker-of-the-year-nominees-6506060?page=2.

69. www.fashion.telegraph.co.uk/article/TMG9965759/Bernard-Arnault-Knighted-by-Prince-Charles.html.

70. www.bloomberg.com/features/2018-richest-families/.

71. Pierre Mallevays, interview, Savigny Partners, Business of Fashion website, 18 November 2009.

72. www.forbes.com/companies/kering/.

73. The Prada Group owns Prada, miu miu, Church's, and Car Shoes. Miuccia Prada's 2012 net worth is $5.6 billion as of June 2021.

74. The shoe company Jimmy Choo was founded in 1996 by the businesswoman Tamara Mellon and Jimmy Choo, a little-known shoemaker. Jimmy Choo left his namesake company and name in 2001 but was reportedly trying to buy them back with help from the Malaysian government in 2011 when Mellon sold to Labelux for over £500 million. In 2017 Michael Kors bought the brand for £896m.

75. https://fashionista.com/2021/06/maeve-reilly-stylist-career-interview.

76. www.businessoffashion.com/articles/luxury/chanel-11-billion-sales-dismisses-rumours.

77. Ibid.

78. McDowell, *The Designer Scam*, p. 5.

79. Thomas, *Deluxe*, p. 163.

80. Ibid., p. 168.

81. Thomas Maier, quoted in www.newyorker.com/reporting/2011/01/03/110103fa_fact_colapinto. The bag designer Luella Bartley also called It Bags 'the beginning of the end of culture in general'. Vogue.co.uk.

82. www.businesswire.com/news/home/20201117005990/en/Global-Luxury-Goods-Market-Report-2020-Market-to-Reach-403.2-Billion-by-2027---ResearchAndMarkets.com.

83. Thomas, *Deluxe*, p. 168.

84. Tansy Hoskins, *What Your Shoes Tell You About Globalisation*, Weidenfeld & Nicolson, 2020, p. 102.

85. www.bloomberg.com/billionaires/profiles/leonardo-del-vecchio/.

Notes

86. www.bain.com/globalassets/noindex/2020/bain_report_chinas_unstoppable_2020_luxury-market.pdf.

87. Faulkner, *Marxist History of the World*, p. 279.

88. Forbes, *Master of the Brand: Bernard Arnault*, 11 April 2010.

89. Richemont CEO Johann Rupert, www.businessinsider.com/how-the-10-biggest-luxury-brands-came-to-dominate-the-world-2012-6?op=1#i xzz2M6Y16Yhk.

90. www.bain.com/globalassets/noindex/2020/bain_report_chinas_unstoppable_2020_luxury-market.pdf.

91. www.vanityfair.com/style/2021/09/diet-prada-roasting-the-runway.

92. L. K. Cheng, 'Li & Fung, Ltd.: An Agent of Global Production', in L. K. Cheng and H. Kierzkowski (eds), *Global Production and Trade in East Asia*. Springer, 2001.

93. H. Faheem and D. Purkayastha, 'Li & Fung: Battling the Global Supply Chain Challenge'. *IUP Journal of Supply Chain Management* 17(4) (2020).

94. Ibid.

95. www.mckinsey.com/industries/retail/our-insights/state-of-fashion.

Chapter 2

1. Quoted in Fiona Sampson's *Two Way Mirror: The Life of Elizabeth Barrett Browning*. Profile Books, 2021, p. 35.

2. www.dazeddigital.com/fashion/article/53877/1/digital-fashion-clothing-industry-saviour-climate-sustainability-the-sims-avatar.

3. Cynthia L. White, *Women's Magazines 1693–1968*. Michael Joseph, 1970.

4. Jenny McKay, *The Magazines Handbook*. Routledge, 2006.

5. Caroline Seebohm, *The Man Who Was Vogue*. Weidenfeld & Nicolson, 1982, p. 38.

6. Ibid., p. 80. Condé Nast's underlining.

7. David Croteau and William Hoynes, *The Business of Media*. Pine Forge Press, 2001, p. 4.

8. Newcombe, interview.

9. Croteau and Hoynes, *The Business of Media*, p. 4.

10. Benjamin M. Compaine and Douglas Gomary, *Who Owns the Media?* Lawrence Erlbaum, 2000, p. 151.

11. Jackie Newcombe, interview, former managing director of IPC Southbank, 16 May 2012.

12. Dallas Walker Smythe, *Dependency Road: Communications, Capitalism and Canada*. Ablex, 1982, p. 37.

13. McKay, *The Magazine Handbook*, p. 200.

14. Olivia Whitehorne, *Cosmo Woman*. Crescent Moon, 2007, p. 82.

15. Eric Clark, *The Want Makers*. Hodder & Stoughton, 1988, p. 350.

16. Robert Merton, *Paul Lazarfeld*, 1948, quoted in Smythe, *Dependency Road*, p. 18.

17. Gloria Steinham, *Moving beyond Words: Age, Rage, Sex, Power, Money, Muscles – Breaking the Boundaries of Gender*. Touchstone, 1994.

18. Richard Shortway, quoted in McKay, *The Magazine Handbook*, p. 200.

19. http://vestoj.com/will-i-get-a-ticket/.

20. I am grateful here to points made by Cameron Joshi, youth engagement officer at Global Justice Now for comments made during a May 2021 Media Reform Coalition event: Protest, Dissent and the Media.

21. I am grateful here to the author Marcus Gilroy Ware for points made at the May 2021 Media Reform Coalition event: Protest, Dissent and the Media.

22. Simone Werle, *Style Diaries: World Fashion from Berlin to Tokyo*. Prestel, 2010, introduction.

23. https://dictionary.cambridge.org/dictionary/english/influencer.

24. https://digitalnative.substack.com/p/onlyfans-and-the-evolution-of-the.

25. Professor Jodi Dean – www.artandeducation.net/classroom/video/174211/jodi-dean-the-limits-of-the-web-in-an-age-of-communicative-capitalism.

26. Ibid.

27. https://dismantlemag.com/2021/05/10/love-island-labor-reality-tv-influencer-pipeline/.

28. Tavi Gevinson, interview, *Business of Fashion*, April 2012.

29. Christian Fuchs, *The Internet: Serving the revolution?* Counterfire. org, 2010.

30. Fuchs, *The Internet*.

31. www.statista.com/statistics/264810/number-of-monthly-active-facebook-users-worldwide/.

32. Jaron Lanier, *Ten Arguments for Deleting Your Social Media Accounts Right Now*. Penguin, 2018, p. 26.

33. Ibid., p. 26. For 'behaviour modification empires' see ibid., p. 8.

34. https://news.harvard.edu/gazette/story/2019/03/harvard-professor-says-surveillance-capitalism-is-undermining-democracy/.

35. https://privacybadger.org/files/pb_journalist_1_pager.pdf.

36. www.eff.org/deeplinks/2009/09/online-trackers-and-social-networks. For this experiment on 19 October 2021, I accepted the suggested cookies and used Google to get into, and move between, sites.

37. www.vox.com/recode/2021/3/3/22311460/google-cookie-ban-search-ads-tracking.

38. www.marxists.org/archive/marx/works/1844/manuscripts/needs.htm.

39. https://newint.org/features/2018/01/01/social-media-mental-health.

40. www.marxists.org/archive/marx/works/1844/manuscripts/needs.htm.

41. https://edition.cnn.com/2017/05/19/health/instagram-worst-social-network-app-young-people-mental-health/index.html.

42. www.wsj.com/articles/facebook-knows-instagram-is-toxic-for-teen-girls-company-documents-show-11631620739.

43. Ibid.

44. Mészáros, *Marx's Theory of Alienation*, p. 144.

45. Ibid., p. 148.

46. Lanier, *Ten Arguments*, p. 27.

47. www.huffingtonpost.co.uk/entry/black-influencer-pay-gap_uk_5ef32959c5b6aa825ac96254.

48. Lanier, *Ten Arguments*, p. 82.

49. https://news.harvard.edu/gazette/story/2019/03/harvard-professor-says-surveillance-capitalism-is-undermining-democracy/.

50. www.creativelivesinprogress.com/article/handsome-frank-instagram.

51. www.theguardian.com/commentisfree/2018/mar/27/pioneer-delete-facebook-addiction-social-life.

52. I recommend this 'Culture Therapist' advice column by Megan O'Grady: www.nytimes.com/2020/03/04/t-magazine/artists-creativity-social-media.html .

53. https://commonconf.files.wordpress.com/2010/09/proofs-of-tech-fetish.pdf and Jodi Dean, *Democracy and Other Neoliberal Fantasies: Communicative Capitalism and Left Politics*. Duke University Press, 2009.

54. www.youtube.com/watch?v=Ly_uN3zbQSU&t=1841s.

55. www.artandeducation.net/classroom/video/174211/jodi-dean-the-limits-of-the-web-in-an-age-of-communicative-capitalism.

56. https://blog.p2pfoundation.net/the-trap-of-communicative-capitalism/2009/07/05, https://commonconf.files.wordpress.com/2010/09/proofs-of-tech-fetish.pdf, and Dean, *Democracy and Other Neoliberal Fantasies*.

57. https://commonconf.files.wordpress.com/2010/09/proofs-of-tech-fetish.pdf.

58. https://commonconf.files.wordpress.com/2010/09/proofs-of-tech-fetish.pdf.

59. Lola Olufemi, *Feminism Interrupted*. Pluto Press, 2020, p. 20.

60. www.theguardian.com/global-development/2021/mar/09/female-workers-at-hm-supplier-in-india-allege-widespread-sexual-violence.

61. www.manchestereveningnews.co.uk/news/greater-manchester-news/nhs-pay-protest-somehow-ended-19985224.

62. https://globallaborjustice.org/justice-for-jeyasre-vigil/.

63. www.artandeducation.net/classroom/video/174211/jodi-dean-the-limits-of-the-web-in-an-age-of-communicative-capitalism.

64. Ibid.

Chapter 3

1. Anne Fogarty, *The Art of Being a Well-Dressed Wife*, 1959. Reprinted V&A Enterprises, 2011.

2. Frederich Engels, *Outlines of a Critique of Political Economy*, 1844.

3. Benjamin Barber, quoted in Hoskins, *Foot Work*, p. 35.

4. www.social-europe.eu/2011/08/the-london-riots-on-consumerism-coming-home-to-roost.

5. www.guardian.co.uk/uk/2011/sep/05/riot-jail-sentences-crown-courts.www.telegraph.co.uk/news/uknews/crime/8695988/London-riots-Lidl-water-thief-jailed-for-six-months.html.

6. www.social-europe.eu/2011/08/the-london-riots-on-consumerism-coming-home-to-roost.

7. www.businesswire.com/news/home/20201117005990/en/Global-Luxury-Goods-Market-Report-2020-Market-to-Reach-403.2-Billion-by-2027---ResearchAndMarkets.com.

8. Juliet B. Schor, Why Do We Consume So Much? p. 3, www.csbsju.edu/Academics/Lecture-Series/Clemens-Lecture-Series/Past-Lectures/Schor.htm.

9. Simonetta Falasca-Zamponi, *Waste and Consumption*. Routledge, 2007, p. 16.

10. www.rt.com/usa/half-poor-america-poverty-909.

11. Alan Tomlinson (ed.), *Consumption, Identity and Style: Marketing, Meanings and the Packaging of Pleasure*. Routledge, 1991, p. 13.

12. www.thesartorialist.com/photos/not-giving-up-nyc.

13. www.threadbared.blogspot.co.uk/2009/09/tramp-chic-and-photo graph.html. Founded by academics Minh-Ha T. Pham and Mimi Thi Nguyen.

14. Engels, 'The Great Towns', in *The Conditions of the Working Class*, 1845.

15. Barnard, *Fashion as Communication*, pp. 107, 145, and chapter 1.

16. An eighteenth-century commentator, quoted in Ibid., p. 107.

17. Tamsin Blanchard, *Green Is the New Black*. Hodder & Stoughton, 2007, p. xi.

18. Juliet Schor, 'In Defence of Consumer Critique: Revisiting the Consumption Debates of the Twentieth Century'. *Annals of the American Academy of Political and Social Science*, 2007.

19. Elizabeth Wilson, *Adorned in Dreams*. Virago, 1985, p. 17.

20. Karl Marx, *The Poverty of Philosophy*, 1847, pp. 41–2.

21. Suj Jhally, *The Codes of Advertising*. Routledge, 1990, p. 2.

22. Nicholas Barbon, *A Discourse of Trade*, 1690. Quoted by Ulrich Lehmann in 'Fashion and Materialism', Marxism in Culture lecture, Senate House, 15 June 2012.

23. Karl Marx, *Outline of the Critique of Political Economy* (*Grundrisse*) www.marxists.org/archive/marx/works/1857/grundrisse/cho1.htm.

24. Ingrid Loschek, *When Clothes Become Fashion: Design and Innovation Systems*. Berg, 2009, p. 135.

25. John Bellamy Foster, Brett Clark, and Richard York, *The Ecological Rift: Capitalism's War on the Earth*. Monthly Review Press, 2010, p. 392.

26. Real value 'existing in a haunted form' – from Marcus Gilroy-Ware speaking at Protest, Dissent and the Media, Media Reform Coalition, May 2021.

27. Bellamy Foster, Clark, and York, *The Ecological Rift*, p. 394.

28. Ibid.

29. www.mckinsey.com/industries/retail/our-insights/state-of-fashion.

30. Jhally, *The Codes of Advertising*, p. 2.

31. https://news.sky.com/story/covid-19-christmas-shoppers-flood-high-streets-in-return-after-lockdown-12152120.

32. Croteau and Hoynes, *The Business of Media*, p. 180.

33. Mészáros, *Marx's Theory of Alienation*, p. 145, quoting Marx.

34. Ashley Mears, *Pricing Beauty*. University of California Press, 2011, p. 75.

35. *British Vogue*, November 2011, p. 111.

36. *Times* Online, Style Article 3304394.

37. www.vogue.co.uk/news/2009/07/17/the-truth-about-fashion-in-a-recession.

38. *Stylist*, Issue 100, 2 November 2011.

39. www.wsj.com/articles/did-catherine-deneuve-design-the-ultimate-zoom-shirt-11607976513.

40. Berger, *Ways of Seeing*.

41. www.dressforsuccess.org/whatwedo_suits.aspx.

42. Joseph Hansen and Evelyn Reed, *Cosmetics, Fashions, and the Exploitation of Women*, Pathfinder Press, 1986, p. 51.

43. Ibid., p. 39.

44. Sandra Lee Bartky, *Femininity and Domination*. Routledge, 1990, p. 75.

45. Ibid., p. 71.

46. G. K. Chesterton, *The New Jerusalem* [1920], 2012, chapter 4.

47. www.statista.com/topics/990/global-advertising-market/.

48. John O'Toole, *The Trouble with Advertising*, quoted in Clark, *The Want Makers*, p. 17.

49. David Norman and Guy Shrubsole, *Think of Me as Evil?* WWF and the Public Interest Research Centre Report, 2011, p. 18.

50. Mészáros, *Marx's Theory of Alienation*, p. 144.

51. Faulkner, interview.

52. Berger, *Ways of Seeing*, p. 125.

53. Ibid., p. 143.

54. Jarrow and Judelle, *Inside the Fashion Business*, p. 256.

55. www.debt.org/faqs/americans-in-debt/.

56. www.wsj.com/articles/SB10001424052748704396504576204553811636610.

57. https://eu.clarionledger.com/in-depth/news/local/2020/01/09/debtors-prison-miss-still-sends-people-jail-unpaid-debt/2742853001/.

58. Lawrence M. Berger, J. Michael Collins, and Laura Cuesta, 'Household Debt and Adult Depressive Symptoms'. *SSRN Electronic Journal* 2013; A. Hiilamo and E. Grundy, 'Household Debt and Depressive Symptoms among Older Adults in Three Continental European Countries'. *Ageing and Society*, 2018.

59. As debt levels rise and the cost of debt becomes unsustainable, crises inevitably arise.

60. Larry Elliott and Dan Atkinson, *The Gods That Failed*. The Bodley Head, 2008, p. 164.

61. 'Ring-a-Ding-Ding', *Sex and the City*, episode 64, season 4.

62. https://tribunemag.co.uk/2020/03/david-harvey-anti-capitalist-politics-in-an-age-of-covid-19.

63. www.manchestereveningnews.co.uk/news/money-saving/martin-lewis-issues-warning-against-19776658.

64. https://tribunemag.co.uk/2021/03/the-fashion-debt-trap.

65. www.stepchange.org/policy-and-research/covid-impact-report-jan-2021.aspx.

66. www.cnbc.com/2020/09/14/klarna-now-europes-biggest-fintech-unicorn-at-over-10-billion-value.html and www.cnbc.com/2021/05/27/softbank-to-back-klarna-in-a-round-that-values-it-at-over-40-billion.html.

67. www.workersrights.org/wp-content/uploads/2020/11/Hunger-in-the-Apparel-Supply-Chain.pdf.

68. Matt Haig, *Brand Success: How the World's Top 100 Brands Thrive and Survive*, 2nd edition. Kogan Page, 2011, p. 117.

69. Jhally, *The Codes of Advertising*, pp. 53–4.

70. Friedrich Engels, *Outlines of a Critique of Political Economy* in Mészáros, *Marx's Theory of Alienation*, p. 158.

71. Dr Juliet Schor, interview, from Hoskins, *Foot Work*, p. 24.

72. Ibid., p. 204.

73. Berger, *Ways of Seeing*, part 4.

74. Marx, in Mészáros, *Marx's Theory of Alienation*, p. 130.

75. Opening lines of Patrick Hamilton's novel *Slaves of Solitude*. Constable, 2006.

76. Hoskins, *Foot Work*, p. 47.

77. Marx, in Mészáros, *Marx's Theory of Alienation*, p. 145.

78. Ibid., p. 158.

79. Raymond Williams, in Bellamy Foster, Clark, and York, *The Ecological Rift*, p. 393.

80. John Bellamy Foster, *Marx's Ecology*. Monthly Review Press, 2000, p. 2.

81. Mears, *Pricing Beauty*, p. 25.

82. www.publiceye.ch/en/topics/fashion/what-makes-up-the-price-of-a-zara-hoody.

83. www.social-europe.eu/2011/08/the-london-riots-on-consumerism-coming-home-to-roost.

84. Ben Fine, *The World of Consumption: The Material and Cultural Revisited*. Routledge, 2002, p. 66.
85. Mészáros, *Marx's Theory of Alienation*, p. 156.
86. www.robertmontgomery.org.

Chapter 4

1. Interview, December 2014.
2. https://tansyhoskins.org/rana-plaza-imperialism-vs-internationalism/.
3. www.livemint.com/Companies/HNZA71LNVNNVXQ1eaIKu6M/British-Raj-siphoned-out-45-trillion-from-India-Utsa-Patna.html.
4. www.ilo.org/dhaka/Areasofwork/working-conditions/lang--en/index.htm.
5. After Percy Bysshe Shelley: 'Monarchy is only the string that ties the robber's bundle.'
6. Interview, December 2014.
7. www.nytimes3xbfgragh.onion/2012/09/10/world/asia/killing-of-bangladesh-labor-leader-spotlights-grievances-of-workers.html.
8. https://i-d.vice.com/en_uk/article/ywv9wg/in-bangladesh-the-people-who-make-your-clothes-are-striking-for-their-rights.
9. www.thedailystar.net/star-weekend/spotlight/news/dispensable-demands-disposable-lives-1688998.
10. Sanchita Banerjee Saxena (ed.) *Labor, Global Supply Chains, and the Garment Indry in South Asia: Bangladesh after Rana Plaza.* Routledge, 2020, chapter 4.
11. Ibid., p. 1.
12. www.businessoffashion.com/opinions/news-analysis/op-ed-preventing-another-rana-plaza.
13. https://bangladeshaccord.org/.
14. www.workersrights.org/wp-content/uploads/2021/05/CGWR2017ResearchReportBindingPower.pdf.
15. Banerjee Saxena, *Labor, Global Supply Chains*, p. 1.
16. www.workersrights.org/wp-content/uploads/2021/05/CGWR2017ResearchReportBindingPower.pdf.

17. https://cleanclothes.org/news/2020/garment-workers-on-poverty-pay-are-left-without-billions-of-their-wages-during-pandemic.

18. Michael Piore, 'The Economics of Sweatshops', in Andrew Ross (ed.), *No Sweat: Fashion, Free Trade, and the Rights of Garment Workers*. Verso, 1997, pp. 135–42, quoted in www.workersrights.org/wp-content/uploads/2021/05/CGWR2017Research ReportBindingPower.pdf.

19. www.workersrights.org/wp-content/uploads/2021/05/CGWR2017ResearchReportBindingPower.pdf.

20. Ibid.

21. Slavoj Žižek, *Violence: Six Sideways Reflections*. Profile Books, 2009, p. 1.

22. Sixty million is an ILO estimate – http://um.dk/~/media/UM/English-site/Documents/Danida/About-Danida/Danida%20 transparency/Documents/U%2037/2018/ILO%20Better%20 Work.pdf?la=en.

23. www.marxists.org/archive/marx/works/1867-c1/ch31.htm.

24. Žižek, *Violence*, p. 8.

25. www.somo.nl/spinning-around-workers-rights/.

26. Bent Gehrt, interview, 2020.

27. Ibid.

28. www.opendemocracy.net/en/oureconomy/report-says-soldiers-shot-three-dead-myanmar-factory-making-us-cowboy-boots/.

29. https://cleanclothes.org/news/2021/clean-clothes-campaign-condemns-silence-of-garment-brands-on-myanmar-atrocities.

30. www.solidaritycenter.org/guatemala-another-union-leader-murdered/.

31. The Red de Defensores de Derechos Laborales de Guatemala (Network of Labor Rights Defenders of Guatemala), *Annual Report on Anti-Union Violence in Guatemala*, 2019.

32. www.wiego.org/informal-economy/occupational-groups/home-based-workers.

33. https://hnsa.org.in/resources/research-violence-against-women-context-home-based-work-nepal.

34. www.metmuseum.org/toah/works-of-art/156.4J23.

35. Engels, *The Condition of the Working Class in England*.

Notes

36. www.radicalmanchester.wordpress.com.

37. Engels, *The Condition of the Working Class in England*.

38. Karen Tranberg Hansen, *Salaula: The World of Second Hand Clothing and Zambia*. University of Chicago Press, 2000, p. 24.

39. Ibid., p. 9.

40. www.bbc.com/future/article/20210316-the-legendary-fabric-that-no-one-knows-how-to-make.

41. Ross, *Slaves to Fashion*, p. 18.

42. Lisa Featherstone and USAS, *Students against Sweatshops*. Verso, 2000, p. 71.

43. V. Roscigno and W. Danaher, 'Media and Mobilization: The Case of Radio and Southern Textile Worker Insurgency, 1929 to 1934'. *American Sociological Review* 66(1) (2001), 21–48.

44. Hoskins, *Foot Work*, p. 228.

45. Jewish Women's Archive: www.jwa.org/encyclopedia/article/shavelson-clara-lemlich; American Postal Workers' Union archive: www.apwu.org/join/women/lbportraits/portraits-labor-triangle.htm; PBS archive: www. pbs.org/wgbh/americanexperience/features/biography/triangle-lemlich.

46. Ross, *Slaves to Fashion*, p. 64.

47. Ibid., p. 54.

48. https://link.springer.com/chapter/10.1007/978-3-030-73835-8_2.

49. www.ecchr.eu/fileadmin/Fallbeschreibungen/CaseReport_KiK_RINA_December2020.pdf.

50. www.guardian.co.uk/commentisfree/2012/sep/14/karachi-factory-fire-pakistan-health-safety.

51. www.spiegel.de/international/world/criticism-over-damages-offered-by-german-discounter-for-pakistani-dead-a-862918.html.

52. Ross, *Slaves to Fashion*, p. 69.

53. Hoskins, *Foot Work*, pp. 55–6.

54. Ross, *Slaves to Fashion*, p. 103. The term 'global scanning' is from Raymond Vernon, 'The Product Cycle Hypothesis in a New International Environment', *Oxford Bulletin of Economics and Statistics* 44(2) (1979): 255–67; global scanning is also used to search for sales sites.

55. Liesbeth Sluiter, *Clean Clothes*. Pluto Press, 2009, p. 39.

56. Cattaneo, Gereffi, and Staritz, *Global Value Chains in a Post-crisis World*, p. 174.

57. Ibid., p. 174.

58. Ross, *Slaves to Fashion*, pp. 140–3. In January 2004, 30,000 Saipan garment workers won a landmark $20 million settlement after 26 US retailers and 23 Saipan factories were sued by labour rights organisations for human rights violations. Retailers included Gap, which was responsible for $200 million of production in Saipan, a fifth of the island's output.

59. Sluiter, *Clean Clothes*, p. 40.

60. Yongzheng Yang, 'The Impact of MFA Phasing out on World Clothing and Textile Markets'. *Journal of Development Studies* 30(4) (1994), 892–915.

61. Cattaneo, Gereffi, and Staritz, *Global Value Chains in a Post-crisis World*, p. 159.

62. www.current.com/shows/vanguard/89785807_battle-of-saipan.htm.

63. Sluiter, *Clean Clothes*, p. 76.

64. Cattaneo, Gereffi, and Staritz, *Global Value Chains in a Post-crisis World*, p. 183.

65. Ibid., p. 198, table.

66. Ibid.

67. Nicholas D. Kristof and Sheryl Wudunn, 'Two Cheers for Sweatshops'. *New York Times*, 24 September 2000.

68. Hapke, *Sweatshop*, p. 1.

69. www.simpletoremember.com/articles/a/jewish_life_in_america. As a result tuberculosis became known as 'the tailor's disease'. Vast commercial laundries were set up, and it was these, with their sweltering, unsanitary conditions, that probably inspired the name 'sweatshop'.

70. Ross, *Slaves to Fashion*, p. 177.

71. www.thenation.com/article/161057/wikileaks-haiti-let-them-live-3-day.

72. www.dawn.com/news/703595/capitalism-a-ghost-story-2.

73. www.fpif.org/articles/rethinking_sweatshop_economics.

74. Faulkner, interview. The concept is from Karl Marx, *Capital*, volume 1. Progress Press, 1887, chapter 25.

Chapter 5

1. Environmental Justice Foundation, http://archive.is/QRrp.
2. IPE, *Cleaning up the Fashion Industry*, www.ipe.org.cn.
3. www.blogs.ei.columbia.edu/2011/05/05/how-china-is-dealing-with-its-water-crisis.
4. IPE, *Cleaning up the Fashion Industry*.
5. www.theaustralian.com.au/news/breaking-news/croc-farmer-decries-carbon-tax-impost/story-fn3dxiwe-1226462688596.
6. www.independent.co.uk/environment/crocodile-farms-is-it-cruel-to-keep-these-wild-creatures-captive-418794.html.
7. Bhopal Medical Appeal, 1994, www.studentsforbhopal.org/node/18.
8. István Mészáros, *Beyond Capital*. Merlin Press, 1995. Capital 'inevitably brings a bitter harvest'.
9. https://ejfoundation.org/resources/downloads/ejf_uzbek_harvest_WEB.pdf.
10. Ibid.
11. www.ejfoundation.org/cotton/white-gold.
12. www.hrw.org/world-report/2021/country-chapters/uzbekistan.
13. www.uzbekforum.org/wp-content/uploads/2020/10/Uzbekistan_Cotton_Harvest_2020.pdf.
14. www.ncbi.nlm.nih.gov/pmc/articles/PMC6056267/.
15. IPE, *Cleaning up the Fashion Industry* and www.ncbi.nlm.nih.gov/pmc/articles/PMC6056267/.
16. www.newsweek.com/river-red-china-1007818.
17. https://edition.cnn.com/style/article/dyeing-pollution-fashion-intl-hnk-dst-sept/index.html.
18. www.cdp.net/en/research/global-reports/interwoven-risks-untapped-opportunities.
19. https://riverbluethemovie.eco/.
20. www.independent.co.uk/environment/crocodile-farms-is-it-cruel-to-keep-these-wild-creatures-captive-418794.html.
21. www.scientificamerican.com/article.cfm?id=croc-unlocked-a-gene-map.

22. https://fashionunited.uk/news/business/hermes-posts-16-percent-revenue-growth-in-q4/2021021953731.

23. www.toxipedia.org/display/toxipedia/Aldicarb.

24. www.bhopal.net/what-happened/that-night-december-3–1984/the-death-toll/.

25. National Research Council, *The Use and Storage of Methyl Isocyanate (MIC) at Bayer CropScience*. Washington, DC, The National Academies Press, 2012.

26. Over half a million people were injured in the disaster and the area remains contaminated. Not until 2010 was anyone convicted of a criminal offence, when eight Indian Union Carbide executives received two-year prison sentences and fines of $2,100. Warren Anderson, CEO of Union Carbide, has not been prosecuted despite attempts to extradite him to India. http://bhopal.net.

27. www.bhopal.org/continuing-disaster/the-bhopal-gas-disaster/union-carbides-disaster/.

28. Carson, *Silent Spring*, p. 16.

29. www.fdacs.gov/News-Events/Press-Releases/2021-Press-Releases/FDACS-Issues-Denial-of-Aldicarb-Pesticide-Usage-Application-in-Florida.

30. www.environmentalhealthnews.org/ehs/news/aldicarb-phaseout.

31. www.bbc.co.uk/news/science-environment-57863205.

32. Kate Fletcher and Mathilda Tham, *Earth Logic: Fashion Action Research Plan*. JJ Charitable Trust, 2019, pp. 22–3. This book is upfront about avoiding 'approaches that are not systemic and holistic' because they aren't radical enough, won't bring actual change, and 'pose the risk of deferring radical change by instilling a false sense of progress'.

33. Azuma Makoto, interview, *Matto Magazine*, Issue 5 (2021).

34. Interview with Dilys Williams, director of the Center for Sustainable Fashion, 23 November 2012.

35. John Bellamy Foster, *Ecology against Capitalism*. Monthly Review Press, 2002, p. 80.

36. Bellamy Foster, Clark, and York, *The Ecological Rift*, p. 78.

Notes

37. David Harvey, quoted in Fred Magdoff and John Bellamy Foster, *What Every Environmentalist Needs to Know about Capitalism*. Monthly Review Press, 2011, p. 97.

38. The environmental ecologist K. William Kapp, quoted in Bellamy Foster, *Ecology against Capitalism*, p. 57.

39. www.theguardian.com/environment/2018/oct/08/global-warming-must-not-exceed-15c-warns-landmark-un-report.

40. Ibid., pp. 105–6.

41. http://changingmarkets.org/wp-content/uploads/2021/06/CM-EX-SUM-FINAL-ENGLISH-SYNTETHIC-ANONYMOUS-WEB-.pdf.

42. Interview quote – Dr Michelle Murphy, February 2022.

43. www.vox.com/the-goods/2020/1/27/21080107/fashion-environment-facts-statistics-impact.

44. https://technoscienceunit.org/people/lab/.

45. https://theconversation.com/why-pollution-is-as-much-about-colonialism-as-chemicals-dont-call-me-resilient-transcript-ep-11-170697.

46. Bellamy Foster, Clark, and York, *The Ecological Rift*, p. 394.

47. Ibid., p. 39.

48. Ibid., p. 64.

49. Juliet Schor, 'The New Politics of Consumption: Why Americans Want So Much More than They Need'. *Boston Review*, Summer 1999, https://pages.ucsd.edu/~aronatas/Schor%20et%20al%20New%20Politics%20of%20Consumption%201999.pdf.

50. www.dailymail.co.uk/femail/article-482849/Pythons-skinned-left-die-The-shocking-reality-fashions-new-obsession.html.

51. https://api.worldanimalprotection.org/country/china.

52. Riley Kucheran with Jessica P. Clark and Nigel Lezama, 'Luxury and Indigenous Resurgence', in Jessica P. Clark and Nigel Lezama (eds), *Decentring Luxury*. Canadian Critical Luxury Studies, Intellect, 2022.

53. https://ifwtoronto.com/.

54. Siegle, *To Die for*, pp. 193–4. Chapter 9 refutes 'fur is ethical/warm/vintage/sustainable' arguments.

55. Magdoff and Bellamy Foster, *What Every Environmentalist Needs to Know about Capitalism*, p. 101.

56. Bellamy Foster, *Ecology against Capitalism*, p. 55.
57. Magdoff and Bellamy Foster, *What Every Environmentalist Needs to Know about Capitalism*, p. 101.
58. Bertell Ollman, *Alienation: Marx's Conception of Man in Capitalist Society*. Cambridge University Press, 1976, p. 135.
59. Bellamy Foster, *Ecology against Capitalism*, p. 81.
60. John Bellamy Foster, 'Marx's Ecology and Its Historical Significance', in Michael R. Redclift and Graham Woodgate (eds), *The International Handbook of Environmental Sociology*, 2nd edition. Edward Elgar, 2000, p. 106.
61. Karl Marx, *The Poverty of Philosophy*, pp. 41–2, quoted in Ibid., p. 383.
62. Bartky, *Femininity and Domination*, p. 72.
63. Falasca-Zamponi, *Waste and Consumption*, p. 48.
64. Bellamy Foster, Clark, and York, *The Ecological Rift*, p. 101.
65. Ibid., preface.
66. www.somo.nl/spinning-around-workers-rights/.
67. Ibid., p. 101.
68. Riley Kucheran, www.cbc.ca/radio/unreserved/indigenous-fashion-the-politics-of-ribbon-skirts-runways-and-resilience-1.6034149 .
69. Jessica P. Clark, 'Putting Canada on the Map: A Brief History of Nation and Luxury', in Clark and Lezama, *Decentring Luxury*.
70. Leanne Betasamosake Simpson, 'The Brilliance of Beavers: Learning from an Anishinaabe World', *CBC Ideas* (2020), www.cbc.ca/radio/ideas/the-brilliance-of-the-beaver-learning-from-an-anishnaabe-world-1.5534706.
71. Leanne Betasamosake Simpson, *Dancing on Our Turtle's Back: Stories of Nishnaabeg Re-creation, Resurgence and a New Emergence*. ARP, 2011.
72. Riley Kucheran, 'Indigenizing Fashion Education: Strong Hearts to the Front of the Classroom', in Ben Barry and Deborah Christel (eds), *Fashion Education: The Systemic Revolution*. Intellect, Forthcoming.
73. https://ricochet.media/en/1863/arthur-manuels-battle-against-the-02-per-cent-indigenous-economy.

74. www.aljazeera.com/features/longform/2021/11/8/the-stench-of-death-life-along-canadas-highway-of-tears.

75. Ibid.

76. 'Land Back', A Yellowhead Institute Red Paper, October 2019, https://redpaper.yellowheadinstitute.org/wp-content/uploads/2019/10/red-paper-report-final.pdf.

77. www.aljazeera.com/features/longform/2021/11/8/the-stench-of-death-life-along-canadas-highway-of-tears.

78. www.theguardian.com/world/ng-interactive/2021/sep/06/canada-residential-schools-indigenous-children-cultural-genocide-map.

79. 'Indigenous Fashionology with Riley Kucheran', *Ologies Podcast*, 11 November 2020.

80. www.cbc.ca/news/indigenous/residential-school-children-deaths-numbers-1.6182456.

81. 'Land Back', A Yellowhead Institute Red Paper.

82. Riley Kucheran, www.youtube.com/watch?v=WRfPKtfVFHI.

83. Kucheran, 'Indigenizing Fashion Education'.

84. Bellamy Foster, *Ecology against Capitalism*, p. 25.

Chapter 6

1. Susie Orbach, *Bodies*. Profile Books, 2010, p. 92.

2. www.iheartthreadbared.wordpress.com/2013/01/07/ashion-and-americas-culture-of-violence.

3. www.mckinsey.com/industries/retail/our-insights/state-of-fashion.

4. Orbach, *Bodies*, p. 7.

5. www.guardian.co.uk/theguardian/2012/feb/04/jo-swinson-interview.

6. www.beateatingdisorders.org.uk/about-beat/policy-work/policy-and-best-practice-reports/prevalence-in-the-uk/.

7. www.mind.org.uk/information-support/types-of-mental-health-problems/eating-problems/types-of-eating-disorders/.

8. www.any-body.org. Orbach, speech to the UN Commission on the Status of Women, 6 March 2012.

9. Orbach, *Bodies*, p. 137.

10. Ibid., p. 89.
11. Ibid., p. 81.
12. Jean Kilbourne documentary, *Killing Us Softly*.
13. Bartky, *Femininity and Domination*, p. 72.
14. www.businessoffashion.com/2013/04/10-of-londons-top-young-fashion-creatives.html#comment-770561.
15. Ibid.
16. Report: *Fashioning a Response: Results from the COVID-19 Survey and a Call to Action* 2020, www.modelalliance.org/published.
17. Ibid.
18. Ibid.
19. Ibid.
20. www.spiegel.de/international/spiegel/spiegel-interview-with-plus-size-model-i-was-asking-how-many-calories-chewing-gum-had-a-653745.html.
21. www.proud2bme.org/node/159.
22. Mears, *Pricing Beauty*, pp. 182–3.
23. Ann Hollander, *Seeing through Clothes*, p. 151, quoted ibid., p. 184.
24. www.independent.co.uk/news/the-model-agencies-say-one-of-these-girls-is-the-proper-shape-and-the-other-is-too-fat-are-they-right-1312076.html.
25. Mears, *Pricing Beauty*, p. 183.
26. www.abcnews.go.com/blogs/headlines/2012/01/most-models-meet-criteria-for-anorexia-size-6-is-plus-size-magazine.
27. Dunja Knezevic, interview, president of The Models' Union, 17 September 2012.
28. Mears, *Pricing Beauty*, p. 183.
29. www.spiegel.de/international/spiegel/spiegel-interview-with-plus-size-model-i-was-asking-how-many-calories-chewing-gum-had-a-653745.html.
30. Knezevic, interview.
31. The World Health Organisation considers anyone with a BMI of 16 or less to be starving. Luisel Ramos's BMI was 14.5 and Ana Carolina Reston's was 13.4. Controversy remains around the usefulness of BMI in assessing health. Recent work by the Model Alliance has found that assessing BMI is less useful than providing proper breaks and food on shoots.

Notes

32. http://fashion.telegraph.co.uk/news-features/TMG10701240/Nobody-wants-a-real-person-on-the-cover-of-Vogue-editor-says.html.

33. www.dailymail.co.uk/femail/article-433829/Size-zero-hysteria-London-Fashion-Week.html#ixzz22qoh8xHZ.

34. Joan Costa-Font and Mireia Jofre-Bonet, 'Anorexia, Body Image and Peer Effects: Evidence from a Sample of European Women'. Centre for Economic Performance, Discussion Paper No. 1098, November 2011.

35. Knezevic, interview.

36. Ibid.

37. Ollman, *Alienation*, p. 166.

38. Karl Marx, *Economic and Philosophical Manuscripts of 1844*, www.marxists.org/archive/marx/works/1844/manuscripts/preface.htm.

39. Marx, *Capital*, volume 1.

40. Eagleton, *After Theory*, p. 42.

41. Knezevic, interview.

42. Bellamy Foster, Clark, and York, *The Ecological Rift*, p. 392.

43. Knezevic, interview.

44. Ross, *Slaves to Fashion*, pp. 21–3.

45. Bartky, *Femininity and Domination*, p. 73.

46. Knezevic, interview.

47. Tansy Hoskins, *Stitched Up: The Anti-Capitalist Book of Fashion*. Pluto Press, 2014, p. 123.

48. www.ellecanada.com/living/culture/can-using-different-types-of-models-benefit-brands/a/58327.

49. Rachel Rogers, Sara Ziff, Alice Lowy, and S. Bryn Austin, 'Disordered Eating Behaviors and Sexual Objectification during New York Fashion Week: Implementation of Industry Policies and Legislation'. *International Journal of Eating Disorders* 54(3) (2020).

50. Orbach, *Bodies*, p. 94.

51. Susie Orbach, 'Ad Men Today Are Wrong on Body Size', www.any-body.org.

52. Orbach, *Bodies*, p. 94.

53. Ibid., p. 89.

54. Ibid., p. 12.

55. Karl Lagerfeld, interview, CNN; www.ellecanada.com/living/culture/can-using-different-types-of-models-benefit-brands/a/58327.

56. www.ellecanada.com/living/culture/can-using-different-types-of-models-benefit-brands/a/58327.

57. Ollman, *Alienation*, p. 135.

58. Magdoff and Bellamy Foster, *What Every Environmentalist Needs to Know about* Capitalism, p. 101.

59. Ruth Frankenburg (ed.), *Displacing Whiteness*. Duke University Press, 1997, p. 13.

60. Bartky, *Femininity and Domination*, p. 65.

61. Ibid., p. 79.

62. www.dictionaryblog.cambridge.org/category/new-words.

63. www.hup.harvard.edu/catalog.php?isbn=9780674049307.

64. www.iheartthreadbared.wordpress.com/2013/01/07/ashion-and-americas-culture-of-violence.

65. Eagleton, *After Theory*, p. 67.

66. https://franklinonfashion.com/challenging-known-fashion-predator-terry-richardson/ and www.artforum.com/news/fashion-photographer-terry-richardson-banned-from-conde-nast-71849.

67. www.dw.com/en/guess-boss-paul-marciano-resigns-over-sexual-misconduct-allegations/a-44198420.

68. www.reuters.com/article/us-american-apparel-charney-idUSK BN0P401420150624.

69. https://wwd.com/eye/people/christy-turlington-burns-harassment-mistreatment-has-always-been-tolerated-in-fashion-industry-11029412/.

70. Knezevic, interview.

71. www.vanityfair.com/online/daily/2012/10/kate-moss-years-of-crying-johnny-depp.

72. www.modelalliance.org/respect.

73. http://blogs.lse.ac.uk/management/2018/03/09/taking-metoo-into-global-supply-chains/.

74. Hoskins, *Foot Work*, p. 212.

75. www.theguardian.com/sustainable-business/sustainable-fashion-blog/fashion-industry-letting-down-disabled-disability-cost-beauty.

76. https://i-d.vice.com/en_uk/article/nengmb/how-do-we-ensure-fashions-diversity-drive-doesnt-just-fetishise-the-new-wave-of-models.

77. Ibid.

78. https://fatshionista.livejournal.com/profile.id

79. www.huffingtonpost.com/jean-fain-licsw-msw/body-image_b_1583322.html.

80. www.kzoo.edu/praxis/what-is-fat-activism/.

81. https://web.archive.org/web/20140210031150/; www.xojane.com/fashion/fatshion-blogging-ate-itself-natalie-perkins.

82. https://observer.com/2013/02/fatshion-police-how-plus-size-blogging-left-its-radical-roots-behind/.

83. Ibid.

84. https://web.archive.org/web/20140210031150/www.xojane.com/fashion/fatshion-blogging-ate-itself-natalie-perkins.

85. www.lesleykinzel.com/how-i-lost-my-appetite-for-fat-politics/.

86. www.bustle.com/articles/149364-body-positivity-needs-to-talk-about-combatting-the-harmful-effects-of-fat-discrimination.

87. www.lesleykinzel.com/how-i-lost-my-appetite-for-fat-politics/.

88. Ibid.

89. 'What Is Fat Activism?' Dr Charlotte Cooper, interview (June 2016), www.kzoo.edu/praxis/what-is-fat-activism/.

Chapter 7

1. Allman, *Fashioning Africa*, p. 2.

2. www.forbes.com/sites/sethcohen/2020/06/10/vouges-anna-wintour-admits-hurtful-mistakes/#1690aec22823.

3. https://edition.cnn.com/style/article/fashion-industry-black-lives-matter/index.html.

4. Ibid.

5. I have selected the term 'models of colour' for this chapter rather than the political term 'Black' in an attempt to show that I am writing inclusively about a multitude of ethnicities who are targets

of racism, including Afro-Caribbean, Latina, Asian, South East Asian, and Native American people.

6. www.nymag.com/fashion/11/fall/china-machado.
7. www.dailykos.com/story/2009/04/04/716393/--Whites-Only-Designers- Reap-What-They-Sew-w-Mrs-O-POLL.
8. www.independent.co.uk/news/uk/home-news/fashion-is-racist-insider-lifts-lid-on-ethnic-exclusion-782974.html.
9. Knezevic, interview.
10. www.independent.co.uk/news/uk/home-news/fashion-is-racist-insider-lifts-lid-on-ethnic-exclusion-782974.html.
11. www.theguardian.com/sustainable-business/black-model-british-vogue-naomi-campbell-racism.
12. Janell Hobson, *Venus in the Dark: Blackness and Beauty in Popular Culture*. Routledge, 2005, p. 114.
13. www.nytimes.com/2008/09/01/business/worldbusiness/01vogue.html.
14. Frankenburg, *Displacing Whiteness*, p. 12.
15. Mears, *Pricing Beauty*, p. 194.
16. Alek Wek, *Alek*. HarperCollins' Amistad, 2007.
17. www.theguardian.com/tv-and-radio/2016/sep/04/thandie-newton-i-wake-up-angry-theres-a-lot-to-be-angry-about.
18. www.theguardian.com/sustainable-business/black-model-british-vogue-naomi-campbell-racism.
19. *British Vogue*, February 2015, p. 127.
20. www.theguardian.com/media/2017/nov/10/former-vogue-editor-alexandra-shulman-find-idea-that-there-was-a-posh-cabal-offensive.
21. Estella Tincknell, 'Always with the In-crowd: *Vogue* and the Cultural Politics of Gender, Race, Class, and Taste', in Laurel Forster and Joanne Hollows (eds), *Women's Periodicals and Print Culture in Britain, 1940s–2000s: The Postwar and Contemporary Period*. Edinburgh University Press, 2020.
22. 'Ill Doctrine, Ugly Shoes and Good Intentions', http://vimeo.com/44343389.
23. Eduardo Bonilla-Silva, *Racism without Racists*. Rowman & Littlefield, 2010, p. 8.

24. Ruth Frankenberg, *White Women, Race Matters: The Social Construction of Whiteness*. University of Minnesota Press, 1993, p. 11.

25. Leila Ahmed, *A Quiet Revolution*. Yale University Press, 2011, p. 23.

26. Ibid., p. 24.

27. Maxine Leeds Craig, *Ain't I a Beauty Queen?* Oxford University Press, 2002, p. 9.

28. Ibid., chapter 1.

29. Ibid., p. 6.

30. Ibid., p. 25.

31. Hobson, *Venus in the Dark*, p. 7.

32. Leeds Craig, *Ain't I a Beauty Queen?*, p. 37.

33. www.iheartthreadbared.wordpress.com/2011/05/05/whats-missing-in-vogue-italias-tribute-to-black-beauties.

34. 'Carine Roitfeld to Depart French *Vogue*', WWD, 17 December 2010.

35. Leeds Craig, *Ain't I a Beauty Queen?*, p. 14.

36. Christopher Boulton, 'Rebranding Diversity: Colourblind Racism within the US Advertising Industry', www.vimeo.com/44500667.

37. Penny Jane Burke and Jackie McManus, 'Art for a Few: Exclusions and Misrecognitions in Higher Education Admissions Practices'. *Discourse: Studies in the Cultural Politics of Education* 32(5) (2011), 699–712.

38. https://missionmag.org/racism-in-the-fashion-industry/.

39. https://i-d.vice.com/en_uk/article/nengmb/how-do-we-ensure-fashions-diversity-drive-doesnt-just-fetishise-the-new-wave-of-models.

40. www.theatlantic.com/health/archive/2020/07/fashions-racism-and-classism-are-going-out-style/613906/.

41. https://qz.com/1971287/why-rihannas-luxury-collaboration-with-lvmh-failed/.

42. www.reuters.com/article/us-italy-fashion-race-idUSKBN26219Y.

43. Oliver Wang, interview, 'Yellow Apparel: When the Coolie Becomes Cool', 2000.

44. Brigette Vézina, 'Curbing Cultural Appropriation in the Fashion Industry'. CIGI Papers No. 213, 9 (2019).
45. 'An Uneasy Cultural Exchange', *New York Times*, 14 March 2012.
46. https://truthout.org/articles/opposing-corporate-theft-of-mayan-textiles-weavers-appeal-to-guatemala-s-high-court/.
47. Ibid.
48. https://i-d.vice.com/en_uk/article/59gq3x/ktz-respond-to-inuit-cultural-appropriation-claims.
49. 'Native Americans Know that Cultural Misappropriation Is a Land of Darkness', *The Guardian*, 18 May 2012.
50. Richard Fung, 'Working through Appropriation', www.richardfung.ca/index.php?/articles/working-through-appropriation-1993.
51. Ibid.
52. Prospect, 'What's in a Name?' http://prospect.org/article/whats-name-3.
53. www.racialicious.com/2011/10/10/an-open-letter-to-urban-outfitters-on-columbus-day.
54. www.alagarconniere.blogspot.co.uk/2010/04/critical-fashion-lovers-basic-guide-to.html.
55. Erving Goffman, *The Presentation of Self in Everyday Life*. Allen Lane/Penguin, 1969, p. 53.
56. www.apihtawikosisan.tumblr.com/post/24815044400/cultural-appropriation-the-longer-article.
57. Kucheran, 'Luxury and Indigenous Resurgence'.
58. Prospect, 'What's in a Name?'.
59. Raahi Reddy, interview, 'Yellow Apparel: When the Coolie Becomes Cool', 2000.
60. www.apihtawikosisan.tumblr.com/post/24815044400/cultural-appropriation-the-longer-article.
61. 'Indigenous Fashionology with Riley Kucheran'.
62. 'Native Americans Know that Cultural Misappropriation Is a Land of Darkness'.
63. Riley Kucheran, written interview. Quoting Andrea Smith, in Audra Simpson and Andrea Smith, *Theorizing Native Studies*. Duke University Press, 2014.
64. Ibid.

65. Andreas Behnke, *The International Politics of Fashion: Being Fab in a Dangerous World*. Routledge, 2017.

66. Kucheran, written interview.

67. Nicola White, *Reconstructing Italian Fashion: America and the Development of the Italian Fashion Industry*. Berg, 2000.

68. 'Five Lessons for the Chinese Fashion Industry from the French'. Accenture Report, January 2012.

69. Edward W. Said, *Culture and Imperialism*. Vintage, 1994, p. xiii.

70. Chinoiserie Query, *Pigeons and Peacocks*, Issue 4.

71. www.vogue.com/article/fashion-leaders-on-the-importance-of-standing-up-against-anti-asian-racism.

72. Catherine Dior was a noted French Resistance member; Christian Dior's niece Françoise a notorious fascist.

73. www.nytimes.com/2011/09/04/books/review/sleeping-with-the-enemy-coco-chanels-secret-war-by-hal-vaughan-book-review.html?_r=1.

74. www.businessoffashion.com/2013/09/chanels-wertheimers-found-11-billion-richer-selling-no-5.html.

75. 'Louis Vuitton's Links with Vichy Regime Exposed', *The Guardian*, 3 June 2004.

76. www.vogue.com/voguepedia/Cristobal_Balenciaga.

77. Paul N. Siegel (ed.), *Leon Trotsky on Literature and Art*. Pathfinder Press, 1970, p. 77.

78. Faulkner, interview.

79. Ibid.

80. Wilson, *Adorned in Dreams*, p. 44.

81. Ibid., p. 204.

82. www.harpersbazaar.com/fashion/trends/a421/coco-chanel-karl-lagerfeld-0909/.

83. Lola Olufemi, *Feminism Interrupted*. Pluto Press, 2020, p. 85.

84. Said, *Culture and Imperialism*, p. xxx.

85. Frankenburg, *Displacing Whiteness*, p. 13.

Chapter 8

1. Karl Marx, *The German Ideology*, Part I, *Feuerbach: Opposition of the Materialist and Idealist Outlook B. The Illusion of the Epoch*, www.

marxists.org/archive/marx/works/1845/german-ideology/ch01b.htm.

2. Barnard, *Fashion as Communication*, p. 39.
3. Steele, *Paris Fashion*, p. 18.
4. Barnard, *Fashion as Communication*, p. 41.
5. Ibid.
6. Fred Davis, *Fashion, Culture and Identity*. University of Chicago Press, 1992, p. 162.
7. Ulrich Lehmann, 'Fashion and Materialism', lecture, 2012.
8. www.scribd.com/doc/38260/Harajuku-Rebels-on-the-Bridge.
9. Davis, *Fashion, Culture and Identity*, p. 168.
10. Wilson, *Adorned in Dreams*, p. 198.
11. Davis, *Fashion, Culture and Identity*, p. 166.
12. James C. Scott, *Weapons of the Weak: Everyday Forms of Peasant Resistance*. Yale University Press, 1985, p. 292.
13. Ibid., p. 293.
14. Ibid., p. 296.
15. Joy James (ed.), *The Angela Y. Davis Reader*. Wiley Blackwell, 1998, p. 277.
16. Steeve O. Buckridge, *The Language of Dress: Resistance and Accommodation in Jamaica 1760–1890*. University of West Indies Press, 2004, p. 95.
17. Ibid.
18. Allman, *Fashioning Africa*, p. 37. Example of Funmilayo Ransome-Kuti of the Abeokuta Women's Union.
19. Kirstin Knox, *Culture to Catwalk: How World Cultures Influence Fashion*. A&C Black, 2011, p. 86. Gauze, the super-fine silk, got its name from Gaza (*gazzatum*), having been produced there from the thirteenth century for export to Europe.
20. www.bmj.com/content/374/bmj.n2168.
21. https://psmag.com/news/we-have-come-to-dance-for-our-people.
22. Kucheran, 'Indigenizing Fashion Education'.
23. Barnard, *Fashion as Communication*, p. 144.
24. Ibid., p. 123.
25. Ibid., p. 130, quoting Dick Hebdige.
26. Ibid., p. 132.

Notes

27. Davis, *Fashion, Culture and Identity*, p. 168.

28. Ahmed, *A Quiet Revolution*, p. 222. While trying to crush women's movements in both Britain and Egypt, Cromer feigned concern for women's rights in Egypt to further imperialism.

29. Ibid., p. 209.

30. Ibid., p. 210. For an interesting discussion of the difference between resistance dressing and the attire of, for example, Hassidic Jews, who are less interested in challenging society than in preserving their way of life, see Davis, *Fashion, Culture and Identity*, p. 181.

31. www.hrw.org/news/2021/07/19/european-union-court-oks-bans-religious-dress-work.

32. Alain Badiou, 'Behind the Scarfed Law there Is Fear', Islam. Online.net, 3 March 2004.

33. Joëlle Jolivet, *The Colossal Book of Costumes Dressing up Around the World*. Thames & Hudson, 2008.

34. Gayle V. Fischer, *Pantaloons and Power*. Kent State University Press, 2001, p. 4.

35. Dexter C Bloomer and Amelia Jenks Bloomer, *Life and Writings of Amelia Bloomer*. Arena Publishing Company, 1895, p. 80.

36. Ibid., pp. 30, 169.

37. www.guardian.co.uk/world/2009/aug/02/sudan-women-dress-code.

38. www.nbcnews.com/shopping/apparel/gender-fluid-clothing-n1270831.

39. www.alokvmenon.com/blog/2020/11/13/degenderfashion-harry-styles-on-the-cover-of-vogue.

40. Ariel Levy, *Female Chauvinist Pigs*. Free Press, 2006.

41. Description of *keffiyeh* print by *Sex and the City* stylist Patricia Fields.

42. Buckridge, *The Language of Dress*, p. 86.

43. Shannon Price, 'Vivienne Westwood (born 1941) and the Postmodern Legacy of Punk Style, Essays from the Costume Institute', Metropolitan Museum of Art, www.metmuseum.org/toah/hd/vivw/hd_vivw.htm.

44. Ibid.

45. Barnard, *Fashion as Communication*, p. 132.

46. Ibid., p. 132.

47. Davis, *Fashion, Culture and Identity*, p. 181.

48. Davis, *Fashion, Culture and Identity*, p. 161.

49. Phrase typically attributed to Werner Sombart (1902) or Elizabeth Wilson (1985).

50. Tim Edwards, 'Express Yourself: The Politics of Dressing Up', in Barnard, *Fashion Theory*, p. 195.

51. Ibid.

52. Elizabeth Fox-Genovese, quoted in Barnard, *Fashion as Communication*, p. 123.

53. Thomas Docherty, *Aesthetic Democracy*. Stanford University Press, 2006, p. xiv.

54. www.youtube.com/watch?v=U1eVAmIPvAU.

55. Buckridge, *The Language of Dress*, p. 86.

56. https://racinewir.com/2021/07/16/why-bother-we-set-out-to-change-the-world-ended-up-just-changing-ourselves/.

Chapter 9

1. Karl Marx, *The Eighteenth Brumaire of Louis Bonaparte*. 1852.

2. James, *The Angela Y. Davis Reader*, p. 244.

3. This chapter is not an examination of small, 'ethical' businesses. There are already numerous books on this subject that readers can find if they are interested.

4. Florence Kelley was a follower of Karl Marx and a friend of Friedrich Engels. Her translation into English of Engels' *The Condition of the Working Class in England* is still used today.

5. www.boisestate.edu/socwork/dhuff/history/extras/kelly.htm.

6. www.rmc.library.cornell.edu/EAD/htmldocs/KCL05307.html.

7. www.socialwelfarehistory.com/people/lowell-josephine-shaw.

8. www.nclnet.org/history.

9. www.source.ethicalfashionforum.com/digital/sustainable-fashion-towards-the-tipping-point.

10. www.thebusinessresearchcompany.com/report/ethical-fashion-market.

11. www.ft.com/content/d174e7d7-97c4-43fc-8765-95075e5fcce7.

12. Riley Kucheran, unpublished essay. Shared with me November 2021.

Notes

13. Duncan Clark, *The Rough Guide to Ethical Shopping*. Rough Guides, 2004, p. viii.
14. www.news.sciencemag.org/sciencenow/2011/10/laundry-lint-pollutes-the-worlds.html.
15. Christina Weil, *Heart on Your Sleeve*. Oxfam Activities, 2008, p. 18.
16. Ibid., p. 18.
17. Blanchard, *Green Is the New Black*, p. 42.
18. Naomi Klein, *No Logo: No Space, No Choice, No Jobs*. Picador, 2001, p. 149.
19. www.ft.com/content/d174e7d7–97c4–43fc-8765–95075e5fcce7.
20. www.mckinsey.com/industries/retail/our-insights/survey-consumer-sentiment-on-sustainability-in-fashion.
21. www.marxists.org/archive/draper/1971/xx/emancipation.html.
22. N. Craig Smith, *Morality and the Market*. Routledge, 1990, p. 6.
23. Mészáros, *Marx's Theory of Alienation*, p. 206.
24. Helen Scott (ed.), *The Essential Rosa Luxemburg*. Haymarket Books, 2007, p. 1.
25. Ibid., p. 89.
26. Hoskins, *Foot Work*, p. 223.
27. Derek Wall, *Climate Strike: The Practical Politics of the Climate Crisis*. Merlin Press, 2020, chapter 10.
28. Scott, *The Essential Rosa Luxemburg*, p. 65.
29. https://labourbehindthelabel.org/report-boohoo-covid-19-the-people-behind-the-profit/.
30. Jodi Dean, 'Communicative Capitalism', in Megan Boler (ed.), *Digital Media and Democracy: Tactics in Hard Times*. MIT Press, 2010, p. 112.
31. Richey and Ponte, *Brand Aid*, preface.
32. Ibid., p. xii.
33. Ibid., p. 187.
34. Ibid., p. 174.
35. Ibid., p. 9.
36. Ibid., p. 152.
37. Ibid., p. 1.
38. Ibid., p. 157.
39. Ibid., p. 3.
40. Ibid., p. 5.

41. Ibid., p. 232.
42. Ching Yoon Louie, *Sweatshop Warriors*, p. 228.
43. Aboriginal Activists Group, Queensland, 1970s, popularised by campaigner Lilla Watson. USAS.org.
44. http://projects.aljazeera.com/2015/08/rana-plaza/childrens-place.html.
45. Scott, *The Essential Rosa Luxemburg*, p. 58.
46. Craig Smith, *Morality and the Market*, p. 40.
47. Magdoff and Bellamy Foster, *What Every Environmentalist Needs to Know about Capitalism*, p. 134.
48. Bellamy Foster, *Ecology against Capitalism*, p. 25.
49. David Harvey, *The Enigma of Capital and the Crises of Capitalism*. Profile Books, 2011, p. 277.

Chapter 10

1. Jason Hickle, *Less Is More*. Windmill, 2020, p. 24.
2. South End Press (ed.), *Talking about a Revolution*. South End Press, 1998, p. v.
3. Mészáros, *Beyond Capital*, p. 812.
4. bell hooks, interview, South End Press, *Talking about a Revolution*, p. 52.
5. Leon Trotsky, 'Literature and Revolution', www.marxists.org/archive/trotsky/1924/lit_revo/intro.htm.
6. Said, *Culture and Imperialism*, p. xiii.
7. Eagleton, *Marxism and Literary Criticism*, p. 68.
8. Ibid., p. 69. Quote about writers from Pierre Mackerey, based on Louis Althusser.
9. Nicholas Bourriaud, quoted in Malossi, *The Style Engine*, p. 271.
10. John Berger, *Art and Revolution*. Writers & Readers, 1969, p. 43.
11. Mészáros, *Marx's Theory of Alienation*, p. 175.
12. Penny Jane Burke and Jackie McManus, 'Art for a Few: Exclusions and Misrecognitions in Higher Education Admissions Practices'. *Discourse: Studies in the Cultural Politics of Education* 32(5) (2011), 699–712.
13. Audre Lorde, *Sister Outsider*, quoted in Hobson, *Venus in the Dark*, p. 143.

Notes

14. bell hooks, interview, pp. 51–2.
15. Ollman, *Alienation*, p. 92.
16. Varvara Stepanova, *Tasks of the Artist in Textile Production*, p. 190, quoted in Stern, *Against Fashion*, p. 55.
17. Mikhail Guerman, *Art of the October Revolution*, quoted in www.marxist.com/ArtAndLiterature-old/marxism_and_art.html.
18. Leon Trotsky, *Literature and Revolution*, pp. 255–6, quoted in www.marxist.com/ArtAndLiterature-old/marxism_and_art.html.
19. Berger, *Art and Revolution*, foreword.
20. Michael R. Redclift and Graham Woodgate (eds), *The International Handbook of Environmental Sociology*, 2nd edition. Edward Elgar, 2010, p. 208.
21. Berger, *Art and Revolution*, p. 30.
22. John E. Bowlt and Matthew Drutt (eds), *Amazons of the Avant-garde*. Guggenheim Museum Publications, 1999, p. 109.
23. Berger, *Art and Revolution*, p. 37.
24. There then followed the loss of the Bolshevik Revolution to Stalinism, which 'expressed itself in one of the most devastating assaults on artistic culture ever witnessed in modern history – an assault conducted in the name of a theory and practise of social liberation'. Eagleton, *Marxism and Literary Criticism*, p. 38.
25. Alexander Laurentier, *Varvara Stepanova*. Thames & Hudson, 1988, p. 81.
26. Ibid.
27. Art critic D. Aranovich, 1926, quoted in ibid., p. 83.
28. Bowlt and Drutt, *Amazons of the Avant-garde*, p. 190.
29. M. N. Yablonskaya, *Women Artists of Russia's New Age*. Thames & Hudson, 1990, p. 115.
30. www.tate.org.uk/whats-on/tate-modern/exhibition/rodchenko-popova/rodchenko-and-popova-defining-constructivism-9.
31. Stern, *Against Fashion*, p. 55.
32. Berger, *Art and Revolution*, p. 47.
33. P. Walton and A. Gamble, *From Alienation to Surplus Value*. Sheed & Ward, 1972, p. 218.
34. www.marxists.org/archive/trotsky/1924/lit_revo/intro.htm.
35. Walton and Gamble, *From Alienation to Surplus Value*, p. 12.

36. Ulrich Lehmann, 'Fashion and Materialism', lecture, 2012.
37. www.somo.nl/wp-content/uploads/2021/05/spinning-around-workers-rights.pdf.
38. Yablonskaya, *Women Artists of Russia's New Age*, p. 156.
39. Lee, *Eco Chic*, p. 82.
40. Reduced from 350,000 tonnes in 2012. https://wrap.org.uk/sites/default/files/2020-10/WRAP-valuing-our-clothes-the-cost-of-uk-fashion_WRAP.pdf.
41. Mészáros, *Beyond Capital*, p. 739.
42. Mészáros, *Marx's Theory of Alienation*, p. 205.
43. Karl Marx, quoted in Orbach, *Bodies*, p. 138.
44. Roland Barthes, *The Fashion System*, Jonathan Cape, 1985.
45. Hoskins, *Foot Work*, p. 194.
46. https://fibershed.org/mission-vision/.
47. Alexandra Kollontai, *Communism and the Family*, 1920.
48. Kucheran, 'Luxury and Indigenous Resurgence'.
49. Vandana Shiva, *Making Peace with the Earth*. Pluto Press, 2012, p. 3.
50. Jason Hickle, *Less Is More*, Penguin, 2020, p. 21.
51. Ibid., p. 22.
52. Ibid., p. 21.
53. Ibid., p. 224.
54. Buddhima Padmasiri, interview, lecturer, Open University, Sri Lanka.
55. Karl Marx, quoted in Mészáros, *Marx's Theory of Alienation*, p. 212.
56. Ibid., p. 211.
57. Karl Marx, *Wage Labour and Capital – What Are Wages? Are They Determined?* 1849.
58. Rosa Luxemburg, *Reform or Revolution*, in Mészáros, *Beyond Capital*, p. 836.
59. Karl Marx, quoted in ibid., p. xxv.
60. Ibid., p. 845.
61. Roy Morrison, quoted in John Bellamy Foster, *The Ecological Revolution*. Monthly Review Press, 2009, p. 264.
62. Andrew Simms, *Tescopoly*. Constable, 2007, p. 232.
63. Mike Cooley, *Architect or Bee*. South End Press, 1982.

64. Max Liboiron, *Pollution Is Colonialism*. Duke University Press, 2021, Introduction.

65. www.wiego.org/informal-economy/occupational-groups/waste-pickers Different regions and languages prefer different terms.

66. 'Why Pollution Is as much about Colonialism as Chemicals', *Don't Call Me Resilient* podcast, https://theconversation.com/why-pollution-is-as-much-about-colonialism-as-chemicals-dont-call-me-resilient-transcript-ep-11-170697.

67. I rewrote this section after an email conversation with Riley Kucheran, to whom I am extremely grateful.

68. https://everydayorientalism.wordpress.com/2021/11/18/the-impossibility-of-decolonizing-anthropology/, quoting Liboiron, *Pollution Is Colonialism*.

69. www.opendemocracy.net/en/decolonisation-comfortable-buzzword-aid-sector/.

70. From Kucheran, 'Indigenizing Fashion Education', quoting Simpson and Smith, *Theorizing Native Studies*.

71. From ibid., quoting Eve Tuck and K. Wayne Yang, 'Decolonization Is Not a Metaphor'. *Decolonization, Indigeneity, Education & Society* (2012), https://clas.osu.edu/sites/clas.osu.edu/files/Tuck%20and%20Yang%202012%20Decolonization%20is%20not%20a%20metaphor.pdf.

72. Ibid.

73. Ibid.

74. Kucheran, 'Indigenizing Fashion Education'.

75. Alan Woods, 'Marxism and Art', www.marxist.com/ArtAnd Literature-old/marxism_and_art.html.

76. Stepanova, 1928, quoted in Yablonskaya, *Women Artists of Russia's New Age*, p. 156.

77. Loschek, *When Clothes Become Fashion*, p. 2; Berger, *Ways of Seeing*, part 1.

78. Berger, *Ways of Seeing*, part 1.

79. Kanye West, *All Falls Down*, featuring Syleena Johnson, 2004.

80. Anna Gough-Yates, *Women's Magazines*. Routledge, 2003, p. 10.

81. Berger, *Ways of Seeing*, part 4.

82. McDowell, *The Designer Scam*, p. 28.

83. Hansen and Reed, *Cosmetics, Fashions and the Exploitation of Women*, p. 53.

84. Bartky, *Femininity and Domination*, p. 71.

85. Juan Juan Wu, *Chinese Fashion: From Mao to Now*. Berg, 2009, p. 2.

86. Ibid., p. 8.

87. Ibid., p. 2.

88. Lehmann, 'Fashion and Materialism', lecture, 2012.

89. bell hooks, interview, p. 50. Attacking 'Left-oriented' art is ideological in itself as an attempt to shut down debate and prevent art from having a social function. People should not have to struggle between their 'political beliefs with their aesthetic and artistic vision'.

90. Debbie Ging, 'Well-Heeled Women: Post-feminism and Shoe Fetishism', webpages.dcu.ie/~gingd/articleslectures.html.

91. Raisa Kabir, www.thefword.org.uk/blog/2013/09/the_veil_debate.

92. Walter Benjamin, 'On the Concept of History', www.marxists.org/reference/archive/benjamin/1940/history.htm, 2009.

93. Raahi Reddy, interview, in *Yellow Apparel*, 2000.

94. Falasca-Zamponi, *Waste and Consumption*, p. 47.

95. Vijay Prashad, interview, *Yellow Apparel*, 2000.

96. www.online.wsj.com/article/SB10001424052970203479104577124613246783618.html.

97. Eagleton, *Marxism and Literary Criticism*, p. 6.

98. Bellamy Foster, Clark, and York, *The Ecological Rift*, p. 103.

99. Alexander Blok, *The Intelligensia and the Revolution*, 1918.

Bibliography

Ahmed, Leila, *A Quiet Revolution*. Yale University Press, 2011.

Albertazzi, Daniele and Cobley, Paul, *The Media: An Introduction*. Pearson Education, 2009.

Aldridge, Alan, *Consumption*. Polity Press, 2003.

Allman, Jean (ed.), *Fashioning Africa: Power and the Politics of Dress*. Indiana University Press, 2004.

Amie, Hardy, *Just So Far*. Collins, 1954.

Anderson Black, J. and Garland, Madge, *A History of Fashion*. McDonald (Black Cat imprint), 1990.

Badia, Enrique, *Zara and Her Sisters: The Story of the World's Largest Clothing Retailer*. Palgrave Macmillan, 2009.

Barnard, Malcolm, *Fashion as Communication*. Routledge, 1996.

Barnard, Malcolm (ed.), *Fashion Theory: A Reader*. Routledge, 2007.

Barrell, Joan and Braithwaite, Brian, *The Business of Women's Magazines*. Kogan Page, 1988.

Barry, Ben and Christel, Deborah (eds), *Fashion Education: The Systemic Revolution*. Intellect, Forthcoming.

Barthes, Roland, *The Fashion System*. Jonathan Cape, 1985.

Bartky, Sandra Lee, *Femininity and Domination*. Routledge, 1990.

Bartlett, Djurdja, *Fashion East: The Specter that Haunted Socialism*. MIT Press, 2010.

Bell, Quentin, *On Human Finery*. Hogarth Press, 1947.

Bellamy Foster, John, *Marx's Ecology*. Monthly Review Press, 2000.

Bellamy Foster, John, *Ecology against Capitalism*. Monthly Review Press, 2002.

Bellamy Foster, John, *The Ecological Revolution*. Monthly Review Press, 2009.

Bellamy Foster, John, Clark, Brett, and York, Richard, *The Ecological Rift: Capitalism's War on the Earth*. Monthly Review Press, 2010.

Berger, John, *Art and Revolution*. Writers and Readers, 1969.

Berger, John, *Ways of Seeing*. Penguin Classics, 2008.

BIS, *Never Leave The House Naked*. BIS Publishers, 2009.

Blanchard, Tamsin, *Green Is the New Black*. Hodder & Stoughton, 2007.

Blyth, Myrna, *Spin Sisters*. St. Martin's Press, 2004.

Bonilla-Silva, Eduardo, *Racism without Racists*. Rowman & Littlefield, 2010.

Bowlt, John and Drutt, Matthew (eds), *Amazons of the Avant-garde*. Guggenheim Museum Press, 1999.

Breward, Christopher and Evans, Caroline (eds), *Fashion and Modernity*. Bloomsbury, 2005.

Buckridge, Steeve O., *The Language of Dress: Resistance and Accommodation in Jamaica 1760–1890*. University of West Indies Press, 2004.

Byrne Smith, Laura, *The Urge to Splurge*. ECW Press, 2003.

Carson, Rachel, *Silent Spring*. Houghton Mifflin, 1987.

Catlaneo, Olivier, Gereffi, Gary, and Staritz, Cornelia (eds), *Global Value Chains in a Post-Crisis World*. World Bank, 2010.

Chan Kwok-bun, Cheung Tak-sing, and Agnes S. Ku (eds), *Chinese Capitalisms*. Brill, 2008.

Chang, Ha-Joon, *23 Things They Don't Tell You about Capitalism*. Penguin Books, 2010.

Ching Yoon Louie, Miriam, *Sweatshop Warriors*. South End Press, 2001.

Chow, Gregory C., *China as a Leader of the World Economy*. World Scientific Publishing, 2012.

Ciochetto, Lynne, *Globalisation and Advertising in Emerging Economies: Brazil, Russia, India and China*. Routledge, 2011.

Clark, Duncan, *The Rough Guide to Ethical Shopping*. Rough Guides, 2004.

Clark, Eric, *The Want Makers*. Hodder & Stoughton, 1988.

Clark, Jessica P. and Lezama, Nigel (eds) *Decentring Luxury*. Canadian Critical Luxury Studies, Intellect, 2022.

Compaine, Benjamin M. and Gomery, Douglas, *Who Owns the Media?* Lawrence Erlbraum Associates, 2000.

Cooley, Mike, *Architect or Bee*. South End Press, 1982.

Croteau, David and Haynes, William, *The Business of Media*. Pine Forge Press, 2001.

Bibliography

Davis, Fred, *Fashion, Culture and Identity*. University of Chicago Press, 1992.

De Marly, Diana, *Working Dress*. Holmes & Meier, 1986.

Dean, Jodi, *Democracy and Other Neoliberal Fantasies: Communicative Capitalism and Left Politics*. Duke University Press, 2009.

Docherty, Thomas, *Aesthetic Democracy*. Stanford University Press, 2006.

Eagleton, Terry, *Marxism and Literary Criticism*. Methuen, 1985.

Eagleton, Terry, *Ideology: An Introduction*. Verso, 1991.

Eagleton, Terry, *After Theory*. Allen Lane/Penguin, 2003.

Elkington, John and Hailes, Julia, *The Green Consumer Guide*. Victor Gollancz, 1988.

Elliott, David, *New Worlds: Russian Art and Society 1900–1937*. Thames & Hudson, 1980.

Elliott, Larry and Atkinson, Dan, *The Gods that Failed*. Bodley Head, 2008.

Engels, Friedrich, *The Condition of the Working Class in England*. 1845.

Falasca-Zamponi, Simonetta, *Waste and Consumption*. Routledge, 2011.

Faulkner, Neil, *A Marxist History of the World*. Pluto Press, 2013.

Featherstone, Liza and United Students Against Sweatshops, *Students Against Sweatshops*. Verso, 2002.

Fine, Ben, *The World of Consumption: The Material and Cultural Revisited*. Routledge, 2002.

Fine, Ben and Saad-Filho, Alfredo, *Marx's Capital*, 5th edition. Pluto Press, 2010.

Fischer, Gayle V., *Pantaloons and Power*. Kent State University Press, 2001.

Fletcher, Kate and Tham, Mathilda, *Earth Logic: Fashion Action Research Plan*. JJ Charitable Trust, 2019.

Fogarty, Anne, *The Art of Being a Well-Dressed Wife* [1959]. V&A Enterprises, 2011.

Frankenberg, Ruth, *White Women, Race Matters: The Social Construction of Whiteness*. University of Minnesota Press, 1993.

Frankenberg, Ruth, *Displacing Whiteness*. Duke University Press, 1997.

Gale, Colin and Kaur, Jasbin, *Fashion and Textiles*. Berg, 2004.

German, Lindsey, *Sex, Class and Socialism*. Bookmark, 1998.

German, Lindsey, *How a Century of War Changed the Lives of Women*. Pluto Press, 2013.

Goffman, Erving, *The Presentation of Self in Everyday Life*. Allen Lane/ Penguin, 1969.

Gough Yates, Anna, *Women's Magazines*. Routledge, 2003.

Granger, Michele, *Fashion: The Industry and Its Careers*. Fairchild Publications, 2007.

Haig, Matt, *Brand Success: How the World's Top 100 Brands Thrive and Survive*, 2nd edition. Kogan Page, 2011.

Hansen, Joseph and Reed, Evelyn, *Cosmetics, Fashions and the Exploitation of Women*. Pathfinder Press, 1986.

Hapke, Laura, *Sweatshop: The History of an American Idea*. Rutgers University Press, 2004.

Harman, Chris, *Economics of the Madhouse*. Bookmark, 1995.

Harvey, David, *The Enigma of Capital and the Crises of Capitalism*. Profile Books, 2011.

Heath, Robert, *Seducing the Subconscious: The Psychology of Emotional Influence in Advertising*. Wiley Blackwell, 2012.

Helen Scott (ed.), *The Essential Rosa Luxemburg*. Haymarket Books, 2008.

Hickel, Jason, *Less Is More: How Degrowth Will Save The World*. Windmill, 2020.

Higham, William, *The Next Big Thing*. Kogan Page, 2009.

Hobson, Janell, *Venus in the Dark*. Routledge, 2005.

Hoskins, Tansy, *What Your Shoes Tell You About Globalisation*. Orion, 2020.

James, Joy (ed.), *The Angela Y. Davis Reader*. Wiley Blackwell, 1998.

Jarrow, Jeanette A. and Judelle, Beatrice (eds.), *Inside the Fashion Business*. John Wiley & Sons, 1966.

Jhally, Suj, *The Codes of Advertising*. Routledge, 1990.

Klein, David and Burstein, Dan, *Blog!* CDS Books, 2005.

Klein, Naomi, *No Logo*. Picador, 1999.

Knox, Kirstin, *Culture to Catwalk: How World Cultures Influence Fashion*. A&C Black, 2011.

Kollontai, Alexandra, *Communism and the Family*. 1920.

Kollontai, Alexandra, *The Autobiography of a Sexually Emancipated Communist Woman*. Herder and Herder, 1971.

Bibliography

Lanier, Jaron, *Ten Arguments for Deleting Your Social Media Accounts Right Now*. Vintage, 2018.

Laurentier, Alexander, *Varvara Stepanova*. Thames & Hudson, 1988.

Lee, Matilda, *Eco Chic*. Octopus, 2007.

Leeds, Craig, Maxine, *Ain't I a Beauty Queen?* Oxford University Press, 2002.

Levy, Ariel, *Female Chauvinist Pigs: Women and the Rise of Raunch Culture*. Free Press, 2006.

Liboiron, Max *Pollution Is Colonialism*. Duke University Press, 2021.

Loschek, Ingrid, *When Clothes Become Fashion*. Berg, 2009.

Lunn, Eugene, *Marxism and Modernism*. University of California Press, 1982.

Magdoff, Fred and Bellamy Foster, John, *What Every Environmentalist Needs to Know about Capitalism*. Monthly Review Press, 2011.

Malossi, Giannino (ed.), *The Style Engine*. Monacelli Press, 1998. Marx, Karl, *Wage Labour and Capital* (pamphlet).

Marx, Karl, *Economic and Philosophical Manuscripts of 1844: Antithesis of Capital and Labour – Landed Property and Capital*.

Marx, Karl, *The German Ideology*. 1846.

Marx, Karl, *The Poverty of Philosophy*. 1847.

Marx, Karl, *Outline of the Critique of Political Economy (Grundrisse)*. 1857–61.

Marx, Karl, *Capital*, volume 1. Progress Press, 1887.

Marx, Karl, *Marx: Later Political Writings [The Eighteenth Brumaire of Louis Bonaparte]*. Cambridge University Press, 1996.

McDowell, Colin, *The Designer Scam*. Hutchinson and Random House, 1994.

McKay, Jenny, *The Magazines Handbook*. Routledge, 2006.

Mears, Ashley, *Pricing Beauty*. University of California Press, 2011.

Mészáros, István, *Beyond Capital*. Merlin, 1995.

Mészáros, István, *Marx's Theory of Alienation*. Merlin, 2006.

Mészáros, István, *The Structural Crisis of Capital*. Monthly Review Press, 2010.

Micheletti, Michele, *Political Virtue and Shopping*. Palgrave Macmillan, 2003.

Naylor, R. T., *Crass Struggle*. McGill-Queen's University Press, 2011.

North, Richard D., *Rich Is Beautiful*. Social Affairs Unit, 2005.

Nystrom, Paul H., *Economics of Fashion*. Ronald Press, 1928.

Ollman, Bertell, *Alienation: Marx's Conception of Man in Capitalist Society*. Cambridge University Press, 1976.

Olufemi, Lola, *Feminism Interrupted*. Pluto Press, 2020.

Orbach, Susie, *Fat Is a Feminist Issue*. Arrow Books, 2006.

Orbach, Susie, *Bodies*. Profile Books, 2010.

Orwell, George, *The Road to Wigan Pier*. Victor Gollancz, 1937.

Pankhurst, Sylvia, 'Communism and Its Tactics'. *Workers' Dreadnought*, 1921.

Raymond, Martin, *The Trend Forecaster's Handbook*. Lawrence King, 2010.

Redclift, Michael R. and Woodgate Graham (eds), *The International Handbook of Environmental Sociology*, 2nd edition. Edward Elgar, 2010.

Rhodes, Leara D., 'Magazines', in Erwin K. Thomas and Brown H. Carpenter (eds), *Mass Media in 2025*. Greenwood Press, 2001.

Richey, Lisa Ann and Ponte, Stefano, *Brand Aid: Shopping Well to Save the World*. University of Minnesota Press, 2011.

Roberts, Paul Craig, *Alienation and the Soviet Economy*. University of Mexico Press, 1971.

Rosenberg, William G. (ed.), *Bolshevik Visions*. University of Michigan Press, 1990.

Ross, Andrew (ed.), *No Sweat: Fashion, Free Trade and the Rights of Workers*. Verso, 1997.

Ross, Robert J. S., *Slaves to Fashion*. University of Michigan Press, 2004.

Said, Edward W., *Culture and Imperialism*. Vintage, 1994.

Scott, James C., *Weapons of the Weak: Everyday Forms of Peasant Resistance*. Yale University Press, 1985.

Seebohm, Caroline, *The Man Who Was Vogue*. Weidenfeld & Nicolson, 1982.

Settle, Alison, *English Fashion*. Collins, 1959.

Sheridan, Jayne, *Fashion, Media, Promotion: The New Black Magic*. Wiley Blackwell, 2010.

Shiva, Vandana, *Making Peace with the Earth*. Pluto Press, 2012.

Siegel, Paul N. (ed.), *Leon Trotsky on Literature and Art*. Pathfinder Press, 1970.

Bibliography

Siegle, Lucy, *To Die for: Is Fashion Wearing out the World?* Fourth Estate, 2011.

Sigsworth, Eric M., *Montague Burton: The Tailor of Taste.* Manchester University Press, 1990.

Simms, Andrew, *Tescopoly.* Constable, 2007.

Sladen, Christopher, *The Conscription of Fashion.* Scholar Press, 1995.

Sluiter, Liesbeth, *Clean Clothes.* Pluto Press, 2009.

Smith, N. Craig, *Morality and the Market.* Routledge, 1990.

Smythe, Dallas Walker, *Dependency Road: Communication, Capitalism, Consciousness and Canada.* Ablex, 1982.

Soper, Kate, *Post-Growth Living: For An Alternative Hedonism.* Verso, 2020.

South End Press (ed.), *Talking about a Revolution.* South End Press, 1998.

Steele, Valerie, *Paris Fashion.* Berg, 1988.

Steger, Manfred B. and Roy, Ravi K., *Neoliberalism: A Very Short Introduction.* Oxford University Press, 2010.

Steinham, Gloria, *Moving beyond Words: Age, Rage, Sex, Power, Money, Muscles: Breaking the Boundaries of Gender.* Touchstone, 1994.

Stern, Radu, *Against Fashion: Clothing as Art, 1850–1930.* MIT Press, 2004.

Strebbins, Robert A., *Leisure and Consumption: Common Ground/ Separate Worlds.* Palgrave Macmillan, 2009.

Thomas, Dana, *Duluxe.* Penguin, 2007.

Tomlinson, Alan (ed.), *Consumption, Identity and Style: Marketing, Meanings and the Packaging of Pleasure.* Routledge, 1991.

Tranberg Hansen, Karen, *Salaula: The World of Secondhand Clothing and Zambia.* University of Chicago Press, 2000.

Tulloch, Carol (ed.), *Black Style.* V&A Publications, 2004.

Turow, Joseph and Tsui, Lohman (eds), *The Hyperlinked Society.* University of Michigan Press, 2008.

Waddell, Gavin, *How Fashion Works.* Blackwell, 2004.

Waldfogel, Joel, *Scroogenomics: Why You Shouldn't Buy Presents for the Holidays.* Princeton University Press, 2009.

Wall, Derek, *Climate Strike: The Practical Politics of the Climate Crisis.* Merlin Press, 2020.

Walton, P. and Gamble, A., *From Alienation to Surplus Value*. Sheed & Ward, 1972.

Weil, Christina, *Heart on Your Sleeve*. Oxfam Activities, 2008.

Welters, Linda and Lillethun, Abby (eds), *The Fashion Reader*. Bloomsbury, 2007.

Werle, Simone, *Style Diaries: World Fashion from Berlin to Tokyo*. Prestel, 2010.

White, Cynthia L., *Women's Magazines 1693–1968*. Michael Joseph, 1970.

White, Nicola, *Reconstructing Italian Fashion: America and the Development of the Italian Fashion Industry*. Berg, 2000.

Whitehorne, Olivia, *Cosmo Woman*. Crescent Moon, 2007.

Wilson, Elizabeth, *Adorned in Dreams*. Virago, 1985.

Wolf, Naomi, *The Beauty Myth*. Random House, 1991.

Wu, Juan Juan, *Chinese Fashion: From Mao to Now*. Berg, 2009.

Yablowskaya, M. N., *Women Artists of Russia's New Age*. Thames & Hudson, 1990.

Žižek, Slavov, *Violence: Six Sideways Reflections*. Profile Books, 2010.

Index

note: brand names by individual designers are indexed under the name of the designer, e.g. Boss, Hugo

Index

body image 68, 159–62, 172–4, 182, 284
Bono 250
Bonvicini, Stephanie *Louis Vuitton: A French Saga* 207
Boohoo 32, 33–4, 40, 84, 146, 239, 248
Boss, Hugo 207
Boussac, Marcel 29
Brecht, Bertolt 17, 260
 'A worker reads history' 11
Britain 25, 29–30, 127, 248
 Factory Act (1833) 124
 Industrial Revolution in 25, 122–3
 riots in (2011) 82
 'Swinging Sixties' 31
British colonialism 108, 218, 276
British Vogue 27, 54, 66, 166, 187, 190–2
Brother Vellies 197
Browne, Cheryl 194
Buckridge, Steeve O. *The Language of Dress* 217
buffalo 155
Burberry 32, 87
Burke, Tarana 177
Burns, Mary and Lizzie 123
Burton, Montague 25–6, 37
Bush, George W. 90
Business of Fashion (website) 50, 54, 66
Business Research Company 239
Buy Nothing Day campaign 91
Buylesscrap.com 235

Calvino, Italo 53, 64
Cambodia 130

Cambridge Analytica 64
Campbell, Naomi 188, 189, 190
Canada 145, 155, 200
 India Act (1876) 155
 removal of Indigenous children to residential schools 155–6
capitalism ix, 4–5, 15, 21, 101, 104, 143, 146, 241, 247, 286
 alternatives to 152
 communicative capitalism 71–3
 creation of false needs by 88, 91
 'just capitalism' 255–6
 post-capitalism 258, 272–4, 280
 surveillance capitalism 64–7, 69
Capri Holdings 43
Carmichael, Stokely 195
Carson, Rachel *Silent Spring* 135
Cartwright, Edmund 122
catwalks *see* fashion shows
'causerism' 242, 243–4, 245
Chamberlain, Neville 26
Chambers, Lucinda 56–7
Chambre Syndicale de la Couture Parisienne 28, 167, 269
Chanel, Coco 16, 42–3, 45, 89, 202, 209–10
 collaboration with Nazis by 206–7
Changing Markets Foundation 144
Chappell, Dominic 38
Charney, Dov 176
Chávez, Hugo 272
Chemical Valley, Canada 145
Chesterton, G.K. 93–4
child labour 9, 124, 137, 237
child models: pornographic images of 176
Children's Place, The 254–5

339

Index

Index

Index

Index

Index

Index